THE PLEASURES OF WINE

THE PLEASURES OF
WINE

SELECTED ESSAYS

GERALD ASHER

CHRONICLE BOOKS

SAN FRANCISCO

The essays in this book have appeared in slightly different form in *Gourmet* magazine.

Library of Congress Cataloging-in-Publication Data available.

ISBN 0-8118-3497-2

Manufactured in the United States of America
Design by Jessica Grunwald
Compositon by Jack Lanning
Cover illustration by Elvis Swift

Distributed in Canada by Raincoast Books
9050 Shaughnessy Street
Vancouver, British Columbia V6P 6E5

10 9 8 7 6 5 4 3 2 1

Chronicle Books LLC
85 Second Street
San Francisco, California 94105

www.chroniclebooks.com

FOR ANDREW TERAN

CONTENTS

INTRODUCTION

IT NEEDS ONLY A GOOD BOTTLE OF WINE FOR A ROAST CHICKEN to be transformed into a banquet. Last night for supper we had a dish of fava beans dressed with the remains of the sauce from the previous evening's osso buco. With a glass of Barnard & Griffin's Columbia Valley Sémillon, it was sumptuous. Need I say: I like to eat and drink—preferably in congenial company.

The novelist Iris Murdoch once said that the purpose of wine is to stimulate the flow of talk. She urged against fine wine in favor of an indefinite supply of something cheaper. I take her point—the spirit of hospitality is better served by a pint of Beaujolais than an ounce of some rarity. But she may have missed an equally important truth: Within reason, the better the wine—and the food—the better the conversation.

A welcoming glass of Champagne and a few freshly toasted almonds can mold six strangers into a dinner party. A bottle (preferably two) of old-vine Zinfandel and a cumin-laced lamb stew will have them predicting the Academy Awards, solving the problems of the ecosystem, and discussing the lives of people they don't know. A few sips of Beerenauslese and a slice of warm apple pie and at least two of those at the table will discover they had a great-grandmother in common.

Imagine then, the flights of fancy at a dinner at Narsai David's house a year or two ago that began with Pol Roger Extra Reserve 1921, disgorged in 1977—still delicately fresh but with a bouquet hinting at the mysteries of the sphinx—and ended with a footnote to history: an 1875 California Angelica, bottled in 1921 for the private San Francisco cellar of Isaias W. Hellman, a founder of the Wells Fargo Bank. In between there were diversions that included fresh caviar from the Sacramento River and smoked salmon from Shanagarry in County Cork, Chilean sea bass in a saffron-hued bouillabaisse broth, a Chardonnay from Iron Horse the color of pale lemons, and wild duck—widgeon and green-winged teal—from the San Joaquin valley, with a brace of silky Chambolle-Musigny '64, one from Veuve Bertheau and the other from Georges Roumier.

At the house of Fran Gage, whose Pâtisserie Française on 18th Street kept San Francisco in *pâte à choux* bliss for years, we segued from a Jepson Blanc de Blancs to a magnum of Pepperwood Springs Pinot Noir, both from Mendocino County and of the 1989 vintage. It was October, a little more than a year ago, and Fran was celebrating the last of summer and the first of fall with a dish of baked tomatoes, served in a fresh tomato sauce vivid with garlic and fennel seeds, followed by cabbage stuffed with minced pork and chestnuts and garnished with young root vegetables, buttered and roasted. The fruit of the Pepperwood Springs wine, elegant and trumpet-pure, sailed above the tomatoes, the garlic, and the parsnips, but rather eclipsed, alas, the gentle harmony of a 1979 Hermitage of the Domaine de l'Ermite that accompanied a creamy Chaource—the cheese of pastoral northern Burgundy. We talked familiarly about children, now adults, reminisced about distant times and far away places, and gossiped about city politics before taking away with us a lingering memory of feather-light pastry, autumn raspberries, and a glass of Moscato d'Asti.

Wine, the thread that binds these essays together, is actually a prism. Through it we see the world—and ourselves—in a different light. If we pay attention, it gives us the measure of Spain's economy and tells us where the money that allowed Chile's first families to establish their prestigious nineteenth-century wine estates around Santiago came from.

Just by tasting the wines we can grasp the difference between classical, rank-conscious Bordeaux and voluptuous, democratic Burgundy. We can read California history in the evolution of its wines, and take the pulse of the organic farming movement by noticing how grape growing is changing. But all of it, eventually, comes back to the table, to the roast chicken and the fava beans and the pleasure we have in sitting together and talking.

CORTON:
THE HEART OF BURGUNDY

WHEN WE CHOOSE A WINE IN A HURRY, WE SOMETIMES DO LITTLE more than pick a name from the list. "That'll do." Yet at times the right choice is so obvious there's no point in hesitating. One evening last year, at dinner with friends in a restaurant where we were snug and safe from a pounding rainstorm, I instinctively turned to the comfort of red Burgundy, barely pausing before I asked for the 1989 *grand cru* Corton-Bressandes from Chandon de Briailles. Corton is called a magic mountain and Les Bressandes is, as Burgundians say, a *climat* on its prime east face. I find Burgundies of the 1989 vintage delicious—they have given me much more pleasure than the vaunted 1988s—and the Chandon de Briailles estate has been a model of well-judged winemaking since Nadine de Nicolay and her daughter Claude took over the management of their family property almost fifteen years ago. In short, I knew this particular bottle was a lucky find that would help us ignore the weather outside. The wine was ready and our glasses filled when the risotto of wild mushrooms, the sauté of sweetbreads, and the roast partridge with glazed chestnuts arrived at the table.

Actually, though it might indeed be magical, Corton is not a mountain at all. It's a massive hill a few miles north of Beaune, thrust forward and almost free from the long slope of Burgundy's Côte d'Or. Though officially in the Côte de Beaune, Corton produces red wines that rival some of the best of the Côte de Nuits. But the hill is aloof from both and seems rather to play the part of a giant hinge buckling together these two halves of the Côte d'Or at the point where the vine-covered slopes of the Côte de Beaune swing back to face the southeast, a subtle but important shift away from the unvarying eastern exposure of the Côte de Nuits. Corton's vines are displayed in a convex half-circle, from east to west, which gives some of them a southerly exposure rare in the Côte d'Or. And the changes in light and warmth from sunrise to sunset and from one part of the hill to another, multiplied by the effect of the vineyards' rapid climb up to twelve hundred feet, impose a diversity in the way the grapes form and ripen that is rarer still within the bounds of a single Burgundian *cru*. Corton is a place where one quickly grasps the significance of the word *climat* in distinguishing one vineyard site from another.

Corton is different in other ways, too—the most significant, perhaps, being that the bed of limestone running uniformly through the *grand crus* of the Côte de Nuits here dips abruptly below strata of chalky Oxfordian marls, clays, and iron-red oolites deposited nearly 150 million years ago, when much of western Europe was covered by Jurassic seas. The manifold layers were shaken up a few million years later when the Alps erupted not far to the east and have been worked on by wind and water ever since. The connections between the tannin in a wine and the clay in the vineyard; between a wine's deep, vibrant color and the effect of iron; and between a wine's full expressive aroma and the presence of chalk in the soil were forged by these distant events. In that sense, the glow of a Corton wine has origins that go back further than most of us can even begin to imagine.

Having said that, I must now admit that on the scale of that great chronological sweep, the vines from which Corton is produced arrived only yesterday. There could well have been a vineyard on the hill in the time of the Romans. The name, after all, is said to be a corruption of Curtis Orthonis, the domain of Orthon, a Roman courtier. But the real push to viticulture in the region started only with the arrival of the Burgundians fifteen hundred years ago. Their king initiated an enlightened policy that allowed men to take lawful possession of any uncultivated land on which they planted a vineyard. So plant they did. In the centuries following

Burgundy's conquest by the Franks in A.D. 534, however, ownership of the vineyards—and often of the men who worked them—was shared between church and nobles. Charles Martel seized church land, including vineyards on Corton, after his defeat of the Arabs at Poitiers in 732, claiming, rightly or wrongly, that the Burgundian churchmen had been lukewarm in supporting his opposition to the invaders.

His grandson, Charlemagne, gave much of it back, including the vineyards of the west and southwest sides of Corton that continue to bear his name. In 775 they went, as the personal gift of the emperor, to the collegial abbey of Saint-Andoche, in Saulieu. In those days the Charlemagne vineyards covered fewer than five acres; yet by the time they were seized during the French Revolution (to be sold as state property along with all other church holdings) they were double that size. In fact, in the thousand years between Charlemagne and the storming of the Bastille, vines had spread slowly over most of the hill. The progression had taken time because the slopes, uncommonly steep for Burgundy, were subject to soil erosion and cleft with open quarries where men had extracted the flat sheets of stone (laves) used in Burgundy for cottage roof tiles. Monks of the Cistercian order planted vines on Corton as early as 1160. Other vineyard proprietors included the cathedral chapter of Autun, the abbey of Sainte-Marguerite at nearby Bouilland, and the Knights Templar. Like the Cistercians, the dukes of Burgundy established a vineyard on Corton in the twelfth century. It's possible to keep close track of it through the ducal accounts: In 1427 it is referred to as the Vigne-Philippe, an allusion to Duke Philip the Good. It wasn't long after that, though, that King Louis XI of France, thenceforth master of Burgundy, sent his personal representative to Beaune expressly to change the vineyard's name in the local register to Clos du Roi. He wanted there to be no misunderstanding about what was now his.

* * * * * *

Corton and Corton-Charlemagne, the hill's twin *grand cru* appellations (one red, from Pinot Noir vines; the other white, from Chardonnay) are divided into roughly twenty of these named vineyards—*climats*. There is more than twice as much Corton produced as there is Corton-Charlemagne. It is the umbrella *grand cru* for red wine produced on much of the eastern, southeastern, and southern slopes of the hill. Charlemagne (Corton was hyphenated to it only in this century) was used historically for vineyards on the west and southwest slopes of the hill that were once associated with the emperor. Straddling the Aloxe-Corton and Pernand-Vergelesses border, they have been replanted any number of times—sometimes with red-wine varietals and sometimes with white—and still exist as the core of the Domaine Bonneau du Martray, the largest producer of Corton-Charlemagne. There is an unlikely legend that the first change from red to white in the Charlemagne vineyard occurred when the emperor's wife, Liutgard, objected to the wine stains on her husband's beard. "It's undignified!" she is said to have protested. In fact, both the soil and microclimate of the Charlemagne vineyards have always been better suited to white wines. The very small volume of red produced there is sold as Corton.

The Corton-Charlemagne *grand cru* appellation extends beyond the original Charlemagne holdings, however, and includes other vineyards recognized for white wines produced in the same terse style. Among them are Les Pougets and Les Languettes (two *climats* adjacent to Le Charlemagne), Le Corton and parts of Les Renardes (farther along the hill), as well as Corton *climats* that obtrude into neighboring Ladoix-Serrigny. All these vineyards also produce red wines sold as Corton, usually with the name of the *climat* hyphenated to it. White wines (and there are quite a number of them, though quantities are small) produced in the other Corton vineyards are deemed not to have Corton-Charlemagne characteristics and are therefore sold—confusingly or not, depending on one's point of view—as *grand cru* Corton Blanc.

What exactly are the characteristics of a Corton-Charlemagne? It's easiest to begin by saying that they include neither the fruit and body of certain Meursaults and Montrachets nor the rapier-keen steeliness of top-class Chablis. A young Corton-Charlemagne opens with a subdued, pebbly aroma and makes a taut and reserved impression on the palate. It's lively, however, and has a firm, elegant texture. Depending on the year, it can seem light and mild (1994), supple and delicately fleshy (1995), mouth filling (1996), or long and nervy (1997). The acids are usually good and help keep the wine fresh for years as it develops an astonishing complexity. With Louis Latour, I had a 1990 Corton-Charlemagne that was the taste equivalent of silk shimmering in light, and a 1985, a wine with an almost honeyed intensity.

I have only once seen a specific vineyard of origin mentioned on the label of a bottle of Corton-Charlemagne; I don't think it's customary. But it is standard practice to show the particular origin of a Corton *grand cru*. When the name is used alone, without indication of vineyard, the wine is almost always a blend drawn from different sites within the *grand cru* or, as in the case of Louis Latour's Château Corton-Grancy and François Faiveley's Clos des Cortons-Faiveley, from an estate vineyard (theirs are at the center of the coveted east face) that doesn't fit neatly into the confines of one specific *climat.*

But whether it's a blend or from a single *climat,* what is it that distinguishes a Corton from other red wines of the Côte d'Or? When I put this question to a number of growers recently, their answers took a similar direction. "A Corton wine is male," says François Faiveley, whose family has long been a proprietor of vineyards there. "It is more vigorous than other red wines of the Côte d'Or." Philippe Senard of the Domaine Comte Senard agrees. "A young Corton is assertive," he says. "There's something violent about it. It's the Burgundy that gains most from aging." Nadine de Nicolay, a woman as graceful as her wines, also sees in her Corton wines qualities she referred to as masculine. "Savigny and Pernand [neighboring villages] are flowery and fruity, but Corton has the darker aromas of the woods—bark and mushrooms," she said.

From my own experience I would say that a young Corton is distinctive among Burgundies for its focus and curious impression of raw energy. I suppose that's the violence Philippe Senard referred to. But when mature, a well-made Corton of good vintage is as sumptuous as it is possible for a wine to be.

Even when differentiating Corton from other Burgundies, however, all the producers I spoke to laid greater emphasis on Corton's own diversity.

"It's so broad," Faiveley said to me when we lunched together in Nuits-Saint-Georges one day, "that I'm always surprised to find Corton existing at all as a single *grand cru.*"

"Each Corton *climat* has such an individual character," Nathalie Tollot, of Domaine Tollot-Beaut & Fils, told me, "that when tasting, one is repeatedly confronting the most basic notions of *terroir.*

"For example," she says, "a wine from Les Renardes is always wild, no matter who grows the grapes."

Senard also finds a savage quality in wine from Renardes. "It makes one think of game, of fur," he told me. "Each site imposes clear characteristics of its own. A Perrières, just as the name suggests, gives a reticent, stony impression. The wines of Bressandes are the most refined of Corton, but they are very muscular, too. Their combination of strength and grace always puts me in mind of a dancer. Wines of Combes are robust, at first even rude, rustic. But it's the wines of the Clos du Roi that, for me, most typically represent what a Corton should be. They have attack, power, and—if you like—a certain majesty."

"To some extent we can impose style on a wine in the cellar," says Jacques Lardière, technical wine director at Louis Jadot. "But we can't impose character, and we can't impose quality either. They come with the vine and the *terroir.* When we try to bring out the expression of a particular *climat* we must take into account the circumstances of the year and, if necessary, modify accordingly both our expectations and the techniques we apply."

"A wine's *terroir* just is," says Nadine de Nicolay. "We do nothing to dramatize it, but we do make an effort to protect it. We avoid the use of fertilizers, which encourages the vine to root deeply and draw on all that is there in the soil. The power and length of a wine comes only from the vine. The kind of power that comes from working the skins and the juice in the course of making wine is superficial; it does not give the wine finesse. On the contrary, it usually destroys any it might have had."

The confidence to react with sensibility to the possibilities of each year comes with experience. "Even if a growing season has been difficult, we make sure that the wine shows as well as it can," Senard told me. "But we must do that without distorting or exaggerating or forcing anything for effect. At each moment I know instinctively what I must do and what I mustn't. But I couldn't explain to anyone else what I am doing or why."

Senard's way of dealing with a vintage, or of approaching a *cru* like Corton, is unlikely to be the same as his neighbor's. That's why two wines from the same site and the same year will always be different. Nathalie Tollot said that the characteristics of the vineyard will always come through—she referred specifically to Les Renardes—"no matter who grows the grapes." She didn't say "no matter who makes the wines" because she knows that every producer has a clear signature. Two wines from one cellar but from distinct sites are likely to show a greater similarity than two wines from grapes grown on one site in the same year made into wine by different producers. There are obvious differences, for example, between the rather massive Cortons of Louis Jadot, where Lardière believes in extracting and revealing the essential *terroir* through long vatting; and the more delicate wines of Louis Latour, who racks a new wine from the skins as soon as he thinks he has what he wants from them, and tames rather than accentuates the *terroir* by tucking in the tannins as discreetly as Beaux Arts architects kept their structural girders hidden from view.

Of recent vintages, perhaps the only one that called for particular restraint on the part of all producers was the 1994. The wines were naturally meager: They lacked flesh, and any attempt to extract more from the grapes would have unbalanced them and made them harsh. Any modest charm would have been lost.

The 1993s, on the other hand, have color and power to excess. Nadine de Nicolay told me that her Clos du Roi was so concentrated that at first it could have been confused with a Cabernet Sauvignon. "The tannins were ripe and soft but they were huge," she said. Almost all the Cortons of this vintage have a distinct suggestion of licorice. The 1995s are supple and fragrant, and I prefer them to the 1996s, though most Burgundians would have it the other way around. In the long term, particularly as far as Corton is concerned, they could be right. But at present I find the 1996s closed in, rather as the 1988s were; they have the same dense tannins and austere acids. The 1997s are already delicious and will continue to be so for a while. Their tannins are fine, their acids moderate, and their fruit flattering. Tollot thinks they'll turn out like the 1989s, "but with more substance."

If she's right, that will suit me very well—I like the 1989s. Their charm was revealed in a 1989 Clos des Cortons-Faiveley offered at my lunch with François Faiveley, as it had been in the Corton-Bressandes 1989 of Chandon de Briailles chosen to accompany my roast partridge and hold a rainstorm at bay. That Corton-Bressandes had been deceptively mellow: Its bouquet and flavor, bringing together the still-youthful elegance of Pinot Noir and sweetly nostalgic reminders of fall (the glazed chestnuts could not have been more appropriate), masked a discreet power that was exhilarating. The wine had finesse—it evolved on the tongue between sip and swallow—and, whatever Mme. de Nicolay might have to say about the distinction of her Cortons in relation to the floweriness of neighboring wines, it left an impression of woodland violets.

It certainly made our evening. I remember thinking how calm the night was when we finally left the restaurant. The rain had stopped and the clouds were drifting away.

LUNCH AT DUCRU-BEAUCAILLOU

A FAMILY LUNCH WITH JEAN-EUGÈNE, MONIQUE, AND BRUNO
Borie of Château Ducru-Beaucaillou began with a glass of Pol Roger
before we sat down to a mushroom flan with Château Haut-Batailly '88;
roast chicken surrounded by young vegetables with Château Grand-Puy-
Lacoste '83; two or three cheeses with Château Ducru-Beaucaillou '78;
and *îles flottantes,* those perennial puffs of soft meringue draped with
threads of caramel, drifting in a light custard.

The wines were there for pleasure not study, but each was typical of
its separate Borie property and summed up the year in which it was
made. The Haut-Batailly, reliably elegant, was classically composed and,
with its mature flavor, seemed more forward than other '88s I'd had
during my visit to Bordeaux. The Grand-Puy-Lacoste, robust as always,
was both supple and generous. It had the concentration of the best of
the '83s, for many growers a commendable vintage that can no more
escape the shadow of '82 than '85 can get round the roadblock of the
acclaimed—questionably, I think—'86.

The '78 had the depth, finesse, and suave assurance expected of a
Ducru-Beaucaillou in its prime. Taking stock now of the wines of the
1970s, I am convinced that, despite some extraordinary '71s (Lafite,
Haut-Brion, Pétrus, Cheval-Blanc, and Cos d'Estournel immediately
come to mind), 1978, a year over which there was originally little fuss,

has proven to be the most reliable vintage of the entire decade. The Ducru-Beaucaillou '78 offered ample justification for such a view.

Later in the day, writing up my notes about those wines with the benefit of perspective, I saw and appreciated more clearly the easy logic with which one wine had prepared us for the next, and the way each dish had underlined the characteristics of the wine it accompanied. I was struck particularly by the artful contribution of the mushroom flan. It had helped draw attention to the mature flavors, woodsy and autumnal, just emerging in the Haut-Batailly '88, by establishing the key—I use the term in its musical sense—in which we would best enjoy them, as well as those of older wines to follow. Some years ago a banquet offered by the Syndicat des Grands Crus at Château Mouton-Rothschild had opened with a mushroom tart and a trio of '79s with the same effect. And last winter, after a morning spent gathering chanterelles and *trompettes de la mort* in the woods of the Santa Cruz Mountains in California, a group of us sat down in the David Bruce Winery to eat them at a feast generously prepared by visiting chefs who had hunted for the mushrooms with us. They accompanied some of the winery's deliciously bottle-aged Chardonnays and Pinot Noirs.

It borders on the precious, perhaps, to talk about the "key" in which we eat and drink—as if we were coming to grips with a sonata rather than a glass of wine and a drumstick—but the first bite and the first sip always shape our expectations of what is to follow. A slice of country *pâté* and a glass of Beaujolais establish one key whereas a dish of sweetbreads in a sorrel cream sauce accompanied by a glass of Meursault-Genevrieres establishes another—even though either, in fact, could be the prelude to roast veal and a bottle of Volnay. Will the veal and Volnay taste the same in each case?

Some of us get stuck in a particular key and taste what is placed in front of us based on inappropriate assumptions. We fail to appreciate it, let alone enjoy it. I think this is what's happened to many people who approach mature red wines in a key dictated by the vocabulary of the analytical tasting notes now bombarding us in newsletters, magazines, and specialist publications. The greater part of the problem is that those notes refer most often to barely stable new wines, only recently fallen bright from the tumult of fermentation. Our eyes glaze over (mine do, at least) as we read the litany of fruit aromas, ranging from black currants to black cherries, punctuated by references to acidity and tannins. A very young red wine will almost always remind us of summer fruits for the good reason that it is still little more than a summer fruit itself. Such information is of use only when it applies to red wine destined for early bottling and immediate consumption—certain kinds of Chinon, for instance, or Beaujolais, a light Zinfandel or a Côtes-du-Rhône *en primeur*. Wines expected to remain in wood for two more years will evolve and bear scant resemblance to what they were when those notes were written. They will, it is hoped, change even more in bottle.

Still, these incessant references to berries and tannins, though of little relevance and even misleading to anyone who will taste the wines fifteen, ten, or even five years later, reverberate in our heads. They establish—inappropriately—the key in which an increasing number of us approach any red wines. We look for bright fruit and broad-shouldered tannins. But a mature red wine in its prime should offer subtlety and nuance rather than a blast of crushed berries. Within its skein of aromas and flavors there should be hints of mushroom and truffle. We should have cause to think of velvet and old silk rather than tannins and acidity. Indeed, if either tannins or acidity is still noticeable after ten years, then the wine is unbalanced. A wine might well take far longer than that to deliver all it promises, but, in maturity, its tannins and acids should be sufficiently in equilibrium to pass without comment.

Any wine, young or old, is more than an amalgam of smells and tastes and organic components waiting to be picked apart, labeled, numbered, and nailed to the wall. A mature wine, particularly, embraces qualities we hardly perceive on a conscious level. Some years ago, a newspaper report of an exhibition of American photographs at the Pompidou Center in Paris compared the best of them, those that captured the intensity of a moment in patterns of light and shade the photographer could not possibly have contrived, with *haiku*, the seventeen-syllable verse in which the Japanese seize a fleeting emotion that is and is gone. Wine, too, changing even as we taste it, delivers a message with meaning only in our response. If we are in the right key when we receive it, our eyes will shine and we shall radiate pleasure. Hence the importance of Monique Borie's mushroom flan.

CÔTE RÔTIE AND CONDRIEU:
A DIVERSION

BEFORE *AUTOROUTES* SWEPT TRAFFIC FROM PARIS TO THE SOUTH
of France in hours, the Beau Rivage at Condrieu was for years a favorite
stopover of mine, close enough to the Route Nationale 7 (known in
those days, with good cause, as *la Meurtrière,* or the Murderess) to be
convenient, but far enough away, across the river, to be tranquil—which
it still is. It's a smarter place than I knew in the '60s, but when I stayed
there I missed the Castaings, the former owners. Or perhaps what I
really missed, in what were still familiar surroundings, was the style
prevalent at small country hotels in France in the fifties and sixties.
There was a simple warmth then, an absence of fuss, but a quick eye for
the details that mattered. At any rate, dinner was good—excellent
cheeses followed a John Dory—and was served by lamplight on the
hotel's enlarged terrace overlooking the river. As darkness fell, the pretty
bridge across the Rhône, a few hundred yards upstream, was softly
floodlit, and its reflection shimmered in the water. Condrieu's dramatically steep vineyards were just behind us.

Just north of Condrieu and extending to either side of the rather
drab little town of Ampuis are the even more steeply terraced vineyards
of Côte Rôtie. The Rhône here flows in a southwesterly direction, and so
these slopes above its right bank face southeast and catch the morning
sun. Recent research at the University of Bordeaux has revealed that vine
leaves use the energy of sunlight more efficiently in the late morning

than in the afternoon, which is perhaps the reason many of the great wine regions of France—in particular the Médoc, the Côte d'Or of Burgundy, and Alsace—have evolved where vineyards have an east or southeastern exposure. On the Côte Rôtie the vines, supported by high tripods of wood stakes rather than by wires, are planted very densely on narrow ledges held in place by walls of unmortared rock first constructed in the time of the Romans.

· · · · · ·

Gilles Barge, president of the association of Côte Rôtie growers, lives a short walk up the hill from the *place* in front of Ampuis' church. An articulate and very friendly man, Barge had come in from his vines to talk to me and was in his work boots and shorts. I asked him about those ancient terraces.

"The terraces keep things here much as they've always been," he began. "Change would be difficult for the Côte Rôtie. When growers elsewhere began to take horses into their vineyards, we couldn't, any more than we can use tractors today. We must work our soil with our hands, as we've always done. The only novelty is that we can sometimes spray by helicopter.

"It's because the work here is largely done by hand that holdings are so small. One man can't cultivate more than two or three acres without help, and it's been difficult for us to find hired labor. Who wants to work with a hoe for eight hours a day?

"At the beginning of the century, there were almost nine hundred acres of vines on the Côte Rôtie, but so many of the young men from these villages were lost in World War I that vineyards were abandoned. The situation was worse after 1945, when our wine sold for the same low price as the ordinary wine being grown down on the plain. It was discouraging. The fruit and vegetable farms by the river were doing well then. Industry was expanding south from Lyon—only twenty miles away—toward Ampuis and offering young people good pay and security. By the beginning of the sixties there were no more than a hundred fifty acres of productive vines on the Côte Rôtie, and not more than a dozen growers."

In the general decline, Barge went on to explain, even the mule tracks on the hillsides disappeared. Everything, including the harvest, was carried up and down on the backs of men. Alfred Gérin, the mayor of Ampuis at the time, thought the vineyards would disappear altogether. The world doesn't lack for wine, after all.

"But, when vineyards are two thousand years old," Barge continued, "and have been nurtured all that time to give a wine of unique character, they have a spirit that must be preserved. We had a responsibility to our children. So in 1963 Gérin built a road up the hillside to improve access to the vineyards. It was a simple, narrow road and very steep in places. But it made such an immediate difference to the growers that Gérin built another, and now there's a network of little roads so that we can get to the vineyards more easily with cars and small trucks.

"Gérin's move saved the *vignoble*. He saved the town. We are now back to four hundred fifty acres of vineyard, and our association has one hundred thirty-two grower members. Forty of them produce enough wine to justify bottling it under their own labels, and about twenty families live from their vineyards alone.

"But in the sixties we were still backward: even our standard of winemaking had fallen. Côte Rôtie wines have always had power and structure, but they had become rustic. We now have a new generation of growers, the majority of them aged under forty and most of them trained at the viticultural high school in Beaune. The resulting change shows both in the vineyards and in the cellars.

"We stick to local tradition. We'd rather warm the must to get a slow fermentation going with our own natural yeast than use a selected yeast from a laboratory. Selected yeasts can make all wine taste the same. We understand better today the why of what we do, and so we do it more appropriately and more effectively."

✦ ✦ ✦ ✦ ✦ ✦

Even those who know little else about the Côte Rôtie know that part of it is called the Côte Blonde and part the Côte Brune. Wine books recount legends of a land inheritance divided between two daughters (one blond and one brunette, of course), but the difference between the Côte Blonde and the Côte Brune is geological rather than legendary. Such topsoil as there is on the Côte Rôtie is a sandy decomposition of granite; but the formation of the quartzlike mica beneath differs from the Blonde to the Brune, giving the vines on either side of the divide different access to water and nutrients. (For the technically minded, it's gneiss on the Blonde side and mica-schist on the Brune.) The difference is made more emphatic by the presence on the Côte Brune of clay rich in iron oxide. The iron not only darkens the soil of that part of the hill but also deepens the color and intensifies the tannin of its wine.

But there is more to the Côte Rôtie than the Côte Blonde and Côte Brune, which together account for only a hundred acres. Most growers have vines scattered along the entire slope, and so the wines made from their assembled grapes, all reds, have traditionally been sold simply as Côte Rôtie. The fact is that the best-balanced wines usually are made from such combinations anyway. Nevertheless, small as the appellation is, the market, it is said, demands an even tighter specificity of origin. To satisfy (and perhaps feed?) this somewhat academic interest, Côte Rôtie's production is increasingly bottled with the names of various sections of its slopes on the labels. One has seen references to the Côte Blonde and Côte Brune, of course, for many years; but some producers now use names taken from old village survey maps that as yet have no legal standing. One official of the Institut National des Appellations d'Origine in Paris told me recently, "The only officially recognized appellation in Côte Rôtie is Côte Rôtie, period."

"We're under pressure from the producers," Gilles Barge said, "to come up with distinctive names for every little part of the hill." He looked hard at me before adding, "The producers know that writers like something they can pick over."

I knew as well as he that dividing the steadily swelling production of Côte Rôtie into many small lots of individual wines, each carefully and separately promoted—with or without the connivance of wine writers, and with or without the support of appellation law—creates scarcities that usually lead in only one direction. It's an old marketing ploy. But I suppose the Côte Rôtie growers have to find the money to keep their ter-races in repair and the hoes busy.

◆ ◆ ◆ ◆ ◆ ◆

Armed with glasses, we went into the cellar where Barge keeps his wine in large and well-matured oak casks, each holding five hundred gallons or more. He seemed to have very few barrels of standard size, and with Columella in mind (in the first century he'd asserted that the particular taste of these northern Rhône wines owed much to the powdered bark of a local tree, used as a preservative) I asked him about the role of oak in making a Côte Rôtie wine.

"New oak barrels certainly add something," he began diplomatically, doubtless remembering his role as president of the association of *all* the growers of Côte Rôtie. Then he warmed to his subject. "But too often they are used to excess, and the finesse of our wines is lost. When oak dominates, the wine is no longer typical of this appellation. So often now one tastes only the oak—the toast, the vanillin—and not the char-acter of this place. That's not in our interest. Anyone can buy new wood and sell the taste of it, even if the wine has no character at all. Obviously it's better to use new wood than old, spoiled barrels. But one must always use it with discretion."

Barge assembles his various lots to make one Côte Rôtie each year. He handed me a sample of the 1992, drawn from wood. It had the aroma and flavor of violets. The wine was full and velvety, yet firm.

In my experience, Côte Rôtie at its best is always more aromatic than Hermitage and more polished than Cornas, the two other major red wines of the northern Rhône. Cornas has more muscle and Hermitage more heart, but the refinement of Côte Rôtie has an almost intellectual appeal. Barge and I went on to the 1991: It was less sumptuous than the 1992 but equally aromatic and elegantly silky. Silkiness is a characteristic of Côte Rôtie when the use of the white grape Viognier is mingled with black Syrah, the grape that is normally dominant in the northern Rhône.

"The appellation law allows us to include up to 20 percent Viognier," Barge explained, "but nobody uses more than 5 percent; most of us prefer much less, and some none at all. Viognier is a very aromatic grape, and when picked fully ripe it adds a roundness and a slightly higher than normal alcohol to our blends, creating the 'fat' that smoothes the edges of the Syrah. The little Viognier in my wine is important—it brings finesse and a certain grace."

Barge's 1990 had a rich color and concentrated flavor. It had been a dry year on the Côte Rôtie, and the vines suffered. Rain in late August helped, but the grapes dehydrated even as they ripened. Knowing this, I expected the wine to be tough. In fact, there was only a suggestion of hardness at the close, and I assumed that it was again a matter of the Viognier tempering any severity.

Although Viognier can now be found in some vineyards in the southern Rhône (and as far afield as California), it is associated with the adjoining appellations of Condrieu and Côte Rôtie more exclusively than any other variety is with any other place. Though some believe Viognier to be descended from an indigenous wild vine, others think that it may have arrived in Condrieu from the Dalmatian coast of the Adriatic in the third century. At the time the emperor Probus had just lifted the edict, issued by Domitian two hundred years before, that limited the extent of vineyards outside Italy, and it's likely that there followed a big rush for cuttings from wherever one could get them. Why not from Dalmatia?

· · · · · ·

As the leading grower in Condrieu, Georges Vernay is, by definition, the world's leading Viognier grower. He said that in Condrieu, too, there had been long years of decline before the present revival. "As recently as 1980 only sixty acres of Viognier were left," he told me. "But there are two hundred now, and we hope eventually to more than triple that number, as the appellation allows.

"We do have a few patches of clay and chalk, where we could, if we wished, make a passable red wine," he went on, "but our sand is really better suited to white. The boundaries for the appellation extend up the hill from the village; that is, we go from 520 feet above sea level up to 975 feet, or 300 meters. Wine produced above that contour and on the plateau at the very top is simply *vin de pays*."

In addition to his seventeen and a half acres of Condrieu, Vernay has vines on the Côte Rôtie, within the Saint-Joseph appellation farther south near Tournon, and on some of the land entitled only to a *vin de pays* designation. With thirty-five acres in all, he has six men working full time with him and his son. "We do everything the old way," he told me. "We even do without herbicides; the grass comes in handy for mulch."

We tasted as we talked, and he got me started with a 1992 Viognier from vines outside the Condrieu appellation. A *vin de pays*, it had the flowery aromas I associate with Viognier, and an attractive but odd suggestion of hazelnuts. It was very good; but, tasting Vernay's 1991 Condrieu immediately afterward, I was reminded once more why certain vines are entitled to an appellation while others are not. The Condrieu was more concentrated and its aroma much more intense, dominated by the smell of hawthorn blossom.

Vernay handed me next a glass of his 1991 Côteau de Veron, a Condrieu he makes with greater emphasis on oak (two-thirds of the wine is fermented in barrel). The wood masks the essential aromas and flavor of Viognier. It was an interesting variant, carefully made to avoid exaggeration, but I did wonder what the advantage was when the other wine, to my taste, was so much more delectable. Vernay wouldn't make it if his customers didn't want it, yet I find this passion for the taste of wood for its own sake perplexing. I find that oak in wine is like garlic in cooking: If it is noticeable as a separate and distinct taste, then it's too strong. Someone should be marketing packets of Columella's oak powder so that those who want oak can add their own, to suit their own taste, and stir. But that would give the game away.

Finally we tasted Vernay's 1990 Condrieu. It was bigger than the 1991: The aroma and flavor were even more concentrated, and it had a fatter, richer texture with a much longer finish. Vernay also has about six acres of vines on the Côte Rôtie, most of which are more than fifty years old, and before I left he showed me the 1991 and 1990 wines made from them. The 1990 was especially remarkable—a sleek, aromatic wine with just a hint of bitter almond at the end. But what interested me particularly was a 1990 Côtes du Rhône bottled under his Saint-Agathe label, which we had tasted only in order to adjust our palates after the Condrieu. It was extraordinarily good—and more reasonably priced, of course, than any of the grander wines of the northern Rhône.

• • • • • •

Prior to going to dinner, I decided to see for myself one of Gérin's roads, so I pointed my rented VW at the hill and went for it. Getting up was tricky: The engine stalled more than once approaching the awkward, unbelievably steep turns. But it was on the way down that the little car earned my respect. The descent was, shall I say, breathtaking, a real test of my steering (and nerves) and of the car's brakes.

Having collected myself, I slipped across the river to La Pyramide, in Vienne, a revered destination in the annals of French gastronomy, for it was here that Fernand Point reigned over what was, in his day, the finest kitchen in France. I had last lunched here a few years before, when the restaurant was being continued by Point's widow, and remembered a pleasant enough lunch served to me under a tree in the courtyard.

Since then the restaurant has been closed, sold and resold, turned into a cooking school, and finally purchased by Dominique Bouillon, a Paris businessman as well as a friend and client of Point's. He couldn't bear to see the repeated degradation of a place he felt should be recognized as the national monument it really is. Bouillon has since sold his share to his partner Patrick Henriroux, a young chef who had previously worked at La Ferme de Mougins near Cannes and before that with Georges Blanc in Vonnas.

I had heard that a vast sum had been spent on restoring La Pyramide to its former splendor. When I arrived I found that, despite other changes, the old graveled courtyard, trees still in place, was much as I remembered it. It had merely been paved over to make a canvas-shaded, summer dining room. The atmosphere was both chic and relaxed, the service impeccable, and the food delicious.

The sommelier at La Pyramide was advertised on the wine list as having won all kinds of awards, including that of the Best Young Sommelier in France. I asked if he could find in the cellar just a half bottle of a Gilles Barge Côte Rôtie older than those I had tasted in Barge's cellar. He wasn't successful in finding the 1985 I was hoping for, but he did find a half bottle of the 1988. Though then still young, of course, it opened up in a decanter, and with my veal chop and sauté of wild mushrooms it brought the day to a fine and fitting close.

The producers of Côte Rôtie and of Condrieu are so few and the volume of wine made by any one of them is so limited that these wines are not in broad distribution in the United States. Occasionally a retailer will have a Côte Rôtie or a Condrieu on display, but the allocation of any single wine is usually so small that it will be kept in the stockroom for those customers who are seriously interested. Often a retailer will sell such wines prior to their arrival through a mailing to account customers or by placing a few telephone calls. Anyone interested in buying Côte Rôtie or Condrieu is well advised to ask to be included in any offering before a shipment arrives.

CAHORS:
AN ANCIENT WINE

IN TODAY'S FRANCE OF HIGH-SPEED TRAINS, NEW ROADS, AND frequently scheduled domestic flights, Cahors—400 miles from Paris and 120 from Bordeaux on the southwest flank of the Massif Central—is uncommonly difficult to reach. It's as if this now tranquil place, once, ironically, a financial and trading hub on the Roman road from La Rochelle to Nîmes and still surrounded by castles that bear crumbling witness to its role in past conflicts, had decided to sit things out for a while. I've known Cahors and its wine, one of the most ancient of France, since the 1950s; and because it seems to be well into a serious revival, I went back there recently to renew my acquaintance.

Made traditionally from Auxerrois grapes (a variety once widely planted in Bordeaux and still found there under its better-known name of Malbec), Cahors wine, noted for its color, distinctive aroma—sometimes I think of violets, sometimes ink—and a firm, tannic grip that loosens with time, was greatly esteemed even in the early Middle Ages. Later, when trade across the English Channel was given a boost by the twelfth-century marriage of Eleanor of Aquitaine to England's future Henry II, it accounted for roughly half the wine shipped from Bordeaux—a port to which Cahors had access via the Lot River, a tributary of the Garonne.

By the early 1300s, however, when the burgesses of Bordeaux won London trading privileges for their wines and expanded their vineyards to take advantage of their luck, they had taken steps to reduce competition from Cahors by restricting its port access during the autumn months, when fleets came to Bordeaux to pick up the year's new wine. Even after the French crown gained control of Bordeaux in 1453, the city fathers knew how to keep their privileges and did so until the revolution of 1789. They excepted a "black wine" made at Cahors by heating crushed grapes in cauldrons before fermentation to concentrate the juice and maximize color. Bordeaux needed it for blending with its own light-colored wines and was ready to pay well for it. It was a concoction, however, never intended for drinking and probably undrinkable. It gave rise to myths that now distort expectations of what Cahors should be. Mention the name of the wine, and someone is sure to respond with a story that purports to explain why Cahors is no longer as black as it once was.

The damage done to Cahors by Bordeaux is well documented, but, in spite of all that, Cahors' reputation, at least, flourished. The wine's greatest success came, at last, in the nineteenth century, when Bordeaux's privileges were finally at an end. The wine, introduced to Russia by Peter the Great, had been adopted for regular use in the Orthodox mass there. Then, in the 1850s, when oidium, a powdery fungus, appeared in the vineyards of Bordeaux with devastating effect, demand for Cahors rose spectacularly, and the wine entered a golden age. It was short-lived, alas. Phylloxera, which had first been seen in the area as early as 1866, had completely destroyed the vineyards by 1884. The Russians, meanwhile, had reacted by planting "Cahors" vineyards in the Crimea, where they continue to this day to produce something called Kaorskoie Vino.

The first attempt of Cahors growers to graft their Auxerrois vines onto phylloxera-resistant American rootstocks failed, leaving many vineyard owners so desperate for income that they planted hybrids to make a red *ordinaire*—and a quick return. By the time Cahors wines were again available, their traditional markets had been lost to the cheap Midi wines surging through France on the recently completed railway system as well as to the *ordinaires* produced in the Lot Valley itself. One setback followed another: The Russian market disappeared with its revolution, economic depression hurt everybody, and two world wars diverted attention from all else. Replanting came to a halt, in fact, and production of authentic Cahors, as opposed to the *ordinaires* from hybrids, became so meager that after the frosts of 1956 and 1957 almost none at all was to be had.

Recovery from that low point began soon after, when a few of the growers persuaded José Baudel, a native of Cahors, to leave his position as chief of the government's viticultural research center in Bordeaux and return to the Lot Valley to help save their wine from extinction. Upon arrival as the newly appointed director of the local cooperative wine cellar at Parnac, Baudel found 95 percent of the vineyards given over to hybrids, with the few hectares still planted with Auxerrois in a sorry state. It took years to propagate the cuttings needed for wide-scale replanting, but his program was eventually completed.

Today the hybrids have disappeared: There are over ten thousand acres of Cahors appellation vineyards, many with twenty- and thirty-year-old vines; and wines from the region's leading estates are again appearing in serious restaurants after an absence of close to a century. Some growers are less enthusiastic than others about the number of more modest Cahors wines to be found on French supermarket shelves. Wine producers, especially when their region is struggling for recognition, are always sensitive about image, but everyone is happy with the present annual production of twenty-five million bottles. Cahors has come far from its former status as a curiosity of the past.

◆　◆　◆　◆　◆　◆

Georges Pompidou, while president of France, had been an early supporter of Cahors. He had a country house in the Lot Valley and his partiality for the wines of Clos de Gamont, in particular, was well-known. It's said that the region attained full *appellation contrôlée* status in 1971 largely because of his personal intervention, though it's perhaps relevant that his minister of agriculture, Bernard Pons, acquired a vineyard property near Cahors at about that same time. In fact, as word of the renaissance of Cahors spread, along with the wine itself, so did the number of its champions.

Alain Senderens, of the celebrated Paris restaurant Lucas-Carton; Alain-Dominique Perrin, president of Cartier's international division; and Margrethe II, queen of Denmark, among others, acquired houses and vineyards locally. Discreetly—there's nothing showy about Cahors—the wine and its region became fashionable.

It was the wine itself that caught the attention of those who invested in the area, but part of the appeal of owning vineyards there is undoubtedly the charm of the Lot Valley. The appellation covers some thirty miles of it—from just east of Cahors down to the village of Soturac—and varies in width, north and south of the river, from one or two miles to five or six. Economic historians will explain the development of vineyards below Cahors by pointing out that the Lot is navigable downstream from that point, allowing the wine to reach distant markets. But more significant is the fact that below Cahors the Lot flows very slowly and loops to and fro to create and almost encircle the tiny peninsulas on which the turrets and old houses of Cahors, Luzech, and Puy-l'Evêque stand in tight formation. Here the river, shifting about in a distant past, deposited sand, silt, and gravel from the defunct volcanoes of the Massif Central, forming gently sloping terraces where vines could be planted. Above the vineyards dense oak woods on hillsides too steep to cultivate hide from view the vines now extending onto the harsh terrain of the plateau—the Causse—that spreads on either side of the valley.

Game, mushrooms, and truffles from those woods have contributed much to the tradition of Lot Valley cooking, founded on the goose, lamb, ham, chicken, *foie gras*, fruits—especially fresh prunes and peaches—tender young vegetables, and flat, creamy-yellow *cabécou* cheeses for which the region is renowned. We shouldn't be surprised that the wine is good, too.

• • • • • •

Jules Guyot, in his multivolume study of the wine regions of France, published in 1876, describes "the symmetry, the regularity, the cleanliness and elegance" of the Cahors vineyards. In his day the vines were planted no more densely than they are today, but they were pruned low, without wires, in what we call a goblet format. Freestanding vines usually carry less fruit than vines supported by wire trellising, and Guyot tells us that those Cahors vineyards yielded, on average, twenty hectoliters to the hectare. In terms of the measures we use in California, that's the equivalent of an extremely low yield of one and a half tons of grapes to the acre.

Growers reestablishing the region's vineyards seem less familiar with Jules Guyot and his low-yielding pruned vines, however, than they are with legends of Cahors' "black wine." Convinced that the area's red wine was once much darker, tougher, and more tannic, they wrote their appellation regulations twenty-five years ago accordingly: Some growers wanted the right to use Merlot, in order to avoid excessively "black" and tannic wine; others, certain that Cahors *should* be black and tannic, asked for the right to introduce Tannat, a tough and late-ripening grape from the Pyrenees. Cahors growers were therefore authorized to blend up to 30 percent of either variety, or a mixture of the two, with the traditional Auxerrois. Most of them introduced both, in proportions based, I suspect, on nothing more than hunch. Many of those same growers are now not sure they need either. Neither had been in use when I last visited Cahors in 1963. At that time, what's more, the Auxerrois vines were often mingled with peach trees. That was the case at Clos Triguédina, where Jean-Luc Baldès is now in charge. He was surprised that I had known and done business with his grandfather and told me he was readopting some of his ideas.

"At present we have 75 percent Auxerrois in our vineyards," Baldès told me, "with Merlot and Tannat making up the balance. But my best *cuvée*, Prince Probus, is made from Auxerrois alone—the way my grandfather did it. If Auxerrois alone gives me my best wine, I don't see why I need the other varieties. So I'm replacing them as I replant. I think Auxerrois is a more authentic expression of Cahors anyway."

The late Jean Jouffreau of Clos de Gamot would have applauded him. A traditionalist who made some of the best wines in Cahors, Jouffreau never used anything but Auxerrois. His son-in-law, Yves Hermann, for many years in charge of Jouffreau's second property, Château du Cayrou, and now of Clos de Gamot too, is also a traditionalist, even if he has used small amounts of Merlot and Tannat at Cayrou. Hermann's wines are sumptuous, perhaps the result of allowing natural yeasts to govern fermentation. "It takes two or three days for indigenous yeast to get started," he told me, "and in the meantime the grape skins, macerating in the juice before alcohol is formed, release color without excessive tannin." What I noticed particularly about the Cayrou wines was the clear way each reflected the style of its vintage: 1990, concentrated but elegant; 1989, more robust (tweed rather than silk); 1988, firmly structured; 1985, powerful but delicate; and 1982, silky, long, and seductive.

Philippe Bernède of Clos La Coutale—"we have made wine here for eight generations"—does not apologize for using supplemental varieties and is happy with what each contributes. "Tannat gives fruit and added strength as well as tannin," he told me. "Merlot gives the wine flesh. Our vines are thirty years old and are all planted on the gravel of the upper terraces, so they ripen well. But I watch the yields of individual vines closely. Forget the hectoliters to the hectare; if a vine is allowed to carry too much fruit, the tannins will not ripen.

"I like a good extraction, and I ferment at a warm temperature to get it. Then, when fermentation is over, I keep the wine warm for another week or so, tasting it daily for flavor and roundness before taking it off the skins. Something happens during that week. I don't know if the skins break down or if the alcohol acts on the tannins ... but I can taste the difference and know when the right moment has come."

Bernède's 1995, then still in wood, was concentrated, harmonious, and surprisingly velvety for such a young wine. "I like elegance," his wife, Andrea, said to me as all three of us were tasting together. "My husband likes substance and character. So we are both happy with this wine."

* * * * * *

If Philippe Bernède is the eighth generation of his family to produce Cahors wine, Alain-Dominique Perrin, of Château Lagrezette, is the first. His is a splendid, money-no-object estate. As if the château itself, all towers and red tiles, were not handsome enough, the cellars, carved from a hillside so that the wine moves by gravity rather than with the aid of pumps from tank to tank on different levels, are spectacular in their efficiency. Everything possible, it seemed to me, had been provided for.

Perrin has done more than most to attract attention to Cahors, but some of his initiatives have been controversial. For example, not everyone agrees with his promotion of "spring wines," *cuvées* of Cahors made to be drunk young and—sin of sins—cool. I was skeptical myself until I tasted his Moulin Lagrezette and found it among the most expressively Auxerrois wines I had tasted all week. True, its lightness and fruit are a departure from the classic Cahors style, but the existence of the one type need not be a bar to the other.

Muriel Delmas, Lagrezette's winemaker, offered to draw three samples of the new 1995 wine for me, each made from just one of the as-yet-unblended component varieties: Auxerrois, Merlot, and Tannat. To my surprise, I found the Merlot more tannic and tougher than the Auxerrois, with little of the flesh so often claimed for it. The Auxerrois, on the other hand, was concentrated, round, and rich in tannins. "Merlot needs Auxerrois more than Auxerrois needs Merlot," was Delmas' dry comment. The Tannat had a dense color but was so sharp it seemed to cut across the tongue, so tannic it puckered the throat. This time the winemaker's response was a shrug. "Perhaps it works synergistically, filling in holes," she offered.

· · · · · ·

There were no vineyards on the *causse* when I visited Cahors thirty-three years ago, but today about a quarter of the present ten thousand five hundred acres of vineyard are up there, properties ranging from Château Quattre, now owned by Champagne Laurent-Perrier (another sign of worldly interest in Cahors), to the tiny Domaine des Savarines, only minutes from Cahors' medieval Valentré Bridge but hidden in wild and isolated country. The proprietor, Danielle Biesbrouck, is making opulent wines (according to the biodynamic theories of Rudolf Steiner, an increasingly popular movement among French winegrowers) by holding down yields to not much more than those reported by Jules Guyot in 1876.

Two of the most distinguished properties on the *causse* were the first to be reestablished after the revival. At Haut Serre, Georges Vigouroux, a leading Cahors wine merchant, has successfully restored a long-abandoned vineyard famous for its wine in the Middle Ages. He is making wine there in the elegantly intense style for which the *causse* has been celebrated. Château Pech de Jammes, the twenty-five-acre vineyard restored by Bernard Pons, is now owned by Americans Stephen and Sherry Schechter. They had been looking for a property in Saint-Émilion to no avail, and were skeptical when told about Pech de Jammes. ("Where's Cahors?" they asked each other.) But they went, and fell in love with the vineyard, the old house, and the Lot Valley. Their wines, deep-flavored, taut, and elegant, are very stylish.

The Lot, even when one has Alain Senderens, Alain-Dominique Perrin, and the queen of Denmark as neighbors, is still *la France profonde*. I asked Stephen Schechter how he feels about his decision to spend so much time there now that he's owned the vineyard for almost a decade. "Let me put it this way," he said. "My business partners have houses in the Hamptons. When they go there, New York goes with them. Cahors is more awkward to get to. But, once here, we can see the stars—and forget the world."

CHINON:
FROM THE GARDEN OF FRANCE

IN THE LAST TWENTY-FIVE YEARS THE AREA UNDER VINES AT Chinon, in France's Loire Valley, has tripled—from roughly fifteen hundred to five thousand acres—and much of its increased production is consumed, logically, in Paris. One evening not too long ago I found myself doing my part, sharing a bottle of Charles Joguet's Chinon, Cuvée Jeunes Vignes, with friends at Le Passage, one of the city's current crop of neighborhood wine restaurants. Tight for space and tucked away in an alley beyond the Bastille Opéra, Le Passage nevertheless draws a crowd most nights because of a wine list, full of surprises, that the proprietor extends on blackboards announcing the day's deliveries. I was eating lamb chops; one friend, a *confit* of duck; another, some grilled salmon. The wine—it was delicious—went happily with everything. I remembered Pierre Couly, of Chinon's Domaine Couly-Dutheil, once saying to me: "A young Chinon is one of the easiest wines to drink. It adapts to just about any food." It certainly did so for us, and perhaps that explains the wine's popularity at Le Passage and similar small restaurants and wine bars.

Paris likes young Chinon. Mature Chinon, available on a much smaller scale, can be a revelation. It's much more than a Chinon with a few years in bottle. In fact, one that presents well in youth rarely repays keeping, whereas a Chinon worth holding usually has a level of tannins that makes it less than seductive when young. This has been true of many wines of recent vintages, including 1989, 1990, 1993, 1995, and 1996. With patience those tannins take on a velvety texture, and at that point the wine—drunk, perhaps, with a braised squab, a jugged hare, roast venison, or even a simple beef stew—really shows what Rabelais was carrying on about.

Charles Joguet, who shares Pierre Couly's view of the adaptability of young Chinon ("It goes well even with certain fish—especially freshwater," Joguet once told me), holds that a fine, mature Chinon is something to marvel at when it accompanies game. "My father and his father were hunters," he said, "and my mother and grandmother would then cook what they brought to the kitchen door. I grew up eating hare and every kind of game bird, and with them we always drank the best bottles from the back of my father's cellar."

Chinon takes its name from the busy little medieval town clustered below the ruin of a massive castle that dominates the valley of the Vienne, a tributary of the Loire in Touraine. From this castle Henry II of England ruled an area stretching from the Pyrenees to the Scottish border long before Joan of Arc came here, in 1429, looking for the Dauphin, the uncrowned Charles VII. She found him hiding among his courtiers while his kingdom was on the point of extinction. Richelieu, Descartes, Balzac, and especially Rabelais are among the others whose names are writ large in local history.

Still, Touraine wears its past lightly, content to be one of the most enchanting regions of France, celebrated not only for the purity of its spoken French and the courtesy of its people but also (Descartes did not live in vain) for the measure, balance, and reason that touches all things there— in particular the kitchen and the cellar. The region, known as the Garden of France, has long been a source of fruits and vegetables for the Paris market, and it was for centuries home to the favorites of French kings, whose handsome Renaissance châteaux adorn the countryside. So no one should be surprised that the Loire's cooking sets a standard for simplicity and refinement. Its food is matched by wines of charm and elegance.

Chinon's red wine is made from Cabernet Franc, a variety that arrived there from Bordeaux, by sea, about a thousand years ago. Cabernet Franc is resilient and does well even at this northern limit of wine production in France, giving wines that are sometimes lean but never less than graceful. They have an aroma and flavor that suggest violets rather than the black currant and plum generally associated with Cabernet Sauvignon.

The rules of the appellation allow Chinon's growers to include in their wine a small proportion of Cabernet Sauvignon; in reality, though, hardly any of them do. Most Chinon is pure Cabernet Franc and, as such, is an example of a classic French wine that is also a "varietal." But, more than that, Chinon is an example of a *vin de terroir* because a wine made from Cabernet Franc, no matter how true to the variety, expresses faithfully the circumstances in which its grapes were grown.

The word *terroir* is confusing to many who limit their interpretation of it to soil alone, for it actually covers an amalgam of past and present that constitutes a vineyard's complete ecosystem. Site and prevailing weather are key factors, obviously; but a vineyard's historical dimension—the long-term effect of man, also an important part of a vine's environment—is equally significant. The way in which land has been worked and fashioned over many centuries, including the progressive selection of those varieties (or the single variety) best adapted to local conditions, contributes as much to the concept of *terroir* as the angle of a vineyard's slope, the direction of its exposure to the sun, and the annual rainfall. The choice of vine variety dictates the density of planting, the manner of trellising, and the cultivation practices necessary to bring into harmony the potential of the site, the needs of the vine, and the balance of the wine. There are social and cultural influences at work, too. The smart worldliness of the Haut-Médoc's *crus classés* is as much a part of their *terroir*—and certainly affects the style of their wines—as an otherworldliness is a part of a more rustic wine region in, say, the Auvergne. A glass of wine is more than the consequence of a summer's day.

· · · · · ·

And that's how it is with Chinon, too. The wine is produced in nineteen communes, including the town itself, that form a compact but varied zone in the valley of the Vienne just before that river enters the Loire. For the few miles before their confluence the two rivers flow almost parallel to each other, with only a narrow peninsula—the Véron—separating them. The tempering effect of so much water—not to mention the Atlantic, just a hundred miles away—establishes a basic parameter for the wine. Another is set by Chinon's intricate geology. All of Touraine is supported by a bed of limestone several hundred feet thick, but as rivers have changed course over millennia (the Loire itself once flowed north from Orléans into the English Channel), they have eroded the chalky rock. Deposits of clay, sand, and flint brought down from the Massif Central have mingled with the debris and sometimes covered it. There is nothing particularly tidy about what lies where: Long ago I learned that a Chinon grower who tells me his vineyard is on chalk and clay, gravel, or flint always means *mostly* chalk and clay, *mostly* gravel, *mostly* flint.

The duality of Chinon—the division between wines to be drunk young and those to be left for aging—springs from this disorder of soils. Wines of the Véron Peninsula are traditionally described as tannic and are considered suitable for aging. Wines from Cravant, a large village east of Chinon with almost a third of the appellation's vineyards, are expected always to be ready for early drinking. But it isn't as simple as that. In general, wines from vineyards on the gravel close to the river are fruity and mild and thus the most quaffable, no matter which commune they come from. Wines from flinty clay—from the slopes near the castle, for example—are sturdier and so likely to give more lasting pleasure. The best wines, though, those that will age for years, developing flavors that unfold and expand on the palate, are from vines growing on stony, chalky clay directly over limestone. "The wines we get passionate about," says Pierre Couly, "come from a few very specific sites."

The effect of a site is modified, in any case, by the vines planted on it. A wine made from the fruit of old vines planted on gravel and clay will probably age better than a wine made from young vines, even if they are planted on the stoniest, chalkiest slope. The origin of the vine wood is important, too. Vines propagated from the cuttings a grower selects from his own carefully observed vines—a practice now forbidden by the National Institute of Appellations of Origin in favor of a limited range of approved clones imposed by decree—produce wines of greater character. ("But how does an individual have a choice in the matter," I asked a grower, naïvely, "if he is obliged to accept—and pay for—the requisite number of officially approved, nursery-grafted clones?" "Once those clones have been delivered," the grower said, a twinkle in his eye, "no one sees what he actually does with them.")

Most growers, in fact, own scattered parcels of land on a variety of soils, with vines of different ages on each. They make both wine to be drunk young and wine to be aged—a strategy that helps their cash flow. Bernard Baudry, a much respected young grower at Cravant, has fewer than fifteen acres of his own, but he both rents parcels of vineyard land and farms yet more on a sharecropping basis. ("An old *vigneron*," he told me, "even if he can no longer work his land, doesn't like to part with it. And he wants to have some wine in his cellar.")

Baudry makes three wines based on his different soils and vine ages. His basic *cuvée*, Les Granges—the quintessential quaffing Chinon—is from Cravant vines grown on sandy gravel by the river. Handled in ways to protect its fruit and freshness, Les Granges spends no time in wood and is bottled in May after the vintage. Baudry makes another *cuvée* without wood, but this one—his Cuvée Domaine—is made from older vines grown on soils that ensure aging potential. A third, Les Grézeaux, is aged in barrel. For this wine he uses the fruit of his oldest vines.

Unlike Baudry, Laurent Gosset, of Château de la Grille, makes only one wine each year. But then he has almost seventy acres, in one lot, of the coveted chalky clay, much of it planted more than forty years ago. "I've little choice in the matter," he told me. "I can only follow where the vineyard leads." Which means he makes all his wine for aging. He was the first producer in Chinon to install fermentation tanks with mechanical treaders—star-shaped paddles that work the mass of skins to help the extraction of color, flavor, and tannin. Not surprisingly, his wines— except for those produced in the occasional light year, like 1992—can be austere when young. Nonetheless, he releases them a full four years after the vintage, and even then recommends waiting another three or four. By the time his wines are ready, they reveal an elegance that was obscured by their youthful inflexibility. The 1989, no longer available at the vineyard but appearing here and there on restaurant wine lists in France, is just now at its silky optimum.

* * * * * *

With several discrete vineyards, Charles Joguet makes a number of wines, including two meant for drinking young. The Cuvée Jeunes Vignes, as the name suggests, is made from the fruit of vines only six to fifteen years old in several of his vineyards. Two-thirds of the fruit presently used for this *cuvée* is from vines planted on flint and clay at Beaumont-en-Véron, an unlikely site in light of the youthful style of the wine. Joguet takes some pains over the Jeunes Vignes; seeing it as different from, but in no way less than, his wines for aging, he respects and protects the difference.

Joguet intends his Clos de la Cure to be drunk young, too. But there is a subtle shift in his approach to this wine, which is made from the fruit of a single vineyard with twenty-year-old vines planted on gravel and clay. Feeling that he shouldn't yet make a wine for long aging from them, he nevertheless recognizes that the elegance and finesse they produce need time to develop in order to be properly appreciated. So he gives the wine a longer vatting time and prepares it for what he calls semi-aging, by which he means a couple of years in bottle.

Three of Joguet's single-vineyard wines are vinified to make the best of their capacity to develop with age: Varennes du Grand Clos (twenty-five-year-old vines on chalky, flinty clay) and Clos de la Dioterie (ninety-year-old vines on chalk and clay), both properties at Sazilly, on the south bank of the Vienne opposite Cravant; and Clos du Chêne Vert, on a particularly steep and historic slope near Chinon that was replanted in 1976 and is part chalky-clay and part chalk and flint. He ferments them in specially designed vats with steel grilles to keep the grape skins submerged. But, unlike other such arrangements, his grilles are linked to motors and move down slowly at regular intervals, forcing the thick layer of grape skins through the must. Tubes allow the juice fermenting below the cap to escape upward as the pressure below increases, gradually finding its way back through the skins as the grille is slowly raised again. This gentle process ensures a generous extraction of supple tannins. Later the wines undergo a malolactic fermentation in barrel, both to soften their natural acidity and to harmonize their disparate elements. They age in wood for two years before bottling.

Charles Joguet leads a double life, as he is also a painter, with an *atelier* in Paris. When his father died prematurely, in the 1950s, he returned from his studies at the École des Beaux Arts to run the vineyard for his mother. "I'd worked in the vines and the cellar all the years I was growing up," he told me. "I knew what a good wine was and understood what had to be done to make it. But I took courses and studied wine seriously. I don't know if my being a painter makes me a better winemaker, or if being a winemaker makes me a better painter. I do my best at both."

Having his other life does encourage him to stand back, think about his winemaking, and be willing to experiment. In 1982 he planted a little over two acres of the Varennes du Grand Clos with direct-rooting Cabernet Franc (that is, vines not grafted onto American rootstock, the usual protection against phylloxera) to compare its wine with what he harvests from the rest of the vineyard. "The directly rooted vines yield half the quantity and a full degree less alcohol," he told me recently. "The vines are planted at the same density as the rest of the vineyard, but the bunches are always smaller and have smaller grapes.

"The difference in alcohol levels is hardly noticeable," he said, "because the ungrafted Varennes du Grand Clos has more substance. It has a special *esprit* too. It develops more slowly but is worth the wait."

A year ago friends gave me a bottle of the 1993 wine made from Joguet's directly rooted vines along with a bottle of his regular Varennes du Grand Clos. I should have held them a while, I suppose; but I was curious to taste and compare them and opened the bottles almost immediately. The wines had more in common with each other than not, but the one made from the ungrafted vines had a decidedly firmer structure, and more obvious acidity, too. I would say that I found it different from the wine derived from grafted vines rather than better, yet I did think it would probably be the more interesting of the two after a couple of years in bottle.

* * * * * *

Joguet's respect for his crop; his determination to extract color, flavor, and tannin with the greatest possible care; and his willingness to allow *terroir*—in the fullest sense—to dictate style is typical of Chinon today. Pierre Couly gives much of the credit for the progress of the appellation to Jacques Puisais, a past president of the International Union of Enologists and now president of the Institut Français du Goût, who came to live in Chinon forty years ago.

"Puisais made us sensitive to the details of quality," Couly told me. "Every year he pushed us a little further. He understood the problems here and discussed them with us in a straightforward way—not in academic or scientific language—and we appreciated his concern both for quality and for tradition.

"When a region has established a style, growers must try—within the limitations of each year—to follow it. When people order a bottle of wine in a restaurant, they have some idea of what to expect and are disappointed when the wine does not conform, even if there is nothing wrong with it. So one must maintain—and improve—quality within certain bounds of style. That is something Jacques Puisais understands and has helped us do."

Couly-Dutheil is the leading producer of Chinon. Created from the fusion by marriage of the Couly and Dutheil families many years ago, the firm leads the appellation not only in the importance of its vineyards and the scale of its production but also in the standard it encourages in others. Each wine follows the precept of showing an aspect of Chinon's *terroir*. My favorites illustrate well the basic styles of Chinon—the youthful and the mature. Les Gravières is a fresh, young wine from vines on gravel terraces at Cravant. And the Clos de l'Echo, from a vine-yard (once the property of the Rabelais family) adjacent to Chinon's castle, is consistently outstanding. The 1990, its color now only just beginning to fade at the edge, has an aroma of preserved fruits. The 1989, rich and, for Chinon, unusually fleshy, is simply magnificent. But I suppose that's as it should be: Gargantua, Pantagruel, and company are quite an act to follow.

* * * * * *

Note: In 1998, in an unwelcome development, Charles Joguet was obliged to cede both his winery and his vineyards to outside investors who had been introduced to him some years previously by his accountant. The wines still bear Charles Joguet's name, but he no longer has any connection with the estate or with the production of its wines.

CÔTES DE CASTILLON:
THE CUTTING EDGE

RÉGIS MORO, A WINEGROWER IN THE CÔTES DE CASTILLON, IN Bordeaux, was astonished when his face made the cover of the French newsmagazine *Le Point*. But neither he nor anyone else was surprised to find that the magazine had placed the Côtes de Castillon among the top ten wine regions of France. Some of the best of Bordeaux's most affordable wines are now being produced there, and they're cropping up in restaurants and on merchants' racks in the United States.

The area takes its name from Castillon-la-Bataille, a small town about six miles east of Saint-Émilion with a street market every Monday, a cycle race every August, and a bridge across the Dordogne. Of its historic past, there is little evidence—an ancient, creeper-strewn gate, vestiges of stone fortifications, and the site of the battle in 1453 that ended the Hundred Years' War. But the hills, the *côtes*, around the town are studded with castles, and the countryside is both pretty and green: Woods bordering the narrow, winding roads and copses tucked among the vineyards shelter an abundance of game—especially dove and boar—and there are always *cèpes* in the fall.

The Côtes de Castillon appellation begins where Saint-Émilion's ends, but there's little to see that distinguishes one from the other: The limestone plateau and chalky clay slopes of Saint-Émilion simply become the limestone plateau and chalky clay slopes of the Côtes de

Castillon. Some growers say that any change in the soil is negligible; it's the gradual shift in climate as one goes up the Dordogne valley that's responsible for any difference one can taste in the wine. The vines break bud, leaf out, and flower as much as two weeks later than they do in some parts of Saint-Émilion—without the tempering effect of the Atlantic, spring is delayed—and although warmer summers sometimes help the vines catch up, picking also often starts a week or two after Saint-Émilion. Others say it's the scattered pockets of Cabernet Sauvignon vines that give the wines their distinct character. Merlot and Cabernet Franc are traditional throughout this side of Bordeaux, but Cabernet Sauvignon, which is widely planted in the Côtes de Castillon, is rare in Saint-Émilion.

Over decades of replanting, the vineyards in the Castillon hills drifted down toward the plain (where cultivation is easier and cheaper). But in the 1970s, as the price of land in neighboring Saint-Émilion and Pomerol rose, any Castillon property that came onto the market was snapped up by someone from the more fashionable appellations next door. The vineyards again climbed to the slopes' higher reaches, where there is more sun and less clay (the limestone up there gives wine of greater finesse).

Local growers had already begun to plant higher, and to modify their winemaking to take advantage of the quality of the fruit, when they were galvanized by events at Château de Belcier, a Castillon estate with about 130 acres of vineyard that had been sold in 1986 to the Macif insurance company. "For years I'd made a light wine from the fruit here," Gilbert Dubois, Belcier's *maître de chais*, told me, "a simple wine ready for early drinking. But the new owners wanted a change. 'We want wine of a quality that justifies our investment,' they said.

"I was eager to go along with them. First, we trimmed the number of buds on each vine. That summer we thinned the leaves to let the light in. We thinned the crop, too, and checked it for ripeness, bunch by bunch, as it came to the crusher. I tried a new approach to fermentation and brought in new barrels—the first to be used anywhere in the Côtes de Castillon for quite some time. Cement tanks had become the norm. The changes cost money, and our customers were taken aback by our price. I thought I'd be looking for new clients, but they were all impressed by the wine and stayed with me."

Belcier's conspicuous success provoked a dramatic shift. By 1989 the market's perception of the Côtes de Castillon greatly improved, and the growers were ready to reclaim its name. For years its official appellation had been Bordeaux Supérieur, with the words *Côtes de Castillon* hyphenated to it almost as an afterthought. The trade liked it that way; the mention of "Bordeaux" in the appellation lowered the price ceiling and therefore allowed them to use the wine to improve their regional blends. In reforming the appellation, the growers dropped the Bordeaux Supérieur and tightened controls to raise quality further. For example, they placed on each grower an obligation to plant his or her vines more densely in the vineyard, increasing the minimum number of plants to five thousand to the hectare (about two thousand to the acre), roughly double the density of vines in many California vineyards. This meant that if the growers were to remain within the permitted yield limit, they would have to reduce the number of bunches ripening on each vine. The result has been consistently riper fruit with flavor more concentrated than ever, and a range of mature tannins that gives the wines a firm yet gentle backbone.

* * * * * *

Confirmation by *Le Point* of the Côtes de Castillon's place in the front ranks of French wines just ten years after the growers imposed these and other changes on themselves has given great satisfaction. When I visited the area in late 1999, I found the growers' enthusiasm exhilarating and the quality of their wines convincing. "What has happened here," said Hélène Lapeyronie of Château Lapeyronie, "is that everyone recognizes more clearly that to make good wine you must have good fruit. There's a limit to what can be done in the cellar to remedy what should have been done in the vineyard. Our work has been transformed."

Lapeyronie and her husband, Jean-Frédéric, have roughly twenty-five acres of vineyard that border Saint-Émilion. Most of it—70 percent, anyway—is planted with Merlot, and the rest is divided between Cabernet Franc and Cabernet Sauvignon. The latter arrived fairly recently. In the 1970s—at the time when there was much replanting—it was the policy of the Institut National des Appellations d'Origine to encourage growers throughout Bordeaux to use Cabernet Sauvignon to improve the quality of the wines, regardless of the varieties they had been using before.

"The trouble with that policy," said Gilbert Dubois, "was that most growers put Cabernet Sauvignon in the low-lying corners of their vineyards, where there's the greatest chance of spring frosts. Because Cabernet Sauvignon breaks bud later than Merlot, they felt it would be at lower risk there. But low-lying sites are often on clay soils that are poorly exposed. Vines there don't get the sun they need to ripen properly. And if Cabernet Sauvignon is to make a contribution to a wine, it must be fully ripe."

Several growers told me of problems they have with Cabernet Sauvignon in all but the most propitious years, even though Hélène Lapeyronie insists that it ripens well in the Côtes de Castillon if it's planted in the right places. "It must be up on the limestone rather than down on clay," she said. "Limestone drains well and warms up quickly. The vines must be well exposed to the sun so that the tannin, the color, and the flavor are really ripe when the fruit is picked. Then Cabernet Sauvignon adds power to the wine and complexity to its bouquet."

To get that perfect ripeness in all three varieties, the Lapeyronies skirmish daily with nature, adjusting the crop loads on their vines as weather conditions change. "We rarely get as much as half the yield permitted for the appellation," she said, "but our fruit is always ripe." And their wines—regardless of vintage—are always densely colored, intensely fruity, and highly concentrated.

So are the wines of Robert Avargues of Château Robin. His were among several I tasted in which the flattering violet perfume of Cabernet Franc came through with unusual clarity. "That's because of picking at full ripeness," he told me. "We wait as long as we have to. And if it rains, too bad." Like most of the other growers, he sorts through his bunches as they move on a belt toward the crusher. Once they are crushed and destemmed, he lets the mass of skins and juice soak together for four or five days at low temperature. "That maceration helps bring out the fruit aromas and deepens the color in the wine," he said. "Fermentation starts naturally once I let the temperature rise. I don't use laboratory yeast. It gives greater security, but it standardizes the wine. I'm not organic or biodynamic or ecological, but I prefer to work with nature. I use organic fertilizer, for example, though it costs more, because I'm not prepared to put chemicals in my soil. When I take that kind of stand in the vineyard, it wouldn't make sense to do anything in the *chais* that smacks of industrial winemaking."

Ripe grapes give healthy lees (the residue that falls as the wine ages in the barrel, not the skins and pips that have been separated after fermentation) that help stabilize the wine. "Lees give the wine richness and nuance," said Patrick Erésué, winemaker at Château de Chainchon, his family's property, and formerly winemaker at Château Canon La Gaffelière, a *premier grand cru classé* of Saint-Émilion. "Richness and nuance, fruit and concentration—these are the qualities that give pleasure in a wine."

When Patrick Erésué talks about the lees of the wine, he parts company with most other Bordeaux growers. It has been a convention there for almost three centuries to draw a young red wine aging in barrel off its lees every three months and transfer it into another, as if the lees— mostly tartrates and spent yeast—were noxious and had to be eliminated. The transfer—known as racking—also allows the wine to pick up some oxygen. A few years ago, it occurred to Patrick Ducournau, a grower of Madiran, a red wine produced in the foothills of the Pyrenees, that the absorption of that small dose of oxygen rather than the elimination of the lees was the real benefit of racking red wine. Indeed, he wondered whether elimination of a red wine's lees was even a good thing. White wines, after all, gain in succulence and depth of flavor when held in a barrel on their lees. They also benefit from the capacity of lees to attract any free oxygen, keeping the wine fresh. But red wines need oxygen to help bring color and tannin together in a way that deepens and fixes one while making the other more supple. Ducournau set up the kind of fine plastic oxygen-supply lines used in hospitals and gave minute, controlled doses to his red wines instead of racking them. The combined benefit of lees and oxygen was astonishing—the wines seemed more full and deeply colored. Côtes de Castillon growers were among the first to accept Ducournau's ideas and to follow his lead. Oxygen lines now trail through most of their cellars.

Régis Moro, the proprietor of Vieux Château Champ de Mars, and *Le Point*'s cover man, put it to me succinctly. "If I want the benefit of keeping my wine in contact with its lees, I can't rack it," he said. "If I don't rack my wine, it will lack the oxygen it needs for the stabilization of color. The lees will have taken it. So I inject micro-doses of oxygen to replace it. Eventually, as the wine develops, the lees are just absorbed into it. They disappear. All that's left are tartrate crystals."

♦ ♦ ♦ ♦ ♦ ♦

Moro and others are installing new, open wooden fermenting vats—the kind that most Bordeaux growers threw out years ago in favor of stainless steel. It hadn't escaped Moro's notice that when Paul Pontallier took over the management of Château Margaux with an enviable budget to update the *chais*, he changed almost everything—except the wooden fermenting vats. Controlled experiments elsewhere in the Médoc a few years ago showed that although analysis reveals no measurable differences between them, two wines made from the same lot of grapes, one fermented in stainless steel and the other in wood, made a completely different impression on nose and palate. The wine fermented in wood was more aromatic and had a longer flavor.

♦ ♦ ♦ ♦ ♦ ♦

In the midst of this enthusiasm for change and innovation I found myself thinking about the events played out at Castillon in 1453. At a time when cannon were still a novelty, the French installed new versions with great explosive force on a slope overlooking the water meadows

outside the town where they expected to be attacked. Then they deliberately drew the English into the trap they had set for them. That simple
ploy brought an end to the Hundred Years' War, shattered forever the
medieval world of chivalry and knights in shining armor, and changed
the direction of European history. The thought helped me put the introduction of cellar oxygen lines and open wood fermenters in Castillon in
perspective.

CHÂTEAU MARGAUX:
TIME RECAPTURED

SHOULD YOU HAVE BEEN GIVEN SEAT 23C ON A DELTA FLIGHT sometime in the spring of 1988, there is a chance that you might have found in the seat pocket in front of you notes of a mammoth two-day tasting of Château Margaux wines from more than fifty vintages spanning two centuries from 1771 to 1984. I was so sure I had gathered them up with the rest of my working papers that I didn't, as we are asked to do, check around for personal belongings. Until this inexplicable lapse, I had been either more careful or lucky.

Usually I rely on my written notes, transcribed and fleshed out, rather than memory, even though recorded impressions of a long tasting can be deceptively skewed. Wines served early, before a taster can set a standard for himself, often have an advantage over those served later. The palate, not yet tuned, let alone jaded, finds delight at that stage in quite simple aromas and flavors, and notes tend to be less critical than they should be. On the other hand, wines served last will often benefit from a palate primed by wines that went before.

Justification of a tasting as opulent as this, surely, is the rare perspective it gives, so perhaps the loss of my tightly focused notes was a blessing in disguise. Forced to rely on key impressions remembered for the insights they had given and for their contribution to the general conclusions I had formed at the time, I was left with a longer view of Château Margaux than would have been possible had I later allowed it to be obscured by a thicket of scribble. That alone was an illuminating experience. Wine writers get bogged down with too many words. There are times when we can't see the wine for adjectives.

Uncluttered perception was more than usually essential on this occasion anyway. In recent years, drawing on the archival treasures of Bordeaux—reports, letters, and accounts lying in attics and forgotten armoires—local historians have shown that the style of Bordeaux wines must have undergone an important change between the late eighteenth century and that point in the mid-nineteenth when the leading châteaux of the Médoc were formally classified for the 1855 Paris Exhibition. With minor reservations, respect for that classification remains strong, implying that the recognizably distinct styles and standards on which it was based have remained broadly constant for more than a century. The reputation of Château Margaux had been unmarred for at least a century before that, however, leaving room to doubt that the transformation could have been of a fundamental nature. Furthermore, eternal speculation rather than resolution of the question seemed inevitable because the château proprietors no longer have stocks of eighteenth-century wines, and even the most indulgent host rarely greets his guests with bottles of eighteenth-century Bordeaux under one arm and wines from the nineteenth century under the other.

We began our weekend with the short series of wines made since the Mentzelopoulos family acquired Château Margaux in 1977. On release, each of these seven vintages had been greeted with a place among the most distinguished classed growths of its year. In fact, Château Margaux's wine had been generally acknowledged as *the* most distinguished of some of those years.

That is what we expect from a *premier grand cru*, of course, but the success in these first years of the Mentzelopoulos proprietorship has seemed the more impressive because of grumbling that the quality of Château Margaux had fallen under the Ginestets, the old Bordeaux wine family obliged to sell the property because of financial reversals in the seventies. It is true that apart from the 1970 (a superb wine), and possibly the 1971, Ginestet vintages at Château Margaux in the seventies had not been brilliant. But that can be said generally of the classed growths of Bordeaux in those years. The weather had been uncooperative. What particularly distinguished the wines of that decade, however, were the depressed prices of a market broken by the collapse of 1974. In such circumstances the usual response to difficult vintage conditions—eliminating with greatest severity all but a few lots from the final blend—would have imposed intolerable hardship and compounded Bordeaux's economic catastrophe.

The wines tasted from the sixties gave a truer picture of the Ginestet stewardship. Then, too, weather conditions had not always been propitious, but the 1962, a year often dismissed for producing light and insubstantial wines in Bordeaux, was both concentrated and balanced; the 1964, one of the few picked that year before the rain that started on October 8 ruined most other wines, was outstanding for depth of color and flavor; the 1966 showed how the Ginestets had preserved Margaux's grace and charm in a year in which most others had presented lean and gawky wines; and the 1961, a wine of unforgettable splendor, presented faultlessly the classic proportion for which Château Margaux is renowned.

· · · · · ·

As we worked our way back through the preceding decades, we were impressed by the consistency of style—elegant bouquet, sustained flavor, sinuous strength—even allowing for the vicissitudes of vintage and for the troubled years of patchwork ownership between the two world wars. We were especially gratified to see how closely the most recent vintages of Château Margaux resembled those from Bordeaux's Golden Age: a period from the late 1840s to the vintage of 1875, when the extensive replanting of the early part of the century had fully matured and phylloxera had not yet devastated the vineyards. Those older vintages included the 1848, the 1864, and the 1870, all still well colored, concentrated, lively, and delicious. The 1847, described when made by the cellar master as having "a lot of finesse, but lacking structure and body," had survived to prove him wrong.

Eventually we came to the two wines from the eighteenth century, from the vintages of 1771 and 1791. The better to set them off, they were presented together with the 1847 and 1848 for comparison. Though twenty years separated the two earlier wines from each other, they were remarkably similar. On the other hand, there was an enormous difference between both of them and the two wines of the 1840s. The color of both the 1847 and the 1848 was unexpectedly dense, and dusky with tinges of brown within the red. The bouquet of each shared those suggestions of chocolate and charcoal common to mature, quality wines based on Cabernet Sauvignon, and both wines had the subtly sweet fragrance of decayed forest undergrowth—a fusion of moss, faded flowers, mushroom, and damp bark—expected in Bordeaux wines of such venerable age. In a thousand years, though, that color could not evolve into the astonishingly vibrant strawberry of the older wines, nor could years alone possibly transform the nineteenth-century vintages' autumnal bouquet and flavor into the voluptuously scented extravagance of the wines from the eighteenth century. We were astonished by the eerie freshness of wines made by men living at the time of the American and French revolutions and confused by their quality—as unexpected as their luminous and perfumed style.

Their color, in fact, would have surprised us less had we been looking with clear eyes at paintings of the period. Most of us assume too easily that an unfamiliar color applied to a familiar object is mere painter's license. Georges de la Tour, Watteau, Nattier—all the seventeenth- and eighteenth-century French painters, in fact—showed the red wine they knew to be a bright, strawberry color. Only in the late nineteenth century did French red wine come to be represented with the dark purply garnets of Fantin-Latour and John Singer Sargent. The change, as we could see from the wines in our glasses, had been real and not an adjustment of artistic convention.

· · · · · ·

What had led to the dramatic contrasts in our glasses? In the decades of upheaval from 1789 to 1848 neither viticulture nor winemaking was spared. In April 1811, when all Europe was embroiled in the Napoleonic Wars, Lamothe, director of Château Latour, wrote to the owner, the Comte de la Pallu, that the naval blockade prevented the shipment of Baltic oak barrel staves, making them both extremely expensive in Bordeaux and hard to come by. "We shall soon have to renounce this quality of wood altogether and make do with what is here, even though the English don't like it." By which he meant, of course, that the taste of French oak, now accepted as integral to the flavor of red Bordeaux, was not at that time appreciated in Bordeaux's traditional market.

Bordeaux had used barrels of local oak only for inferior wines unsuited for export. Wines of the first quality went into heavy barrels made from oak shipped from Poland, Lithuania, and Latvia, from the old ports of Stettin, Danzig (now Gdansk), Memel (now Klaipeda), and Riga. Wines of lesser quality went into barrels from Lübeck in northern Germany, not far from Hamburg. Discussion about variations of flavor resulting from the choice of oak from one provenance rather than another was as passionate and as inconclusive then as it is now, when California winemakers argue their preferences for Limousin rather than Nevers, or Vosges rather than Tronçais, all of them oaks from France.

The substitution of French oak for Baltic had been prompted by the same difficulties that had separated Bordeaux from its overseas markets where wine matured in Baltic oak was preferred, so the change was probably seen at the time as a temporary inconvenience of small long-term consequence. When peace was restored, however, there seems to have been only a partial return to the use of Baltic oak barrels, though their use as late as the 1840s is clear from a paper presented to the city's Academy of Science, Literature, and Art by a Bordeaux pharmacist reporting on his analyses of imported and local oaks. Describing his experiments with pulverized samples of each combined with red and white Bordeaux wines, he claimed to have found that certain northern oaks transmitted a balsamic odor to wine.

Be that as it may, few would dispute that Baltic oak has a milder effect on wine than does French. It neither loads a young wine with tannin nor imposes so heavily the oak flavor to which we have now become accustomed.

Tannin, in oxidizing, and, later, in breaking down, encourages both the brown tinge of aging red wine and that slightly decadent, woodsy bouquet redolent of what the Viennese call, in macabre fashion, the sweetness of death. It is possible to hypothesize, at least, that time in Baltic rather than French oak had allowed those eighteenth-century wines to retain, even today, their youthful purity of color, bouquet, and flavor. In the eighteenth century, after all, wine was not bottled with a view to further aging but for preservation.

* * * * * *

While French was replacing Baltic oak in the cellars, an equally extreme change was taking place in the vineyards. Cabernet Sauvignon, with its characteristically pungent aroma and flavor, had been present in Bordeaux vineyards since the seventeenth century. It had played a minor role compared to Malbec, an early maturing, abundantly fruitful variety, and Petit Verdot, a vine with grapes that ripen late to give a highly colored, spicily flavored red wine that ages well.

The quality of Cabernet Sauvignon was recognized, but its spreading use in the Médoc in the first half of the nineteenth century, according to the reminiscences of Edward Lawton, the most distinguished Bordeaux wine broker of his day, was simply in response to a series of wretched summers in which Malbec vines had flowered badly and failed to set fruit—to the growers' great loss. Cabernet Sauvignon, a hardy vine that buds late and therefore presents less risk of damage from spring frost, will set from flower to fruit even in conditions too adverse for other varieties. By the late 1840s, its assertive and unmistakable flavor had come to dominate the style of Médoc wine. Perhaps because Merlot gives a fuller, firmer, and fruitier wine than Malbec (even if it shares its viticultural disadvantage of failing to set in difficult conditions), it was also used to replace Malbec in those colder Médoc soils where there was a risk of Cabernet Sauvignon failing to ripen adequately. There are no known references to Merlot in the Médoc before this time.

With Cabernet Sauvignon and Merlot replacing Malbec, there was less need of the backbone previously supplied by Petit Verdot, though remnants remain in most Médoc vineyards. There are still small plots of Malbec, too, throughout Bordeaux, especially in the Graves and Saint-Émilion. In addition, many properties (but not Château Margaux) have an important acreage of Cabernet Franc, a variety that brings color and aroma. But the change from a predominantly Malbec and Verdot blend matured in mild, Baltic oak barrels to an essentially Cabernet Sauvignon and Merlot blend, its pungency reinforced by the flavor of French oak, took Bordeaux wine in a flying leap from the classical restraints of the eighteenth century to the vigorous flamboyance of the nineteenth.

It is possible that other, marginal, practices might have contributed to the differences between the two pairings of wines in front of us. In the early nineteenth century Bordeaux growers began adding proportions of deep-colored Hermitage from the Rhône to intensify in their wines those sturdy characteristics evolving with the growing proportion of Cabernet Sauvignon and the use of French oak. For a time there were experimental plantings of Syrah, the grape used for Hermitage, even in vineyards as prestigious as those of Château Latour. Perhaps such adjustments had contributed to the density of the 1847 and 1848 Château Margaux. On the other hand, reflecting, perhaps, the greater artifice of fashionable French life in the eighteenth century, the practice of perking the then more delicate aroma of Bordeaux with powdered orrisroot, the rhizome of iris, became commonplace. It was used, as it is today in the making of perfume, to contribute a scent of violets. Perhaps its presence partially explains the powerfully exotic bouquet of the 1771 and 1791 wines, though I prefer to attribute that not to man's alchemy but to divine intent.

SAINT-VÉRAN:
A SIMPLE LUXURY

A FRIEND WHO HAD THE ART OF LIVING DOWN PAT ONCE SAID, "There is no such thing as a cheap luxury." I sometimes remember her words when I look at the prices of the finest white Burgundies and get a feeling close to vertigo. But if luxury is never cheap, pleasure need not be expensive. As far as white Burgundies are concerned, there are, in fact, delicious and even distinguished wines out there at reasonable prices. They're just not obvious to us because we are dazzled by Meursault and Puligny-Montrachet and distracted by the flood of wines from the various Mâcon cooperatives.

I enjoy wines from the Côte Chalonnaise—essentially Mercurey, Rully, and Montagny. The area was considered an extension of Burgundy's Côte d'Or until revolutionary France, dividing former provinces into administrative departments at the end of the eighteenth century, put it in the Saône-et-Loire, on the wrong side of an arbitrary line. But the white Burgundies I drink most often are from Saint-Véran, a small appellation (covering little more than twelve hundred acres) carved out of the Mâconnais in 1971. These wines are usually fleshier than other Mâcons, with a brighter aroma and more intense flavor. Depending on the age of the vines—always Chardonnay—and the grower's attitude toward barrels, among other things, a Saint-Véran can have exuberant fruit or the silky complexity we normally associate with far grander wines. I take advantage of the differences by serving the bolder style of Saint-Véran (fermented in a steel tank) as an apéritif and, at table, with fresh and uncomplicated dishes—pastas, curries, or any kind of mixed salad. But the Saint-Véran I like best is one fermented in barrel and aged a couple of years in bottle. It's delicious with a creamy *blanquette* of veal, poached fish, or chicken braised with fennel and garlic.

Although the appellation is fairly new, the special area it covers has always been recognized for the quality of its wines. The great medieval abbey of Cluny had vines at Davayé. That particular hillside is now part of the teaching and funds-generating vineyard attached to the *lycée viticole*—the viticultural school. Indeed, the larger part of Saint-Véran's appellation that lies within Davayé was originally to be included within the 1936 boundary proposed for Pouilly-Fuissé. (Pouilly-Fuissé is sandwiched between Saint-Véran's two halves.) But the whole idea of controlled appellations was new then, and many growers were still suspicious of it. To them it smelled of government regulation, limited yields, and higher taxes at a time when wine prices were at rock bottom. Many of them simply wanted to be left alone to make what they could of a difficult situation. In Davayé, at a time before widespread refrigeration, that meant producing more red wine than white—and they didn't see how being part of the Pouilly-Fuissé appellation would be of any help to them. So they turned the proposal down.

* * * * * *

The area I'm describing is at the southern tip of the Mâconnais, just before it merges into the granitic mass of the Beaujolais. In fact, it collides rather than merges: The bed of limestone that runs through all of Burgundy breaks asunder here into a series of abrupt escarpments of which two, Solutré and Vergisson, dominate the skyline for miles around. Vines cover their lower slopes, drawing what sustenance they can from a bleak mix of clay and limestone. Those of Pouilly-Fuissé— that appellation draws together the villages of Vergisson, Chaintré, Fuissé, and Solutré (with its dependent hamlet of Pouilly)—are on steep, well-exposed slopes where the considerable presence of clay means the wine will have body and structure. In the Saint-Véran villages, especially Davayé and Prissé, the slopes are less precipitous and the clay, less pervasive, often gives way to solid limestone.

There are differences between the particularly supple Saint-Véran wines of Davayé and Prissé, two villages north of Pouilly-Fuissé, and those of the four villages that lie to its south: Chasselas, Leynes, Chânes, and Saint-Vérand. Because of incursions of the Beaujolais' granitic sand, experts of the Institut National des Appellations d'Origine are said to have checked carefully which parcels in those more southerly villages were to be included in the Saint-Véran appellation and which were not (some white wines of the area have the compromise appellation of Beaujolais Blanc). But I sometimes wonder. I've been told often enough that the wines from that side of the appellation simply need time to come round, but to my palate they're hard when young and not much improved as they age. Fortunately, Davayé and Prissé produce more than half the wine of the appellation, and their wines are the ones I always buy.

The name Saint-Véran comes from what is now known as Saint-Vérand, even though, ironically, it's the village with the smallest acreage devoted to the cause. Formerly "Saint-Véran-des-Vignes," it was obliged by the French postal service to accept a distinctive final *d* some years ago in return for being allowed to shorten it name. The commune had thought the "des Vignes" suffix cumbersome (and perhaps too quaint) but is now fighting the bureaucrats—so far without success—to have it restored. The battle is perhaps no more than a sign of wanting to be more closely identified with the growing reputation of the wines. Yet it's also a symptom of the changing attitude to vines and wine in rural France. Burgundy's Côte d'Or and Bordeaux's Haut-Médoc enjoy international reputations that reflect glory on their vineyards' proprietors. But the lives of most French winegrowers have never been particularly glamorous. They are small farmers—twenty-five acres is a fair-sized holding—with a very labor-intensive crop. They live in their overalls.

Their sons and daughters, obliged to help with the pruning and picking, often choose to become pharmacists and engineers rather than work in all weather for such uncertain rewards and so modest a life. But *their* sons and daughters, sometimes raised in cities, perhaps loved the summers they spent in their grandparents' vineyards; and as the wine-growers of the hour have taken their place with the *chefs du moment* on the covers of magazines, they now see a life with vines rather dashing. So when one generation, comfortably settled well away from the tribulations of agriculture, shows little interest in taking over the family vineyard, the next is frequently keen to take its place. Educated—usually they've had professional, technical, or business training—and often with experience in sales or administration, they know a thing or two about marketing and raising capital. Twenty or even fifteen years ago, there would have been little in a new and as yet unknown appellation like Saint-Véran to hold the imagination of ambitious young men and women, let alone draw them back from the opportunities of Paris and Lyon. But the modem and fax machine have redrawn the parameters of the winegrowers' world and allowed them to be masters of their own fate.

＊ ＊ ＊ ＊ ＊ ＊

Gilles Morat, now a Saint-Véran grower, left his village when he was twenty to follow a career in electronics. Yet when his father retired several years ago, he seized the chance to return. "I was successful in my work," he told me, "and I enjoyed it. But when my second child was born, I realized I was spending too much time away from my family, constantly on the road, constantly under pressure. I never thought I would want to come back to take on my father's vineyard. But I am now so totally engrossed in it, it's as if the fifteen years of my other life hadn't happened."

When he first returned, Morat spent a year at the *lycée viticole* of Davayé, mastering the theory of what his father had simply absorbed while working at his own father's side. It was essential for Morat to go back to school: A diploma of professional competence or its equivalent is a requirement in France to qualify for the generous assistance provided to young farmers by the state, including the guarantees for low-interest loans to reequip outdated cellars and to extend holdings if and when land is available. These days a good third of the student body at the Davayé *lycée*—a hundred or more—are men and woman with professional qualifications in other fields taking special courses in enology and viticulture while getting involved in properties for which they had neither intended nor expected to assume responsibility.

It's a sign of the dramatic changes at Saint-Véran. Thirty years ago the growers had no direct access to the market. The wine they produced—already by that time most of it white—was sold in bulk at the going rate for Mâcon Blanc. It disappeared into the blends of local *négociants,* so the quality and character were of little account. The grower was paid on the basis of volume and alcohol degree; therefore, every experiment, development, and change in the vineyards in the decades after World War II had but one objective: to increase yields. It was the establishment of the Saint-Véran appellation that turned things around by giving the wine an identity, a name by which its quality could be recognized and remembered. The growers invested in replacing old equipment and in replanting.

"We reverted with passion to the traditional methods of our grand-fathers, as if they were something new and extraordinary," Jean-Luc Terrier of the Domaine des Deux Roches told me. "Here we are, making our own compost again instead of using chemical fertilizers. And far from boosting yields, we prune severely and then go out into the vineyards again in summer to thin the fruit for perfect ripeness and better quality. We've found our way back to what had worked for us before. It has been our salvation."

Gilles Morat was able to add a bit of land to his father's holding and has a sharecropping arrangement on a few acres more. As yet, there's very little space for barrels in his winery—though equipped with as much polished steel as a dairy, it's not much bigger than a suburban garage. But his tank-fermented wine, long and supple, starts with an enticing burst of fruit on nose and palate that defies criticism. Though Morat is constrained by his circumstances, there are Saint-Véran growers who quite deliberately use no wood at all.

Richard Martin of the Domaine de la Croix Senaillet, for example, ferments his grapes in separate lots in small, enamel-lined tanks and never puts them into barrels. He pointed at the crumbled mass of limestone in his vineyard and said, "That's what makes our wines smell and taste of fruit and flowers. Saint-Véran is not just a superior Mâcon or a lesser Pouilly-Fuissé. It has a character of its own. My job is too preserve it.

"When friends my age took over family properties where the wine had always been made in tank," he said, "many of them promptly introduced barrels. I did the opposite. My father had used barrels, even though he sold most of his wine in bulk. I got rid of all the wood. I sell 80 to 90 percent of my production in bottle, and I want my wine to show as much fruit and freshness as possible."

Jean-Luc Terrier, like many other Saint-Véran producers, avoids the use of wood for his basic, estate Saint-Véran so that it can be enjoyed young. He ferments the wine in stainless-steel tanks and holds it there until he is ready to bottle it. The 1998 opens with very seductive fruit. The wines he produces from his old vines and his best vineyard sites, however, are fermented or aged at least partially in wood. Part of his 1998 wine from the Terres Noires vineyard is fermented in steel tanks and part in barrels. It has an aroma of honey and flowers and the texture of silk. The wine he makes from Les Cras, which is sold out almost as soon as it's released, is fermented and aged in wood alone.

"The wine can be relied on," he said, "to have a good weight and feel. It simply doesn't need the spurt of fruit that stainless steel preserves in our other wines." When I tasted the 1997, it showed just the beginning of bottle bouquet, but the flavor was already deep and long.

◆ ◆ ◆ ◆ ◆ ◆

Roger and Christine Saumaize of the Domaine Saumaize-Michelin are among those who use only wood for their wines. "Stainless-steel tanks allow a very close control of fermentation temperature," Christine Saumaize told me. "And fermentation at a very low temperature retains primary grape aroma. But it does so at the expense of any expression of *terroir* and robs the wine of real personality. Fermentation in barrel presents obvious problems, and temperature control is only one of them. But if the lees are left in the barrel and stirred from time to time, the wine will have a fatter texture and a length and depth of flavor that become increasingly important with age. That primary aroma, so attractive in a young wine, soon fades, and often there's nothing much to take its place."

Some growers who ferment their wine in tanks also hold it there a few months on the fine lees. Apart from any other benefit, a wine stays fresher in the presence of its lees: They protect it by absorbing free oxygen. But the surface area of lees settled in the bottom of a 10,000-liter tank, relative to the volume of wine, is less effective than lees that have spread over the lower part of a 220-liter barrel. Most Saint-Véran growers try for the advantages of both steel and wood by combining a proportion of wine fermented in each.

Quite a number do achieve that kind of balance, though Christine Saumaize says she doesn't find the result satisfactory. "When we bought our first barrels in 1985," she told me, "we used them to make wines we could combine with the wine we had fermented in steel tank. But the *cuvée* lacked harmony. We tried again and again, and finally we came to the conclusion that we had to choose tanks or barrels, one or the other, and we chose wood."

· · · · · · ·

I soon learned that it wasn't so much a matter of choosing wood or tank, but doing what the fruit dictated. "If you're going to ferment a wine in wood," Bénédicte Vincent of the Château de Fuissé explained, "it must have concentration to begin with. That means old vines, low yields, a privileged site, or all three. The wines we make from our vineyards in Saint-Véran, where the vines are young, are never in wood. (To satisfy our American customers, who like a barrel-fermented style, we buy grapes from a Saint-Véran grower with old vines to make a wine we bottle under our merchant label.) And, in turn, we know that a wine with substance from older vines needs to have time in wood if it is to reach its potential."

Roger Saumaize's cousin, Guy Saumaize, of Domaine des Maillettes, like many another, makes what he calls a "traditional" Saint-Véran, fermented and held in stainless steel on lees routinely stirred until he bottles the wine in the March following the harvest. ("Even in tank," he says, "the lees give a fatter texture.") He also produces a Grande Réserve, from old vines and fermented and matured in wood alone, and when I tasted the wine I could almost feel its power and intensity.

"There's a call for both kinds of wine," Guy Saumaize said. "A wine fermented in stainless steel has a dashing immediacy. But it's out of place with certain foods. A barrel-fermented wine is more complex, more nuanced, and eventually more satisfying. You must be willing to wait for it, however. And then take the time to appreciate it."

And that's part of the art of living.

LE BEAUJOLAIS NOUVEAU
EST ARRIVÉ!

EVERY YEAR ON THE THIRD THURSDAY OF NOVEMBER, BARS, CAFÉS, and bistros all over Paris revel, with varying degrees of decorum, in the new harvest's Beaujolais. The cynical would say that the success of Beaujolais Nouveau—almost as great in Brussels, Amsterdam, Frankfurt, and New York as it is in Lyons—is a triumph of marketing and promotion. But commerce merely cashes in: The gaiety is spontaneous, and the joy a response to something beyond posters and bar streamers. A mouthful of wine that was grapes just weeks before, and earth, rain, and sunshine only weeks before that, is an exhilarating reminder of what really makes the world go round.

Well over half the annual production of Beaujolais and Beaujolais-Villages together is sold, shipped, and presumably paid for before Christmas. This is not an unhappy situation for the growers to find themselves in. Unfortunately, the intense but fleeting attention distorts our perception of the wine: It is more than a nine days' wonder. The phenomenon of Beaujolais Nouveau also means that wines of the ten Beaujolais *crus* are often considered stale news when released the following spring (Brouilly, Côte de Brouilly, Chénas, Chiroubles, Fleurie, Juliénas, Morgon, Moulin-à-Vent, Saint-Amour, and Regnié may not be sold as *vin nouveau*). They can hardly re-create the excitement generated the previous November, when the vintage made its debut. The result is that some of the region's best wines slip onto the market unannounced and unnoticed.

Once (and I mean centuries ago), when all wine was sold from the barrel and no one knew how to keep a part-empty container's contents from deteriorating, each new vintage was so eagerly awaited that it would be shipped off to market still seething its way through the final stages of fermentation. Most of those wines were boisterously rough; few could have been as delectable, drunk in their infancy, as wine made from the Gamay grape of the Beaujolais. Even without the help of controversial techniques to expand the wine's aromatic potential or boost its power, young Beaujolais, tender yet sprightly and, left to itself, redolent of peonies in full flower, is as seductive as any wine can be.

Growers were still shipping barrels of new (and probably fizzy) Beaujolais to Lyons as recently as the 1930s. The wine was set up on bistros' zinc counters and, once tapped, run off directly into the pitchers from which it was served. In Paris, too, there were bars known for the new Beaujolais that arrived each fall with much local fanfare. Such wine, with "beaded bubbles winking at the brim," brought to the shabbiest hole-in-the-wall a vision of distant countryside, of vines in sunlight, and, who knows, perhaps of Dionysus himself. Jubilant.

There was nothing either formal or official about the dispatch of these wines: no release date; no organized promotion; and, even when the machinery of controlled appellations had already been put in place, no trail of certificates. Eventually, however, bureaucracy stepped in to tidy things up. In 1938 the practice of selling a Beaujolais freely outside the bounds and documentation of the new appellation laws was curtailed, and then wartime measures that controlled the release of all wines broke the tradition altogether—at a time when it might have done most good.

The restrictions inaugurated under the Vichy administration (how fitting for that lot to have put pain to one of life's simple pleasures) were not revoked until 1951, when the authorities fixed December 15 as an annual date on which controlled appellation wines of the new vintage could be released for sale. Growers in regions that had traditionally sold some of their new wine earlier immediately lobbied for appropriate exceptions. On November 9, 1951, permission was given for Beaujolais growers, among others, to release certain wines for sale *en primeur*—which meant, specifically, one month earlier than the standard date.

That, then, was when Beaujolais Nouveau (or Beaujolais Primeur, as some people prefer to call it) was first given official recognition. In 1985 the *primeur* release date of November 15 was changed, as far as Beaujolais was concerned, to the third Thursday of November so that arrival of the new wine in far-flung places could be tied to a weekend during which everyone could enjoy it. Sales of Beaujolais Nouveau, which had grown to almost half a million cases by 1960, now exceed six million cases a year.

* * * * * *

The Beaujolais region lies west of the Saône, just above Lyons. Though now perceived as an appendage to Burgundy (at the northern limit, Beaujolais vines fraternize with those of the Mâconnais), the Beaujolais and Burgundy have never been, historically, connected. In fact, rivalry between the Beaujolais and the Mâconnais was so extreme in pre-Revolutionary France that it erupted regularly in drawn-out legal actions and appeals to the courts and councils of the crown.

The Beaujolais, protected by Lyons' powerful archbishops, had been allowed to sell that city its wine free of taxes, an advantage denied growers of the Mâconnais, regarded as denizens of the duke of Burgundy. This snub became all the more galling to Mâcon in the seventeenth century, when improvements to an ancient road west from Belleville, the small Beaujolais port on the Saône River, across the watershed to Pouilly-sur-Loire, gave Beaujolais producers easy access to Paris, a market the Mâcon growers had worked hard to open for themselves. On convoys of barges that passed through the newly constructed Briare canal, linking the Loire and the Seine Rivers, Beaujolais made its appearance in the capital.

The town councillors of Mâcon relied on the archaic configuration of the revenue system under the *ancien régime* in desperate attempts to crush Beaujolais with taxes. But in 1694, after years of squabbling, the mayor of Villefranche (the Beaujolais' own "capital") and his supporters were granted a ruling in their wine's favor. They won their case on a legal nicety but had suggested anyway that the crown's income would in fact increase at a faster rate if no additional taxes were imposed. It's the standard argument, of course, in such situations (*plus ça change,* and all that); but the Beaujolais growers gave weight to it by predicting that, left alone, they should be shipping to Paris at least 8,000 hectoliters of wine a year by 1700. Their claim proved to be incredibly modest: A report published in 1769 shows that Beaujolais growers were by then shipping to the city 160,000 hectoliters a year—equivalent to 1.75 million cases of wine. (This result eventually persuaded the growers of Mâcon to drop Pinot Noir in favor of the Gamay they had sneered at in their litigation.)

This growth of sales caused a dramatic expansion of vineyards in eighteenth-century Beaujolais and led to the spread of a system of share-cropping already prevalent in the area. Groups of a dozen or more small growers each held and tended ten to twenty acres of land—both vineyard and arable—for an owner with whom they were obliged to share their harvest. The system still exists on some large Beaujolais estates; I some-times see the great casks the French call *foudres* lined up, each identified with the name of the grower whose crop is destined to fill it. As for the Beaujolais' privileged relationship with Lyons, that still exists, too, but in a different and curiously modern form: Anyone driving down the *autoroute* from Paris to the Mediterranean discovers that there is no toll for using the stretch of road between Villefranche and Lyons.

· · · · · ·

The Beaujolais no longer has a political boundary. Partly in the adminis-trative *département* of Saône-et-Loire and partly in the *département* of the Rhône, it is defined viticulturally by the French appellation laws. Villefranche is a convenient hub from which to explain the layout of the various appellations that make up the Beaujolais. More confusing than the article, which distinguishes "the" Beaujolais region from Beaujolais wine, is use of the word Beaujolais to refer broadly to the wines of the entire region; they include Beaujolais-Villages and wines of the ten *crus* as well as plain Beaujolais itself. As a result, one often hears wine from the basic Beaujolais appellation referred to (as above) as "plain" Beaujolais, "simple" Beaujolais, or "ordinary" Beaujolais, when it may not be plain, simple, or ordinary at all.

The 22,000 acres of vineyard southwest of Villefranche where "plain" Beaujolais is produced form both the largest and the most varied of the appellations. Beaujolais-Villages is produced northwest of the town in a region of wide, undulating hills. Its 15,000 acres of vines lie adjacent to, and sometimes surround, the vineyards of the ten *crus,* which vary in size from Chénas, with 600 planted acres, to Brouilly, with 3,000. Together, the *crus* comprise some 13,000 acres of vineyard.

Those Beaujolais-Villages hills are the last outcroppings of the Massif Central, a granite formation far older than the Alps or the Pyrenees. Millennia of rain and wind, heat and ice, have reduced them to a coarse sand that now presents a deceptive softness of contour. Though never seeming so, the hills can be both high and steep. Their soils are less homogeneous than their common profile might suggest. Granitic sand predominates, but there are everywhere gradations and mixtures. In the Beaujolais-Villages, the sand, mostly gray-colored, is often mixed with clay. At Brouilly, Fleurie, and Regnié the sand, mostly pink, is fairly pure. On the Côte de Brouilly the vines are planted on a splintered blue-black rock (reputed to be among the hardest in France) that recurs, mixed with pink granite, at Juliénas. In Morgon, there's schist beneath the upper vineyards—notably its Côte de Py—and clay lower down, and Moulin-à-Vent has deposits of manganese so heavy that in the last century they were mined commercially. The relative toughness of Moulin-à-Vent wines is thought to be connected to this presence.

• • • • • •

As might be expected, each *cru* has distinctive characteristics. One such might be no more than a particularity of aroma—Brouilly, it is said, is grapey, while Fleurie smells of violets, Saint-Amour of peach, and Chénas of spices. These differences are harder to pin down, however, than the sharper divisions based on body and structure. It's far easier to see that, whereas Brouilly, Côte de Brouilly, Regnié, Fleurie, Saint-Amour, and Chénas have in common their elegance and fragrant delicacy, Juliénas, Morgon, and especially Moulin-à-Vent possess greater generosity, deeper flavor, and more lasting power. Chiroubles, of which there is very little anyway, stands apart from the others: Less aromatic than some, and without the fleshiness of others, it has a lacy texture and a sleek charm.

Markets usually show a marked preference for one *cru* over another. "Lyons traditionally prefers a Beaujolais with a firm edge," Paul Jambon, of the Pavillon de Chavannes on the Côte de Brouilly, told me. "The Lyonnais like structure, and they don't like the aroma to be too exuberant. Lyons drinks Morgon and Moulin-à-Vent. But Paris, which appreciates lighter red wines with fresh aromas, drinks Fleurie and Brouilly. The Swiss, too, have a passion for Fleurie, which is why it is now one of the most expensive of the *crus*."

Site—*terroir*—is important everywhere in establishing the personality of a wine, but Claude Geoffray of Château Thivin, also on the Côte de Brouilly, feels it to be especially so in the Beaujolais because Gamay itself is such a low-key varietal. A Gamay wine expresses the character of the vineyard or it expresses nothing. Which is why, Geoffray says, the yield of grapes from each vine must be severely restricted and the winemaking as nonintrusive as possible. With roughly 4,000 vines planted to the acre, Geoffray expects to harvest no more than 1.5 pounds of grapes from each. In comparison, most California vineyards carry 1,000 vines to the acre, with which they rarely harvest fewer than 4 tons of grapes. That's about 8 pounds of fruit from each vine.

Château Thivin's *cuverie*, built against a hillside, was planned to allow its winemaking to flow not with pumps but by gravity from the tanks—where the whole bunches are allowed to ferment and macerate in a manner unique to the Beaujolais—to presses below and then farther down into the cellar. Fermentation is completed in old wooden *foudres*, each with a capacity of about a thousand gallons.

In a tradition imposed, in fact, by the appellation regulations, the harvest must be brought to the *cuverie* in whole bunches. There they are dumped into reception tanks, preferably no higher than they are wide. The weight of the mass crushes the bottom bunches, which begin to ferment and release carbon dioxide. It fills the crevices between the rest of the bunches, stifles the yeast, and inhibits the spread of fermentation. But even in these conditions, the warmth generated affects the uncrushed bunches in ways that extract color and flavor from the grape-skins without releasing tannin (not that the Gamay grape has much). Malic acid is also substantially reduced—a reason for the softness of new Beaujolais—and the grapes' sugars are freed for a more rapid and complete fermentation later, once the bunches have been removed from the vat and crushed. First, however, they spend from three to ten days in this state of anaerobic metabolism, a process basic to the universally appealing style of Beaujolais.

* * * * * *

Each grower handles the maceration phase differently, of course, and distortions do occur. Usually they are the result of a grower's taking a shortcut, hoping to get quality results while boosting yields, or of his allowing the success of *primeurs* to influence the way he makes a *cru* wine. Or they are an exaggeration to attract star ratings from the more-is-more school of wine critics. One technique is to heat the grapes to 60° or 70° C, thereby increasing the extraction of color, before cooling them to a temperature at which a yeast culture can be introduced. Wines made this way are round and big but lack both vivacity and personality. Another technique is to push yields to the limit, despite the risk that the fruit will then not ripen fully. A heavy hand with chaptalization—adjustment of sugar levels from sacks held ready for the purpose—and the introduction of yeasts that generate powerful, if short-lived, aromas during fermentation mask the wine's inherent deficiencies. On the other hand, there are many growers—young ones especially—whose approach to winemaking is practically in step with that of their grandfathers.

Olivier Ravier, of the Domaine de la Pierre Bleue and president of the Beaujolais growers' association, says that people accept clumsy wines made with exaggerated chaptalization and monster yeasts when they lose their ability to taste and appreciate subtlety.

"French children," he told me, "once went from water to water-and-wine, to wine-and-water, and, eventually, to wine. It was part of growing up, and they learned to appreciate the taste—and the use—of wine. Now our children drink heavily advertised sugary soft drinks with phony fruit flavors. One day they learn from their friends to add alcohol to it. And eventually they leave out the soft drink. This has led to both social and economic problems. We winegrowers have difficulty tempting such impaired palates back to wine. But it's the same with food. Too much of what we eat is processed and tastes of manufactured flavors. How can we expect anyone to understand and enjoy the infinite range of tastes and aromas that real wine and real food offer? These are things one must learn in childhood."

To get to the root of the problems, Ravier and other Beaujolais growers started a program—L'Univers du Goût—for Villefranche elementary schools, which teaches children how to taste. One of the most basic lessons for very small children involves each child's bringing to school a particular vegetable—a carrot, a leek, and so on—which the class tastes and then puts in a pot for making, with the help of the teacher, a soup that they all get to eat. Gradually the lessons go deeper. A discussion on varieties of pears, for instance, will include a simple history of the fruit, an explanation of how it is cultivated, the uses for each variety, and, of course, a chance to taste and compare them.

Forty-four of the town's schoolteachers have taken the voluntary training course for the program so far, which covers all fruits, vegetables, herbs, and spices. There is a Villefranche center for the program with its own reference library, but much of the teacher training is done in the well-equipped tasting room at Ravier's vineyard. There, each session ends with a wine tasting. Ravier just smiled when I asked if that might have contributed to the program's phenomenal success. The agricultural college of the next *département* has asked for his group's assistance in starting a similar program.

• • • • • •

Food is important in the Beaujolais: The style of cooking has a solid, country quality. The serious reputation of the *auberge du cep* in Fleurie attracts a clientele from Paris as well as Lyons, whereas the *coq au vin* in Juliénas, with its slightly more flamboyant appeal, is presently popular with the local smart set. Other restaurants with excellent—and typical— food include Chez Christian Mabeau at Odenas, elegant and welcoming and with a large shaded terrace for lunching and dining in summer; Ann de Beaujeu, a small reasonably priced hotel and restaurant in an attractively appointed former private mansion in Beaujeu; and Le Morgon, a simple-looking restaurant, up a lane away from the village of Villié-Morgon, with a wide selection of Morgon wines listed by producer.

Visitors to the area may also enjoy a tour of George Duboeuf's Hameau du Beaujolais, a transformation of the former railway station at Romanèche-Thorins. Its hour-long mixed-media overview of the region includes exhibits (as well as a slow-motion film of fermentation shot with an endoscopic camera, the kind surgeons use to take a look where the eye cannot go) on everything from geology to the history of making bottles. The show ends with a wine tasting accompanied by local bread and sausage.

The chalk-clay soil of the southern Beaujolais, rich in iron, has a golden color that has earned it the name of *terres dorées,* or golden lands. The terrain is precipitously abrupt and strewn with old castles, tawny Romanesque churches, and impossible legends. The clay and the iron, especially, lend the wines here—the plain Beaujolais—a natural rusticity. Good examples are the wines from Jean-Paul Brun's Domaine des Terres Dorées and Pierre-Marie Chermette's Domaine du Vissoux at Saint-Vérand.

On this area's back roads a succession of villages, each prettier than the last, has cafés and bistros offering a simple country lunch and a carafe of wine from the vineyard outside the window. Those looking for more refined cooking will find that too, at restaurants like the Vieux Moulin at Alix and Les Marroniers at Lozanne. Everyone hopes, one day, to find a corner of France, true to itself, easily accessible, but overlooked by tourism. Here it is. Just turn right off the *autoroute* at Villefranche.

LES CHEVALIERS DU TASTEVIN

OF THE TWELVE THOUSAND MEMBERS OF BURGUNDY'S CONFRÉRIE
des Chevaliers du Tastevin, two thousand live in North America. From
Halifax to San Diego they are attached to groups known rather forbid-
dingly as *sous-commanderies,* the oldest and probably the largest of which
was founded in New York in 1940.

No doubt more than a few Americans will be among the five or six
hundred *chevaliers* and guests, black-tied and robed *du soir,* who will sit
down on a June evening to dine at candlelit and flower-bedecked tables
in the twelfth-century wine cellar of the Château du Clos de Vougeot.
According to the calendar of the Confrérie, they will be gathered there
for its annual *chapître* in honor of the flowering of the vine. In fact,
Burgundy's vines, heeding no calendar, are sometimes disobligingly
unpunctual, and so it is just possible that those assembled will be antic-
ipating rather than celebrating the blossom in the vineyards. Either way,
their enthusiasm, you can be sure, will be great.

A *tastevin* (the *s* is pronounced in English but is silent in French) is
a Burgundian taster, a shallow silver dish perhaps three inches across
with a thumb grip at the side to give it the misleading appearance of an
ashtray. The slightly convex bottom and the traditional pattern of dim-
ples and fluting on the sides are more than decorative: Their refraction
of light through a few drops of wine reveals secrets of quality and style
to the initiated. An old, family *tastevin* wrapped in cotton cloth is sure to

be in the pocket of any Burgundian winegrower, merchant, or broker. It is for his or her professional use, of course, but it is also a sort of discreet talisman that the possessor would be unhappy to lose, or even to have left behind when leaving home.

The original intention of the founders of the Confrérie had been neither more nor less than to foster an occasional evening of good cheer to amuse their friends. Georges Faiveley, a wine merchant from Nuits-Saint-Georges, and Camille Rodier, then president of the local tourist office, had the idea in the early thirties. Times were difficult. Economic depression and the social upheaval of World War I had not helped Burgundy's wines. The benign art of the table that is based on good food and wine as enhancements of the company of others rather than as ends in themselves was in decline. "As our wines are not selling," they concluded, "let's ask our friends to come and drink them with us."

· · · · · ·

In the seventeenth and eighteenth centuries, drinking clubs and fraternities were as common in France as in England. In Burgundy the Ordre de la Boisson, with statutes written in verse, was founded in 1703. Its rule of punctuating gastronomic evenings with music and singing was carried over by a colonel of the Twelfth Hussars when, in 1812, he revived the order as the Confrérie des Francs Buveurs Bourguignons to enliven his retirement in Dijon. A manuscript on which he had recorded its procedures and formalities was unearthed by Faiveley and Rodier, who used them as a model for their new fraternity. Its first "chapter" took place in an old cellar in Nuits-Saint-Georges in 1934 and followed by and large the patterns retrieved from the Francs Buveurs, sparged with additional ceremony lifted from Molière's *Le Malade Imaginaire* and illuminated by a pageantry of scarlet and gold costumes loosely adapted from the robes and caps of the pre-Revolutionary French parliamentarians. It made quite a show.

Even in those early days, the Confrérie used the same sense of purpose and quality in picking its guests as its members would use in picking their grapes for a good *cuvée*. Photographs of prewar *chapîtres* show leaders of the gastronomic world—André Simon, founder of the International Wine and Food Society, for example, and Curnonsky, *"prince des gastronomes"*—breaking bread with key members of the French government, of the Académie Française, and of the Paris diplomatic corps. In 1937 the then United States' ambassador to France, William Bullitt, was inducted into the *Confrérie*. (It was much later, at a *chapître* of the Confrérie in October, 1951, that Curnonsky gave new life to Brillat-Savarin's rather lugubrious declaration that a meal without cheese was like a beautiful woman with only one eye.)

Over the years, *tastevin* in hand and possibly tongue in cheek, the Confrérie has succeeded in winning an ever-widening circle of influential friends, not just for Burgundy but for France itself. Those of celebrity in government, business, science, and the arts have been delighted, and more than a little flattered, to be invited to a *chapître* of the Confrérie at Clos de Vougeot; to eat and drink sumptuously; to shout, clap, and wag fingers to the rhythm of the *ban bourguignon*. A guest at a past chapter might have been seated beside Alfred Hitchcock or Ingrid Bergman; Chancellor Helmut Kohl or the Comtesse de Paris, wife of the Pretender to the French throne; Mstislav Rostropovich or Sir Christopher Leaver, Lord Mayor of London; Peter Ustinov or Yehudi Menuhin; the president of Volkswagen or the chairman of Crédit Lyonnais; the Netherlands minister of finance or the British ambassador. Here might have been Mary McCarthy, there General Norstad; here a prince of Sweden, and there an American astronaut, a French Olympic equestrian, a German philosopher. So broad has been the reach of the Confrérie that, in not much more than half a century, it has become a French national institution.

◆ ◆ ◆ ◆ ◆ ◆

The *chapîtres* continued to be held regularly in that old cellar beneath Nuits-Saint-Georges until the outbreak of World War II, but Etienne Camuzet, owner of the Château du Clos de Vougeot and from the first a supporter of the Confrérie, occasionally made the vast wine cellar there available for gala events, when the *caveau* in Nuits-Saint-Georges would have been impossibly small. The château had long been under separate ownership from the vineyards that surround it, and, after the liberation of France in 1944, Camuzet offered it to a group of the *chevaliers,* himself among them, with the specific intention of leasing it to the Confrérie. Classified as a *monument historique,* the château has long been what the French call an *haut-lieu,* not just of Burgundy but of France. For two hundred years now, all French troops passing the Clos de Vougeot are obliged by tradition to present arms. In terms both of its form— majestically solid, elegantly severe—and its history, it is symbolic of the two forces that have shaped Burgundy: the region's agricultural wealth and an intellectual brilliance that in the late Middle Ages radiated throughout all of Europe from the monasteries at Cîteaux and Cluny.

Clos de Vougeot's origin lies in a scrap of land—less than an acre— given to the monks of Cîteaux early in the twelfth century. (The Cistercians began as a community of extreme ascetics, devoting their time to prayer and rigorous field labor in reaction to what they saw as the soft monastic life practiced elsewhere at the time. They had settled in a desolate and swampy area a few miles from Nuits-Saint-Georges in 1098.) By the fourteenth century, as the order prospered, the Cistercians had expanded their holding to 125 acres of vines, the largest single vine-yard in Burgundy. In 1336 they enclosed it within a wall—hence, *Clos de Vougeot.* Of the original buildings they erected there in 1150, the vat hall and the wine cellar—a stone barn rather than an underground chamber and now the dramatic setting for the Confrérie's dinners—are still standing. The better-known buildings visible from the road and more often seen in photographs and drawings were built in the mid-sixteenth century and judiciously restored around the turn of the nineteenth.

◆ ◆ ◆ ◆ ◆ ◆

Each *chapître* dinner—there are seventeen of them every year—is timed with the precision of a rocket launching. I quote from Lucien Boitouzet's *Histoire de la Confrérie:*

> 8:10 P.M. The first white wine is served
> 8:15 P.M. Trumpets and hunting horns

8:20 P.M. The first speaker gives the Rabelaisian grace

8:30 P.M. The waiters enter with the first dish

8:40 P.M. Trumpets and the entrance of the Cadets de
Bourgogne . . . and so on until . . .

11:20 P.M. The Cadets de Bourgogne depart

11:25 P.M. Coffee, *marc*, and *prunelle* are served

11:30 P.M. Orchestra

11:40 P.M. Entrance of the Grand Conseil, and the
ceremony for the induction of new members
begins.

* * * * * *

Attendance at a *chapître* of the Confrérie is, clearly, not to be undertaken lightly.

To say that the Cadets de Bourgogne are a group of Burgundian folk singers is like describing the Compagnons de la Chanson as a barber-shop quartet. Though they appear dressed in the black caps and aprons of Burgundian cellarmen, the Cadets (a term to be understood figuratively; many are grandfathers) are from numerous walks of life. They jolly the evening along with ballads, old Burgundian drinking choruses, and whatever else might seem appropriate. Not so long ago, for a group of Houston astronauts, they donned ten-gallon white hats to render "The Yellow Rose of Texas," and for Yehudi Menuhin they sang a three-part chorale composed for the occasion by the director of Dijon's music conservatory.

The group began, under their earlier name of Chanteurs Bourguignons, back in the 1920s, when a dozen or so men within the Cercle Rameau, a Dijon choir, all of them as partial to wine as to music, would meet over a bottle to sing. They were soon a part of every wine event and celebration of the region and performed regularly at the Caveau Bourguignon in Dijon. There they expanded their repertoire by introducing new songs, often Burgundian poetry set to music and harmonized for them by the talented assistant director of the Cercle. Their presence at the Confrérie's first *chapître* in 1934 was as inevitable as the wine in the glasses, and so it has since remained as one generation of Cadets has replaced another.

But singing is thirsty work. When the Cadets break to moisten their throats, their Burgundian *confrères* take over and bring the assembly up to date with satirical news and stories of Burgundy and of the world beyond its borders. The pace is fast, the wit is sharp, nothing is sacred. The seemingly contradictory French qualities of measure and hilarity, charm and mockery, grace and ribaldry, pursue and complement each other. Both an urbane Molière and an earthy Rabelais would feel at home at a *chapître*. So would a worldly Talleyrand, the master statesman who lost neither time nor ground in adroitly managing his career from the reign of Louis XVI to the revolutionary government's and from Napoleon's to the restored Louis XVIII's. At the Congress of Vienna he is alleged to have said that the art of diplomacy is largely the successful deployment of a good cook and a battery of saucepans. Had he added "and a cellar of good Burgundy" he would have nailed the Confrérie's formula pretty well. Because it must be said that the delicious wine and the good-natured songs and the funny stories rest on the foundation of an impeccable kitchen.

* * * * * *

The Confrérie originally relied on outside chefs, usually a local restaurateur, for its banquets. Lucien Boitouzet explains: "At the beginning there was a mobile kitchen, which was in itself a challenge. The food was cooked in the kitchens of the Croix-Blanche restaurant in Nuits-Saint-Georges and then transported in vans to the Château du Clos de Vougeot. An unexpected bump in the road could upset the sauces. Should the vans be late, the organizers had to improvise a speech to entertain the waiting guests...."

The château's medieval kitchen would have been perfect for roasting a whole ox but not for preparing more subtle dishes. A new kitchen was finally installed in 1953, however, and in 1956 Georges Garin, the new owner of the Croix-Blanche, raised the standard of Confrérie dinners immeasurably. (Garin left in 1960 to go to Paris. The restaurant he opened near Notre Dame, Chez Garin, quickly earned two rosettes from *Michelin* and for more than a decade, until he semiretired to the south of France, was one of the most distinguished, fashionable, and successful restaurants in Paris.)

Garin's successor at the Croix-Blanche, Jean Fargeau, accepted the challenge of maintaining the standard. When he left in 1968, the Confrérie hired a full-time chef of its own, with two *sous-chefs* and a kitchen staff of some twelve others to support him. Harry Yoxall in his book *The Wines of Burgundy* gives the menu of the dinner Fargeau prepared for the 1967 Chapître du Printemps, at which he was promoted to *commandeur* in the Confrérie. It is impossible to convey in translation the Rabelaisian flavor of the original French, but the list of wines and dishes alone suggests the style of a Chevaliers du Tastevin dinner:

Cold suckling pigs in jelly and
parsleyed ham served with
strong Dijon mustard and
Bourgogne Aligoté '64
from Magny-les-Villers

Truffled soufflés of pike Nantua
with Puligny-Montrachet,
Les Combettes, '64

A fricassee of young
cockerels and morels
Beaune '64

Baked gammon
Nuits Clos de la Maréchale '64

Cheeses
Clos de la Roche '62
Strawberries from Meuilly
served en Melba

I had enjoyed several of Fargeau's dinners as a guest at various *chapîtres*, but by the time I was myself inducted as a *chevalier* of the Confrérie in 1981, his toque had passed to Hubert Hugot, the chef who now presides over the kitchens at Vougeot. The occasion was the Chapître de la Saint Hubert, always the first dinner of December, which is dedicated to the patron saint of hunters and is preceded by a mass at the old village church of Gilly-lès-Cîteaux. The note in my diary reads:

> Chapître de St. Hubert, began with mass at Gilly
> church, a hunting horn sextet, and a blessing of dogs.
> Priest said his church usually too big: The St. Hubert
> mass was only day in the year he wished it bigger. We
> were six hundred, not including the dogs. Reassembled
> later in courtyard of Vougeot, decorated with huge
> fir trees that seemed to be growing there, transforming
> it into a forest glade. By torchlight, a stag (actually a skin
> filled with chunks of meat) was given to the dogs. Dogs
> obviously already too well fed and not much interested.
> Endless hunting calls on the horns. Bitterly cold,
> but cups of hot chicken broth handed round. Inside, bril-
> liantly organized, vastly entertaining and superb dinner.

Would I be pushing it to quote the menu?

Roulade *of* foie gras
with a Bourgogne Aligoté of the
Hautes-Côtes de Nuits

Biscuit *of Salmon* [a cream of salmon mounted like a
soufflé and nothing to do with biscuits as we understand the term] *with Meursault-Chevalières '78*

Chicken Gaston-Gérard with Côtes de Nuits-Villages '77
[Gaston-Gérard was a minister of tourism, the first
member of a French government to be made a *chevalier*

of the Confrérie. I wish I could remember how he cooked
his chicken, but I can't; I know the sauce was based on
Dijon mustard, but the details are lost in a happy blur.]

Haunch of Venison Grand Veneur
with Chambolle-Musigny
Premier Cru '74

Cheeses
Latricières-Chambertin '74

Pears poached in red wine,
with petits fours

Wines served at *chapître* dinners are identified by no more than the label
of the Confrérie, are selected twice a year, and are drawn mostly from
wines already submitted blind for the approval of an independent jury
now assembled twice a year at the Château du Clos de Vougeot to assign
the right of *tastevinage*. The mix of the roughly two hundred jurors varies
somewhat from session to session but includes wine professionals,
restaurateurs, officials of government departments concerned with
wine, and specialist writers, as well as connoisseurs at large. Never are
officials or members of the Grand Conseil of the Confrérie included, and
the work is divided so that the jurors taste in groups of five or six and no
one has to judge more than fifteen to eighteen wines.

A wine that is approved—*tasteviné*—by a jury is allowed to carry the
boldly decorative arms of the Chevaliers du Tastevin in association with
the name of the grower or of the merchant who bottled it. As a support
it is less important, perhaps, to growers and merchants with established
international reputations. But the insignia gives the consumer the guarantee that the wine of a small or unknown grower is worthy of attention.
It can even help a well-known merchant when he is offering a wine from
an unfamiliar appellation. The insignia of the Confrérie encourages a
consumer who might otherwise have hesitated to take a risk.

It should go without saying that any wine submitted must be from Burgundy, but it must also be of a specific appellation and of a single vintage. Jurors are expected to judge a wine by asking themselves whether it accurately corresponds to type for the appellation and vintage given. They must be confident that it will mature well—otherwise the Confrérie's label could be discredited. And they should be sufficiently impressed by the wine to feel they would be proud to serve it at their own tables. The tastings are not competitive, and no medals are awarded. Jurors are not expected to submit notes on the wines they approve, but they are required to give a specific reason when refusing a wine the privilege of the Confrérie's label.

This judging activity of the Chevaliers is the one most in the public eye. Bottles bearing the arms of the Confrérie can now be seen on wine lists all over the world. The growing value of such endorsement has led to a steady increase every year in the number of applications for *tastevinage*. In 1950, the year of the first jury, 133 wines were submitted and 103 accepted. In 1987 the number of wines submitted to the jury had increased more than tenfold to 1,429, and 773 were accepted.

Through the *tastevinage*, one might say, the Confrérie des Chevaliers du Tastevin has been able to extend its reach and its chances of making even more friends for Burgundy and for France. In a way, every bottle with the Confrérie's coat of arms carries the message of the Chevaliers du Tastevin. Of those who have been touched more directly by being honored at Vougeot, none has responded more aptly than Maurice Chevalier when promoted from *chevalier* to *grand officier* at a *chapître* at the Château du Clos de Vougeot in October 1960. In thanking the Chevaliers du Tastevin and their guests assembled in that great wine cellar, he said, "My profession, ladies and gentlemen, has been since childhood to be a sort of commercial traveler for French friendship. In other words, it was my job to make friends for my country wherever I went, rather like the wines of France...." And rather like, he could have added, the Chevaliers du Tastevin.

FRANCONIA:
GOING FOR BAROQUE

A FEW YEARS AGO, AT THE END OF MAY, I WAS IN THE GERMAN city of Würzburg for the final night of the annual Baroque music festival. While dusk gathered over the rose garden of the Residenz, the sumptuous eighteenth-century palace of the former prince-bishops, its scented arbors and pathways illuminated by flickering torches, three hundred of us, decorously black-tied or discreetly bejeweled, sat under the vast Tiepolo ceiling of the Imperial Hall listening to soloists of the Leipziger Gewandhaus Bach Orchestra play, as a prelude to dinner, music by Corelli, Handel, Bach, and Vivaldi.

It was a brilliant performance, and as we moved to our candlelit tables in the adjoining White Hall (the room's every surface encrusted, by Antonio Bossi—who later went mad—with the world's most extravagant display of Rococo plasterwork), I wondered what wine on Earth, let alone what dish, could possibly make an impression against the competition of all this splendor. I need not have been concerned. Dinner began with a succulent terrine of smoked trout, from streams on the Spessart mountains to the west of Würzburg, accompanied by a memorably stylish Franconian wine, a Würzburger Stein Sylvaner '91, grown just a few hundred yards from where we sat and made in the palace cellars beneath our feet. After a pigeon consommé and a pause for a glass of prize-winning Eschendorfer Lump Sylvaner Spätlese '89, we went on to

99

enjoy a 1990 Bürgstadter Centgrafenberg Spätburgunder Kabinett, one of Germany's rarest red wines, with a fillet of young venison, cranberry sauce, and sesame-strewn potatoes.

• • • • • •

Mention Würzburg or its region, Franconia, and most Americans (other than members of the United States Third Infantry Division stationed there) draw a blank. Yet Franconia—the storybook Germany of forests and vineyards, venerable castles and comfortable old inns, Baroque palaces and Rococo churches—is little more than an hour's drive east of Frankfurt's steel-and-glass metropolis. Those who go there find gingerbread houses and cobblestone streets within the walls and turrets of medieval villages; delicious food garnered from local farms, rivers, and woods; and of course Franconian wine, to enjoy in a grower's snug parlor or in a wisteria-draped courtyard.

Franconia's art treasures and architectural riches are a legacy of the time when packhorses and mule trains carrying the world's luxuries—silks, dyes, pepper, saffron—wound their way from the Alpine passes and the upper reaches of the Danube to the valleys of the Main and the Rhine and to the headwaters of the Weser and the Elbe. From Genoa to Lübeck, from Constantinople to Antwerp, and from Venice to Hamburg, all roads passed through Franconia. (Wagner, which means "wagoner" or "teamster," is one of the region's most common family names.)

Great trading and banking dynasties were founded there. To get goods from one watershed to the other, bills of exchange and letters of credit were as essential as horses. Taxes, dues for right of passage, commissions, and profits on reworked commodities enriched Franconia's merchant families and paid for the adornment of their cities. These were people who lived well and drank well. The religious institutions they supported established the area's vineyards, first mentioned in seventh-century documents, on the sites best calculated to provide them with the finest wine.

In 1802, when Napoleon deposed the ruling prince-bishop of Würzburg in the course of bringing the map of Germany's principalities closer to his own taste in political geography, Franconia was annexed to Bavaria, a German state distinguished for beer rather than wine. But Franconia has remained faithful to the vines that line the valley of the Main River as it meanders from the hills of the Steigerwald in the east to a gap south of the heavily forested Spessart in the west. (The Main then flows past Frankfurt to join the Rhine.)

The Spessart's mountainous mass protects the vineyards from the rain of the prevailing westerlies, but it cuts them off from maritime influence, too, leaving the Main valley exposed to an extreme continental climate. Summers are hotter, winters colder (the Main freezes over regularly), and both spring and fall are shorter than they are on the Rhine. Late spring frosts are common and can damage a potential crop severely—as happened in 1985. Ideally, Franconia needs grape varieties that bud late and ripen early, to reduce the risk of damage by spring frosts and to make the most of the short span of an intense Franconian summer.

But the Main valley, compressed and convoluted between the Spessart and the Steigerwald, encompasses a series of subtly changing weather patterns as it twists repeatedly to and fro, ensuring, in its turns, the benefit of many sheltered and south-facing slopes. The valley's soils are varied as well. In the west, a reddish sandstone (which reappears on isolated sites farther east) gives full white wines and, from Pinot Noir, Germany's most reputed reds. Closer to Würzburg, in the middle section of the valley—known as the Triangle (*Dreieck*) because the river there follows the form of a giant V—a particularly active limestone formed from seashell fossils promotes in the wines a characteristically sturdy finesse and the delicate but intense fragrance most associated with the best of Franconian wines. Farther east, the vineyards on the gypsum and heavy clay of the Steigerwald give firm wines of greater substance that, though slower to disclose themselves, age well.

◆ ◆ ◆ ◆ ◆ ◆

Mature Franconian wines have always been keenly sought out, jealously hoarded, and highly prized. In his book *Vintage: The Story of Wine*, Hugh Johnson tells of being one of a privileged few who tasted, in London in

1961, a wine grown on the Stein vineyard at Würzburg in 1540, a hot, dry year in which, records show, there was no rain from April to October. Under those conditions, the wine was probably as difficult as it was concentrated. At any rate, it spent more than a hundred years in a regularly replenished cask in the cellar of the prince-bishops before being bottled in the late seventeenth century. In the nineteenth century, following Franconia's complete absorption into Bavaria, the bottles were transferred to the royal cellars. From there they were eventually sold off at auction, along with much else, during Germany's republican era after World War I. Even though four hundred years old, the wine, Johnson tells us, was still lively, reflecting, as it were, "the sun of that distant summer."

The vigorous elegance of Franconian wines has been their chief attraction. They were favorites of Goethe (whose last recorded words, in 1832, came in the form of a question about the Franconian wine being offered him: "You haven't put sugar in it?" he is said to have asked). André Jullien, in his reliable *Topographie de Tous les Vignobles Connus*, first published in Paris in 1816, described the wine of Würzburg as "a dry wine with spirit, perfumed and very agreeable" and, making much of the high prices it fetched, ranked it with the most esteemed of Germany. Henry Vizetelly, in his 1875 report on the wines of the world presented at the International Exposition of 1873 in Vienna, said much the same, praising its "flavour, fullness, and delicacy" as well as its "singular vigour and fire." He, too, ranked Franconian wines among the greatest.

High praise of Franconian wine continued into this century: Morton Shand, in his *Book of Other Wines—Than French*, published in 1929, was as enthusiastic as Goethe, Jullien, and Vizetelly. Usually a carefully observant writer, hardly given to purple prose, Shand got carried away when writing of Franconian wine. (He mentions *Steinwein*, incidentally, using as a generic term a name that should have been—and now is— legally restricted to wines from the Stein vineyard in Würzburg.) While telling of German writers who compare Franconian wine to madrigals, Shand outdoes them with an embarrassingly fey comparison to "a dewy posy of wild flowers, fresh picked by fairy fingers," but settles down to describe, more matter-of-factly, the wines' "subtle delicacy of flavour and ... rare, if almost evanescent, bouquet."

· · · · · · ·

The world virtually lost sight of Franconian wines after Shand's book. For years they were all but unobtainable in Germany and quite impossible to find elsewhere. There are many reasons why the area under vines had shrunk severely by the early twentieth century—chief among them the cost of replanting Franconia's steep hillsides after phylloxera struck in the 1870s. Vestiges of the Napoleonic inheritance law that divides vineyards—and divides them again with each succeeding generation—had already imposed an awkward and expensive pattern of cultivation as families struggled to deal with their many minute and widely scattered parcels of vines acquired through past marriages. The problem exacerbated the already high risk of growing grapes in a region where a year's crop could be lost in a single spring night's frost.

By the 1960s, the production of Franconian wine did not meet local demand. A vintner had only to provide a few tables and benches in his leafy garden in summer or a cozy wine room with candles and checkered tablecloths in winter for customers to arrive to spend a pleasant hour with a *Schoppen* (traditionally a quarter liter of young wine) and a snack of bread and sausage. Inevitably, a case or two of wine would leave the house with each visit. Even when the vintage had been abundant, the cellars were soon empty.

Changes in Germany's wine laws in 1971 and a program that helped consolidate Franconia's vineyards into workable holdings through an officially sponsored exchange among growers of widely separated small plots revived interest in viticulture. In the last twenty years the area under vines in Franconia has increased from barely five thousand acres to fifteen.

The steadily rising production has been further swollen recently by a series of exceptionally abundant harvests. For the first time since anyone can remember, there is presently not only enough wine for Franconians but wine to spare. This statement is all the more significant if one bears in mind that a fear of running out of wine is of such long standing in Franconia that there were times in the eighteenth century when growers were forbidden by decree of the prince-bishop of Würzburg from selling any wine at all outside his territory.

Almost 90 percent of all Franconian wine is still consumed within Bavaria, but a number of growers are now making small shipments to other parts of Germany and even to the United States. I have seen the distinctive *Bocksbeutel* (the flattened, round-bellied flagon in which Franconian wines are sold) on merchants' shelves as far apart as Santa Monica, California, and Amagansett, New York.

· · · · · ·

In Franconia, the wines are generally drier than elsewhere in Germany, though their labels sport the same classifications—Kabinett, Spätlese, Auslese, and Beerenauslese—to denote the maturity of the grapes, or at least their level of natural sugar when picked. Franconia's hot summers reduce acidity, making residual sugar less important to the wines' overall balance; that's why the growers there can allow a drier fermentation, imposing on themselves a stricter parameter of dryness for wines labeled *Trocken* (dry) and *Halbtrocken* (semi-dry) than Germany's national law requires of them.

Though almost half the vines planted in Franconia are Müller-Thurgau—since World War II the most widely planted variety in Germany because of its large yields and low-risk cultivation—the classic grape of the region is Sylvaner. The new plantings show a steady return to it. "Consumers here have had a fling with all the new varieties," Jochen Freihold, director of the Franconian Winegrowers' Association, told me recently, "and it's interesting to see that those who really appreciate their wine eventually return to Sylvaner."

Sylvaner has a long history in Franconia. In fact, the variety made its German debut there in 1659 in the vineyards of Schloss Castell in the Steigerwald. It is thought to have found its way into Franconia by way of the Danube, just like the silks and spices that preceded it. The earliest

Sylvaner wines must have made an impression, because the variety spread rapidly.

Riesling is grown only on the most favored sites in Franconia. (It covers just 3 percent of the region's vineyard acreage.) The structure imposed on Franconian wine by climate and soil—a structure that gives Franconian Sylvaner its uncommon elegance without affecting its natural tenderness—can be too severe for the inherently steely Riesling. That's why Riesling is planted only on vineyard sites—such as the Würzburger Stein, the Würzburger Abtsleite, and the Randersackerer Teufelkeller—where summer starts earlier and finishes later. When a Franconian Riesling succeeds, however, whether thanks to site or summer or both, it succeeds with rare magnificence.

Other traditional German grape varieties are grown in Franconia, but the area became known, in the first years of its revival, for its considerable acreage of new crossings, many of them specially developed in response to the region's short, hot summer. Each of them has its supporters, but mostly their wines have the quick and easy appeal of pop music—and pall as rapidly. Some say it's simply that the newly crossed vine varieties are highly prolific, and that their wines would have a more classic style if the yields were more strictly controlled. But small yields—and therefore smaller revenues—raise other issues in a place such as Franconia, where production costs are high. Rieslaner, a cross between Riesling and Sylvaner as its name suggests, is one new variety that works well there, especially when used for rich Auslese and Beerenauslese wines. Its intense bouquet, almost like fresh apricot, and deep, lasting flavor become particularly attractive when supported by luscious sweetness.

· · · · · ·

Even after the consolidation of land holdings, the average vineyard in Franconia remains small: The 15,000 acres of vines are divided among 7,735 registered growers. Those figures must be carefully interpreted, however, because a few large estates reduce yet further the average for others. A third of the growers, usually those with less than an acre or so of vines, take their grapes to a growers' cooperative, where the quality of wine will depend on the vineyards of its members and on their diligence. The cooperative at Thüngersheim, just north of Würzburg, shows how well the system can work if local vintners so will it. A selection of wines from Thüngersheim, the best being from the Johannisberg vineyard, a great block of red sandstone thrusting through the limestone of the Triangle, is now being distributed in the United States.

Of the large estates, the most significant are those of Würzburg's Bürgerspital, founded in 1319, and Juliusspital, established in 1576. Both are charitable foundations supporting—with the revenues of their vineyards, farms, and timberland—homes for the elderly, mental institutions, and hospitals. The holdings of the Juliusspital make it the second largest wine estate in Germany. And the vineyards bequeathed to both the Bürgerspital and the Juliusspital by their original founders and by later benefactors are the finest in Franconia. The Bürgerspital's highly privileged sites have allowed it to specialize in Riesling (the variety makes up roughly thirty percent of its production), and a Riesling style—tight, austere—is the hallmark of its wines.

The Staatlicher Hofkeller, formerly the private domain of Würzburg's all-powerful prince-bishop, is now the property of the state of Bavaria. (Some of its vineyards are used for research and teaching.) I have never seen a more spectacular cellar than that beneath the Würzburg Residenz. The long, vaulted aisles, wide and high enough to take a bus, are lined on both sides with enormous and beautifully carved oak casks. Lit by candles, as they are for special occasions, they make an unforgettable sight.

Two of Germany's noble families also have extensive vineyards in Franconia, in the Steigerwald. Schloss Hallburg is the property of Count von Schönborn, and the domain of Schloss Castell has belonged to the family of Prince (and eminent banker) zu Castell-Castell for almost a thousand years. In addition to fine dry wines, weightier and more intense than those of the Triangle, the Castell domain produces exceptional dessert wines—Spätlesen, Auslesen, and Trockenbeerenauslesen—from Rieslaner and Scheurebe grapes grown on its Casteller Kugelspiel vineyard. A 1979 Casteller Kugelspiel Trockenbeerenauslese the color of dark amber, offered to me at the close of a lunch at Schloss Castell, smelled and tasted of praline and rose petals, apricots and honey. Count zu Castell-Castell, the prince's nephew and estate manager, told me that 1992 had produced the best wines in Franconia since that spectacular 1979 vintage.

What's extraordinary is that all these great estates make a score or more wines every year (the Juliusspital makes sixty) by separating grapes according to variety, provenance, and quality, and each one is worthy of representing that estate as if it were the only wine it produced.

♦ ♦ ♦ ♦ ♦ ♦

There are smaller estates making superb wines, too. For example, though I'm not enthusiastic about German red wines, I acknowledge that if the best in Germany are from Franconia, then the best in Franconia are from the Weingut Fürst in Bürgstadt. Paul Fürst makes Germany's most distinguished Pinot Noir—in German, *Spätburgunder*—but I prefer his superb Pinot Noir *Weissherbst* (the word used for white wine made from red grapes). Light gold in color, subtly flavored, and remarkably full-bodied, Fürst's *Weissherbst* is a favorite in Germany's top restaurants.

Outstanding producers in the Triangle include Artur Steinmann and Ernst Gebhardt, both of Sommerhausen, a community of artists and writers a few miles upriver from Würzburg. There, in a tiny but perfect theater above the village gatehouse, are regular performances of plays, concerts, and late-night political cabaret (a German tradition). The local inn offers such delicacies as lilac-blossom, rosebud, and fir-tip ice creams from a sort of homeopathic dessert trolley.

Steinmann lives nonchalantly with his family in the house where Francis Daniel Pastorius was born in 1651. Pastorius, as German Americans know, brought thirteen families to Pennsylvania in 1683, the first Germans to settle in what was to become the United States. On summer weekend afternoons Steinmann plays his accordion for the visitors who sit at tables on the grass in front of his house or has local writers and musicians give poetry readings and recitals. The most popular entertainment, though, is the occasional concert by the band of the U.S. Third Infantry—in homage to Pastorius, one could say.

. . . .

Iphofen, in the Steigerwald about twenty miles southeast of Würzburg, is one of the most charming of the wine towns, with a Renaissance council house, pretty squares, tree-lined streets, and fine Baroque doorways. Two of the region's leading growers are based there: Hans Wirsching and Johann Ruck. Wirsching has made a specialty of Pinot Gris (*Grauburgunder*) from his holdings on the town's Julius-Echter-Berg— where the Main valley's red sandstone appears amid the Steigerwald's deep clay—but is best known for his powerful Riesling and Sylvaner wines. Ruck prides himself on his old vines and the backbone they give his wines. "They have a deeper root system," he says, "and are more consistent in yield and quality." He, too, makes Riesling and Sylvaner— enticingly spicy—from his vines on the Julius-Echter-Berg and on the Kronsberg vineyard. (An Iphöfer Kronsberg from the Juliusspital was one of the wines served to Queen Elizabeth at her coronation banquet in London in 1953.)

Iphofen is a center of good cooking as well as fine wine, with two outstanding restaurants. The reputation of Kammer, a tiny restaurant on the marketplace, draws customers from as far as Frankfurt and Nuremberg. The Zehntkeller, an old tithe barn divided into intimate rooms with no more than three or four tables in each, specializes in typical hearty Franconian dishes, including a local style of *pot-au-feu* made with kid and young vegetables and a venison soup served with mushroom dumplings.

But then one eats well almost everywhere in Franconia. The Juliusspital, the Bürgerspital, and the Hofkeller at the Würzburg Residenz all have restaurants where their wines are available with a choice of simple but well-prepared dishes. Zur Stadt Mainz, also in Würzburg, has a family atmosphere and a Franconian kitchen—wild boar and red cabbage, oxtail in red wine, and some kind of meat dumplings with onions are usually on call. Zum Stachel, Würzburg's oldest wine tavern (it opened in 1413), has an astonishing list of Franconian wines and is so popular in summer that guests happily share tables with strangers just to have a place in its magically beautiful courtyard. And at the Bären, in the town of Ochsenfurt, braised veal and potatoes becomes a dish fit for a king.

Those who go to Würzburg for the Baroque music festival at the end of May or for the Mozart festival a week later—or both—arrive in the middle of asparagus season. (For the Mozart festival, the Würzburg City Philharmonic plays on the terrace of the Residenz for an audience that can choose between folding chairs on the gravel or bring-your-own-blanket on the grass.)

From around early May until late June, German restaurants vie with each other to see which can offer the most tender, the most creamy-white, and the thickest asparagus stalks. Special menus offer dishes that are simply excuses to serve each customer a full pound of white asparagus, usually with a bowl of steamed, freshly dug new potatoes on one side and a bowl of melted butter or hollandaise on the other. The season starts whenever the first asparagus is ready to be cut, but no matter when that might be, whether late or early, it ends punctually on June 23, the Feast of Saint John. The day always comes too soon; but if the season has been satisfactorily long and the asparagus particularly good, one can hear, on June 23, all the way from the Spessart to the Steigerwald, a great sigh of contentment as each and every person swallows the last bite of his or her last pound of asparagus for the year. Any regrets are then drowned in a glass of Franconian Sylvaner.

SCHOOL DAYS ON THE RHINE

"GOOD MORNING!" SAID DR. OTTO CURRLE, COUNSELOR TO THE regional Chamber of Agriculture. "I hope you ate a good breakfast!" Thirty-six of us, some rumpled from the bus, some from lingering too late the night before in a local vintner's parlor, were on the brink of our fourth day of lectures, tastings, and visits in a week-long course on German wines. We had been disgorged into the morning mist of Alzey, near Mainz in the Rheinhessen, and stood at the door of the official testing station where local wines, once they are approved for sale, are certified with their batch number.

"We shall show you how we do it," promised Dr. Currle. "We shall show you the problems. We shall teach you. We shall also test your ability to taste. I hope you ate a good breakfast!"

We had indeed eaten a good breakfast. We had learned by then that a copious breakfast, a solid lunch, and an ample dinner were essential bulwarks against the course's four or five daily tasting sessions. A wholesomeness altogether appropriate to scholastic endeavor seemed to be the guiding principle in the choice of food served. When one's days started with a foundation of ham, cheese, sausage, and eggs, one was later able to sustain boiled beef with onion sauce, roast pork tenderloin, braised beef with red cabbage, stewed chicken with *Spätzle*, or boiled salt pork with mashed potatoes. No one picked at the food, and no one had need to send desperate messages home for care packages.

Every year the German Wine Academy conducts one of its courses in English. It runs from Sunday evening to Saturday morning. It's based at Kloster Eberbach, a former Cistercian monastery in the Rheingau, but students are housed nearby in the comfortable seventeenth-century beamed and gabled Hotel Schwann in the pretty Rhine-side village of Winkel.

The lectures and tastings are given in locations as diverse as the Baroque refectory of Kloster Eberbach; the old stables of the Deinhard estate at Deidesheim; cellars probably first burrowed into the Moselle hillsides by retired Roman veterans; and around barrelheads among the vines of the Liebfrauenstift-Kirchenstück at Worms, the vineyard that lent its name to Liebfraumilch. By bus and river steamer, the course meanders from Winkel to Worms, from Bernkastel to Bad Kreuznach, and from Rüdesheim to Heidelberg.

The programs are really directed at those with a serious interest in German wine, but each session is subtly modified to suit the needs of the particular group. The course is a bargain for anyone who enjoys wine, offering (for the modest cost of about a thousand dollars, excluding airfare) an experience of Germany beyond the casual traveler's usual bounds—a chance to meet and be involved with Germans at their work; to learn something that, however imperfectly remembered, will enhance life's pleasure; and to taste a greater variety of German wines in a week than most wine buffs would in a year. The arrangements run like clockwork, of course. The bus is always waiting, speakers have their notes prepared, glasses are in place, wines are chilled and listed on a tasting sheet, and in every inn or restaurant along the way, meals are ready to be served the moment the group arrives.

◆ ◆ ◆ ◆ ◆ ◆

On the first evening, we gathered at the Schwan for dinner and found, over a glass or two of sparkling wine, that though English was to be our common language, we were in fact from Sweden, the Netherlands, Canada, Denmark, the United States, Norway, Britain, and New Zealand. Professionally we ranged from sommerliers and wine distributors to bank managers, engineers, civil servants, accountants, teachers, physicians, journalists, secretaries, and designers. Two young women from a Norwegian hotel school had won scholarships to be with us. You could say we were a mixed bunch. Helmut Jung, director of the academy, welcomed us officially with an exhortation to be punctual.

We soon understood why. Every day was crammed with visits to cellars, vineyards, and research stations. There were lectures, tastings, and instructions in everything from current trends in grape breeding by Helmut Becker, head of Germany's renowned State Research Institute of Viticulture and Oenology at Geisenheim and one of the wine world's major figures, to an illuminating tasting of faulty wines conducted by Dr. Currle, who made sure we would never again confuse mishap for character.

Though no two days were the same, the first gives the flavor of them all. We set off for Kloster Eberbach, the academy's headquarters, at 8:30 *sharp*, with the far bank of the Rhine still lost in early morning fog. Kloster Eberbach is also the administrative center of the Hessian state vineyards. Originally ecclesiastical property, it was ceded to the dukes of Nassau when the estate was secularized in 1803 and was then transferred to the Prussian royal domain. The buildings, impressive for their scale and severity rather than their ornament, are enfolded in a wooded valley so unspoiled that they were used for scenes in the movie *The Name of the Rose*, a story of fourteenth century monastical mayhem. On long oak tables in the splendidly paneled refectory, a fat binder of information was waiting for each of us. It was packed with answers to questions we hadn't even known to ask, from production statistics, distribution flow charts, and extracts from German wine-labeling law to schedules of the annual value of German wine exports worldwide and drawings that showed us how to prune a vine.

In an introductory session, Helmut Jung, assisted by Dr. Hans Ambrosi, director of the state vineyards, painted in broad strokes the background of German viticulture and its place in Europe and the world at large. From the many numbers we were given, two struck me as particularly significant: one hundred thousand hectares of vines and one hundred thousand growers. The average vineyard holding in Germany is no more than a hectare—two and a half acres. German viticulture is highly fragmented and therefore essentially an artisan's occupation.

Jung explained how Germany's northern climate influences the styles of wine produced there. He discussed the grape varieties grown in Germany and explained where and how they were used and what to expect from their wines. All we had been told was then illustrated by a tasting of wines carefully selected to point up the differences among the German wine regions, grape varieties, degrees of dryness, and degrees of grape ripeness when picked. After a brief tour through Kloster Eberbach, we returned to the refectory to find that the staff had removed our glasses and replaced them with the same series of wines, but this time unmarked and jumbled. We retasted them "blind" and enjoyed that first rush of confidence in finding that we could recognize for ourselves what we had earlier been taught to identify.

After lunch at the *Kloster's* own tavern-in-the-trees, and just as soon as the last of the group could be retrieved from the medieval labyrinth of cellars and dormitories where they had managed to lose themselves, we were off to Schloss Johannisberg.

· · · · · ·

It is said that Charlemagne himself first ordered vines to be planted on the steep hill now dedicated to Saint John the Baptist. From the palace at Ingelheim across the Rhine, Charlemagne had seen that this was where the snow melted first every spring. By the eighteenth century the hillside estate belonged to the prince-abbots of Fulda, who replaced the monastery on the site with an elaborate priory. In restoring the vineyards, damaged and neglected during the Thirty Years' War and its aftermath, the current prince-abbot ordered the best of them to be planted exclusively in Riesling vines, the first time vineyards anywhere had been planted solely with this variety. Riesling in California is referred to still as Johannisberg Riesling because of this association with Schloss Johannisberg.

Records have been kept of every harvest of Schloss Johannisberg since 1716. Those detailed accounts support the story of the 1775 incident that led to the discovery of the benefits of late-harvested grapes. That year the courier, returning from Fulda with the prince-abbot's permission to begin picking, was delayed. The grapes were already overripe and shriveled; by the time the harvest was under way, they showed signs of the rot we now know to be *Botrytis cinerea*. The result was an astonishing success. In the two hundred years since then, wines made with deliberately late-picked grapes—*Spätlese, Auslese,* and *Beerenauslese*—have made the reputation of this section of the Rheingau.

At the beginning of the nineteenth century, Schloss Johannisberg passed in rapid succession from the prince-abbots to the Prince of Orange, to Marshall Kellermann as a gift from a victorious Napoleon, and finally, on Napoleon's defeat, to the Emperor of Austria, who presented it in perpetuity to his chancellor, Prince Metternich. The widow of Metternich's great-grandson still lives in the house.

After we had admired a statue of the tardy courier, the view from the terrace, the fiftieth parallel marker (the fiftieth parallel is considered the northern limit of tolerance of *Vitis vinifera*), and the handsome buildings of the *Schloss,* largely reconstructed because of heavy damage in an air raid during World War II, we trooped down a long, stone stairway into a vast, ancient cellar, a remnant of the original monastery.

German wines travel perfectly. If handled correctly, they will taste the same in Kansas City as in Koblenz. But any wine tasted in the cellar where it was made, within yards of the vines that bore it, has an extra dimension, a magic that has nothing to do with balance or critics' approval. We knew we should not expect any Schloss Johannisberg wine we might meet elsewhere to taste quite the same as the three we sampled that afternoon. On the other hand, did any of us realize that it would be impossible from then on to take even a sip of a Schloss Johannisberg wine, anywhere in the world, and not be reminded of how it had been, standing in pools of candlelight among shadows a thousand years old?

We took a short break in Rüdesheim before continuing to Schloss Vollrads in Oestrich. Those who wanted to went in search of coffee or tea. (I looked in vain for the pastry shop where forty-five years ago, as a wine trainee, I used to stuff myself on Sundays with fruit tarts and whipped cream.) Others shopped for postcards, souvenirs, and family gifts or went to gawp at the Drosselgasse, a noisy Rüdesheim alley crowded at all hours of day and night with wine pubs, sausage stalls, oompah bands, and flush-faced polka dancers.

♦ ♦ ♦ ♦ ♦ ♦

The Schloss Vollrads property was in the Greiffenclau family for at least eight hundred years. Sales of wine by the Knights of Greiffenclau from their vineyards at Oestrich are documented as far back as 1211, and the family is known to have been in possession of part of the property for at least a century before that. Such a long tradition imposed its own responsibilities on the late Count Erwein Matuschka-Greiffenclau, who lived at Schloss Vollrads and devoted himself to managing its affairs.

In an elegant gilt- and brocade-paneled salon there, we tasted in sequence a dry 1986 Schloss Vollrads, a semidry 1985, a 1985 *Kabinett*, and a 1975 Hallgartener Schönbell *Spätlese* from the Fürst Löwenstein estate, a neighboring property acquired by the family in 1979. Count Erwein talked to us about the wines, the estate, and, a subject close to his heart, the common misconceptions about German wines with food.

It is best to choose wine, he said, to suit the intensity of flavor or the texture of the food or its sauce. These are more important considerations than whether the meat is light or dark. He accepted that there were occasions when a red wine was needed to achieve balance but thought such a limited choice occurred less often than we were led to believe. We knew how well medium-dry German wines went with pâtés, mousses, and terrines, but not all of us understood how easily the fruity acidity and barely perceptible sweetness of these wines harmonize with the slight acidity and similarly moderate sweetness of many vegetables and sauces.

♦ ♦ ♦ ♦ ♦ ♦

The wines Count Erwein had chosen for us to taste were delicious and established for us high criteria for the last tasting of the day—a comprehensive selection of about a dozen Rheingau wines waiting for us a few miles away at Schloss Reinhartshausen, formerly the estate of Prince Friedrich of Prussia and still the property of his sons, the great-grandchildren of Kaiser Wilhelm II. The tasting was introduced and conducted by Dr. Karl Heinz Zerbe, managing director at the time of the Schloss Reinhartshausen estate. He gave such a comprehensive account of the Rheingau that I could barely take notes fast enough.

All the tasting sheets handed to us during the week gave details of the alcohol level, acidity, and residual sugar of each wine presented. At first I had thought it a pity to distract us from the wine with numbers, but I soon realized how subtly we were being taught that a number out of context meant very little. We came to see for ourselves that residual sugar and acidity had to be read together to be understood, one always modifying the other; and even so, intensity of flavor could shift their effects considerably. At the Schloss Reinhartshausen tasting, for example, a 1986 Geisenheimer Mönchspfad Riesling *Kabinett* from the Weingut Schumann-Nägler, rich with almost 3.2 percent residual sugar and only .75 percent acidity, had such deep, intense flavor that it seemed in perfect, lively balance. But another grower's 1986 Lorcher Schlossberg, with less residual sugar (2.4 percent) and a higher level of acidity (.89 percent), lacked flavor, and, despite the crisper definition promised by the numbers, it tasted flat and zestless.

There were many remarkable wines given to us to taste that evening, but I shall mention only two more, both from Schloss Reinhartshausen's own vineyards: a superbly ripe 1976 Erbacher Schlossberg Riesling *Auslese* and a rare and curious Erbacher Rheinhell '87 made from a combination of Chardonnay and Pinot Blanc vines planted on an island in the Rhine. Under German wine law, Chardonnay may be planted in Rheingau vineyards only by special permission and for controlled experiments. The wine had an austere, pebbly style, not unlike a Chablis, and was a great curiosity among so many floral and fruity Rhine wines.

We drove back to Johannisberg to eat dinner at a small restaurant perched in the vineyards above the village. There should have been a romantic view of the vines and the river by moonlight, but the rain that had been threatening all day came down in torrents. At last, tired after a very full day, we climbed into the darkened bus, ready for our sleepy ride back to Winkel. The engine started, the door swung closed, and then suddenly from speakers overhead came the unmistakable twang of Willie Nelson: "On the road ageeeeehn...."

. . . . . .

Note: For more information about the German Wine Academy, write to the German Wine Information Bureau, 245 Fifth Avenue, New York, New York 10016, or call (212) 896-3336.

SOAVE:
A HOUSE DIVIDED

THOUGH IT HAD BEEN RELEGATED, NOT SO LONG BEFORE, TO COR-
ners reserved for straw-covered flasks and dusty bottles of retsina, Soave
became, in the 1970s, one of the most popular white wines in the United
States. Restaurants of all kinds offered it by the glass as their house wine,
and it was stacked prominently in two-liter jugs in markets and stores.
To some extent, of course, Soave's success sprang from its low price and
from Americans' readiness in that decade to try whatever was different
or new. But the demand for Soave was above all the first obvious result
of changes that had swept through Italy after the introduction of new
wine laws in the 1960s. Newly defined appellations had encouraged
Italian growers to extend and rationalize their vineyards. (Vines had
often been mingled with other crops, especially fruit trees, and sometimes
still are.) Furthermore, in helping to finance a modernization and refit-
ting of Italy's wine cellars, the government had stimulated a formerly
uncharacteristic obsession with technically fault-free winemaking. The
well-packaged, polished wines that began to flow from Italy quickly
attracted attention and gave Italian growers, merchants, and exporters a
renewed commercial energy.

As far as Soave was concerned, the 1968 law defining what it was and
where it came from tripled the area of production defined by ministerial
decree in 1931 by extending it from hills that separated and surrounded
the small towns of Soave and Monteforte to include great stretches of

adjacent flatland. At one time much of this land had supported cereals, especially corn, and the road from Soave to Verona, the nearest city, is still lined with the bakeries and processing plants that once had drawn their raw material from those fields. Vines had begun to displace grains on the plain at least ten years before the 1968 law, and wine produced from the new vineyards had already been accepted as Soave of sorts. As vineyards had not previously been planted on the flatlands—the ancient custom had always been to put them on hills—there was no other name in current usage, and to those concerned it had probably seemed easier to enlarge an existing *denominazione* than to create a new one.

The original vineyards of what is now described ominously as "historic" Soave still cling to their terraces on slopes too steep for mechanized cultivation. They are rooted in a meager, friable volcanic tufa, porous with tiny air bubbles that were trapped when lava cooled who knows how many millennia ago. Officially these hills have been reborn as Soave Classico in the hope that this slight distinction of name will be enough to alert consumers and therefore protect their hardworking proprietors, who have been obliged since 1968 to compete directly with the fifteen thousand acres of parvenu Soave surrounding them on the fertile plain of the Adige River. No one can say that things have gone well for "historic" Soave since the change. Though there is now renewed interest in the hillside vineyards, and considerable rejuvenation among them, it is said that more than a thousand acres of their vines have been more or less abandoned since the enlarged, 1968 definition took effect.

Unlike vines in other regions, secured to stakes or trained along wires, vines for Soave are spread horizontally across arbors, called *tendoni* and *pergole*, a few feet above the ground. The difference between the two is slight: A *tendone* is a single, narrow, flat beam about six feet across, supported by posts on either side of the alley that runs between the rows, whereas a *pergola* is an open arch formed by two poles, each attached to an upright stake and the whole arrangement resembling a pair of honor guards, swords slanted overhead, at a military wedding. Both came into general use in the 1840s, but only after much debate on the advantages of these then-newfangled ideas compared with the known merits of training vines up and between trees. Seen from above, the vines present a vast green canopy smoothing and smothering everything except an occasional clump of trees and the towers and tawny-colored rooftops of the two towns and their adjacent hamlets.

· · · · · · ·

I have heard that there were once as many as two dozen grape varieties grown in this part of Italy, but today, in principle, just two are used to produce Soave. One of them, Garganega, is unique to the region and is known to have been cultivated there since the thirteenth century. It gives Soave its structure and its characteristic, slightly almondlike aroma. It is a vigorous vine that fruits prolifically; growers know that a Garganega vine will produce more fruit, if allowed to, than it can fully ripen. The poor soil of the hillside vineyards serves to restrain growth, but even so the growers have always had to be careful to graft the vines onto root-stocks calculated to discourage the bearing of excessive fruit. Such does not seem to be the case on the plain. "If God gives abundance," one plains grower said to me, "why should we refuse it? It would be perverse." The truth is that the plains growers, most of them suppliers of grapes by the ton to the cooperatives and big production houses, learned long ago that, even if a bigger crop meant the quality of their grapes could command only a lower price per kilo, the volume alone would more than make up the difference. Green grapes pay one's debts, runs an old Italian proverb.

The second variety planted for Soave is, in theory, the Trebbiano di Soave. First used in the early nineteenth century, it boosts the wine's strength while refining its flavor. From the beginning, Trebbiano di Soave has often been mixed (and confused) with Trebbiano Toscano, its common but high-yielding cousin. Trebbiano Toscano, unlike Trebbiano di Soave, brings nothing to a wine except volume. Yet as vineyards spread across the plain in the 1960s, the Trebbiano planted there was more often Toscano than di Soave. It has always been said that the vineyards expanded faster than local nurseries could supply vinewood for Trebbiano di Soave. But it is common knowledge that growers on the plain were less impressed by Trebbiano di Soave's qualities than they were influenced by its drawbacks: It is less productive than either Garganega or Trebbiano Toscano; it is more susceptible to rot, a serious consideration on the humid flatlands; and its grapes ripen considerably earlier than those of the Garganega, raising logistical problems because the varieties are commingled for planting and hired teams must pick them together.

The law requires that any Soave blend include a minimum of 70 percent Garganega. Many of the vineyards in Soave Classico are a 100 percent Garganega—as are the wines made from them—but no one knows how extensively the Trebbiano Toscano is planted in the plains, due to the practice there of planting varieties promiscuously. It would take an army of qualified officials to identify each vine.

In the 1960s, when the transformation of Soave was barely under way, I remember tasting a marvelously compact, deeply flavored wine made from a grape called Durella. Though once in high favor among the growers of the region, it is rarely used now except as the base of a locally consumed sparkling wine. It is thought to be too homespun, too coarse, for the "new" style of Soave. That sleek, high-tech style, an important factor in Soave's success in the 1970s, resulted from applying winemaking techniques introduced worldwide in the 1960s— essentially, fermentation at a low temperature in stainless-steel vats—to grapes planted where the very conditions that ensured ease of cultivation would also guarantee unobtrusive characteristics in the wine. One could say that everything about the new Soave led logically and as if by design to the production of a clean dry wine, inexpensive to produce and simple to promote. Nicolas Belfrage, in his book *Life Beyond Lambrusco*, describes the new Soave as a "product whose greatest asset is the improbability of its causing offence," while Victor Hazan, in *Italian Wine*, dismissed it with faint praise so exquisitely deadly that a Borgia would have been thrilled: "[It] is such an inoffensive wine," he writes, "that to reproach it for not having a bolder personality seems peevish."

· · · · · ·

Of course, Soave's an easy target now. But that is because we have already forgotten how difficult it was twenty-five years ago to find just such a consistent, refreshing Italian white wine to drink as a straightforward mealtime beverage, at a price comparable to that of a beer or a soft drink. There was much to be said for the brave new Soave then, and there is much to be said for it now. The mistake, and from the point of view of the hillside growers of "historic" Soave perhaps the word should be misfortune, was to grant it a distinguished name and thereby all but eclipse the original.

Luckily, some extraordinary wines have continued to be made as Soave Classico throughout this period of change, though in this country, by and large, they have been difficult to find. Changes in Italy itself—laborers who drank copiously of inexpensive wine as a source of calories no longer need to do so, while their grown children share what are now international tastes in wine as in much else—have brought quality and character rather than quantity and anonymity back into focus. Even the large production companies are now setting aside special lots for separate bottling and are establishing Soave Classico blends from specific vineyards where their interest begins with the choice of clone of the vines to be planted. Bottling companies are forming contractual associations with the owners of vineyards of repute whereby they provide financial and technical assistance in return for marketing rights.

For instance, starting with the 1984 vintage, Pierluigi Borgna, cellar master of Santi, a small, fine wine subsidiary of the Gruppo Italiano Vini (owners of Folonari and many other important Italian wine companies), began to set aside selected lots of grapes from Monteforte for a distinctive Soave Classico, Vignetti di Monteforte. He has experimented with it constantly over the years since then, at one point fermenting 10 percent of it in small oak barrels—a practice discontinued because it interfered with the expression of the vineyard.

He has also experimented with the current fashion of cold grape-skin maceration—allowing skins to soak in the juice at low temperature for a few hours after crushing and before pressing to extract flavor—using a blanket of nitrogen to avoid the perils of oxidation. "In the sixties we introduced the French method of pressing to separate skins and juice completely as soon as the grapes were picked, and this was a great improvement on previous, clumsy practices. Some character and individuality were lost, but the Soave was lighter, more agreeable, more consistent—and more popular. But that very consistency has also been one reason that Soave, traditionally a handcrafted wine with a longtime reputation for individuality as well as quality, has begun to be perceived as industrially produced. Grape-skin maceration is not in itself the whole answer. But we need to restore character to our wines."

Bolla, for its part, has developed Soave Classico Tufaie, made from a combination of grapes from selected sites, about twenty acres in all, on the slope of Foscarino near Monteforte. Bolla's production director, Elio Novello, like Borgna, has been a keen proponent of cold-maceration techniques to boost flavor, and his Tufaie is a wine that adds authority to the firm's customary lively style.

Perhaps Masi, a small, family-owned company at San Ambrogio di Valpolicella, has gone to the greatest lengths with the concept of wines from particular sites. The owners, brothers Sandro, Dario, and Sergio Boscaini, have formed relationships with growers owning favored sites: Masi supplies cash and technical help to build or improve the winery facilities as well as year-round viticultural guidance. (Dario Boscaini, the man who provides this counsel, not only is responsible for Masi's own vineyards but is also the director of viticultural studies at the Valpolicella Agricultural College.)

Last summer I accompanied Dario Boscaini on one of his visits to Benvenuto Pra, owner of Col Baraca, a remote vineyard producing a wine with which Masi has had particular success. The vines at Col Baraca, I was told, are virtually all Garganega, with perhaps 1 or 2 percent of old Durella and an even smaller proportion of ancient Trebbiano di Soave that survived a devastating hail storm in 1960. Pra, an energetic man in early middle age, is proud of the well-equipped but no-frills winery that now adjoins his house.

"I invested along with Masi," he told me, "but I now have more profit, more security, and more satisfaction. Before I built the winery, I was obliged to sell my grapes. The price I got for them was never affected by any extra effort I made. Now the return I get is a direct function of the quality of the wine.

"It is not easy for a small farmer like me to set up such a winery. Even supposing that I had had the resources to do it alone, I had no access to the market. Which is why this collaboration has been so important to me. It has added value to my crop and to my land."

If you were to ask local growers and winemakers like Pra, who among their colleagues are presently producing particularly distinguished Soave—in addition to their own, of course—Roberto Anselmi and Leonildo Pieropan would certainly be among the first names to be mentioned.

Pieropan and Anselmi, opposites and competitors but friends and allies in the defense of Soave, have sometimes attracted the resentment as well as the admiration of their peers. There was more than muttering when they recently worked with Luigi Veronelli, Italy's most respected wine writer, to persuade the Italian minister of agriculture and the president of the Italian National Wine Committee to block a recommendation of the local *consorzio* to raise Soave's present maximum production limits per hectare.

"The *consorzio*'s solution to every problem has been to increase production," said Anselmi, with more than a touch of scorn, puffing on a cigar. "I have a problem with the *consorzio*."

Others, calmer and perhaps more cynical than Anselmi, have suggested, however, that the *consorzio*'s objective in easing the level of the maximum permitted yield was not to increase production but merely to bring the regulation closer to what is actually being harvested and thereby to make more palatable the start of a long-overdue enforcement of the law.

The *consorzio* is the body charged with implementing wine regulations and with making recommendations to Rome for any modifications generally supported by growers or merchants. Every *denominazione* has a *consorzio*. I could see how the Soave *consorzio* would have a hard time keeping everyone satisfied, obliged as it is to look to the interests of growers as diverse as those who push their vines for tonnage and those who, like Anselmi and Pieropan, are constantly pruning to reduce their crops. Anselmi's concerns and projects are such that it would have been amazing if he hadn't had a problem with the *consorzio*.

• • • • • •

With more than a hundred acres of his own, and another sixty acres of rented land under his control, Anselmi has taken a radical approach in his search for quality. For a start, he is passionately opposed to the traditional *pergola*, for he believes it leads inevitably to overcropping each vine and therefore sees it as the most primary of all evils. He already has ten acres of Chardonnay and Sauvignon Blanc, trained along wires according to the Guyot method commonly used in France and planted four thousand vines to the acre. (The customary density in the region, even for Soave Classico, is a thousand vines to the acre.) In order to comply with the legal tonnage regulation, the level of pruning required is severe.

Even more controversially, because it challenges the most sacred of Soave tenets, he has planted a vineyard of wire-trained Garganega with a density of twenty-five hundred vines to the acre. "The law does not require me to use the *pergola*. Which is not to say," he went on darkly, "that the *consorzio* won't try to introduce such a rule."

Actually there is more skepticism than hostility directed at Anselmi's vineyard practices. "It's not just that it goes against what we were taught," one neighbor told me. "I believe it is more than chance and blind tradition that have led us to use the *pergola* system through several generations. To plant vines so densely means that pruning will have to be extreme. And, given the exuberant vigor of Garganega, I don't see that the vines will survive such drastic treatment very long. If we all trained our vines that way, we would never again have old vines or the quality of wine we get from them. Even so, I raise my hat to his courage."

One gets the impression that Anselmi has deliberately sought to distance himself from whatever is conventional Soave wisdom. Still—and despite the Chardonnay and the Sauvignon Blanc, the controversial density of planting, and his experiments with barrel fermentation—Anselmi's Capitel Foscarino, a traditionally made wine based on grapes grown on traditional *pergole,* is without doubt one of the greatest of all Soaves. (Foscarino is the volcanic hill that dominates Soave, and Anselmi has a vineyard on its summit.) At its best, the wine offers a perfect example of what the French call a peacock's tail: a long elegant shimmer of flavors. I can't say that I have always been as impressed by the barrel-fermented Capitel Croce; it is an interesting wine made from pure Garganega, but its character is sometimes overwhelmed by oak.

Anselmi uses his French oak barrels to much greater advantage in aging his superb Capitelli, his version of Recioto di Soave. Before it was known for anything else, Soave was famous for Recioto, wine made from the most sugar-concentrated grapes on the vine. (André Jullien, the Paris wine merchant and author of the classic *Topographie de Tous les Vignobles Connus,* referred to Soave's Recioto in 1816 as "a well-regarded *vin santo*" but was so unfamiliar with Soave that he mentioned only "a fairly good red" of the Soave hills, about which he might have been confused, and said nothing of the white.) To make Recioto, the ripest and most perfect bunches are allowed to dry on reed trays, to concentrate the grape sugar, before they are pressed and undergo their long, slow fermentation. The practice probably goes back to antiquity, but it is usually accepted that the Venetians encouraged Recioto's production in the sixteenth century after Ottoman encroachments on their eastern empire had deprived them of similar dessert wines from the Greek Islands. In any event, Anselmi's Capitelli, with its rich flavor of praline, coffee, and conserved fruits, is an unqualified delight.

· · · · · ·

Leonildo Pieropan, who also makes a Recioto, as well as an experimental late-harvest Soave, took on the family vineyard and cellar in 1967. He inherited from his father and his uncle not only ten acres of vines—

since increased to fifty—but a passion for excellence. The Pieropan vine-yards are well placed, something he himself would emphasize as the source of all else; but it is clear from talking to him that the style of his wines is an expression of the man. Unlike Anselmi, Pieropan comes across as a prudent traditionalist even though he has tried, and contin-ues to try, every new fad if only to be sure that there isn't a better way. He has rejected in turn barrel fermentation ("the Soave character just dis-appeared"), grape-skin maceration (it was the old peasant way of mak-ing wine; it gives a good aroma at first, but the wine doesn't stand up in bottle"), and fertilizers ("we chop up and put back everything we take from the vine, including what we prune. We don't need to add anything more except some sheep dung every two or three years").

On the other hand, though with nothing like the density of Anselmi's vines, he has planted his vines at eighteen hundred to the acre as opposed to the standard thousand so that each vine, pruned back, need ripen fewer bunches. Not content with that, he always counts his potential crop after flowering and further removes any bunches he con-siders excessive. His press wine, 20 percent of his yield, is separated and sold off in bulk.

Some years ago I lunched with Leonildo Pieropan and his wife, Teresita, at Lo Scudo, a popular restaurant on the main road outside Soave. He poured for me the 1989 and 1988 wines from the Calvarino vineyard we had visited earlier that day. (The name Calvarino—Calvaire in France—sometimes refers to the site of the crucifix among the vines. It is more commonly the name given to the steepest, most backbreaking, but, as likely as not, most rewarding section of a vineyard.)

The food—*sopressata* sausage with grilled polenta and some veal medallions in a Soave-based sauce—was delicious, but my attention was taken entirely by those two wines. The 1989, youthfully vibrant, had that rare intensity of flavor we have come to expect only in wines bearing appellations of far greater international prestige than Soave. The 1988, aromatic and ample, was confirmation, if any were needed, of everything a true Soave could—and should—be.

· · · · · ·

Note: Since the 1999 vintage, Roberto Anselmi has abandoned the geographic appellation Soave for his wines. "It was like divorcing a much-loved wife," he told me. The last straw for him was the consorzio's *using the cover of an application for Soave to be raised to the high quality status of a DOCG—*denominazione di origine controllata e garantita—*to slip into the revised statute a clause raising the permitted yields of grapes per hectare, the very change already attempted and blocked by the minister. In the ensuing row, the application was modified but the public differences between Anselmi and the* consorzio *had become too bitter for him to continue as a member of the group. His wines now carry a regional geographic appellation—much as the super-Tuscan reds did twenty years ago at the start of the battle to reform the quality of Chianti—and to sell them he relies on his own reputation rather than that of what he sees as a discredited* denominazione.

THE NOBLE WINE OF MONTEPULCIANO

PAOLA DE FERRARI'S FATHER, EGIDIO CORRADI, WAS BORN IN Cervognano, a Tuscan village tucked into hills that start at the very walls of Montepulciano, southeast of Siena, and descend in a great rolling spread to the floor of the Valdichiana, many hundred feet below. The upper reaches of the slopes are covered with a patchwork of olive groves, wheat fields, and vineyards—the customary Mediterranean trinity of oil, bread, and wine—stitched together by seams of tall cypresses that shade the cart tracks leading to farmhouses hidden from the unpaved roads. Both tracks and roads are banked, in spring and summer, by a profusion of yellow broom and sweet-smelling acacia blossoms. By autumn the vines are mottled with russet and brown, the wheat fields are no more than a dusty stubble, and a pungent aroma of fermenting grapes drifts among the trees.

From his home in Genoa, Egidio Corradi used to go back to Cervognano every year to buy a supply of the local wine, tasting his way from vat to vat and from cellar to cellar to find the right Vino Nobile di Montepulciano. "His enthusiasm for Vino Nobile was really a symptom of his nostalgia for Cervognano itself," says Signora de Ferrari. "Every year he used to complain that the wine was no longer as he remembered it.

"But a wine from Cervognano, even when it was not as good as he thought it could be, was still, in his opinion, the best Vino Nobile, better than the wine from the other villages around Montepulciano. He said it had always been that way. Eventually, to be near the village, he bought two small adjoining farms and combined them to make what is now our Boscarelli property."

Paola de Ferrari and her late husband, Ippolito, inherited Boscarelli. "We restored one of the farmhouses—it was a ruin—and then, starting in 1964, we put in two or three acres of vines. We planted them in rows, as a true vineyard should be, not mixed with fruit trees. We intended to grow just enough grapes to make some good wine for ourselves and our friends.

"But then, almost in spite of ourselves, we gradually expanded the vineyard, selling the grapes we didn't need. Some new vats and barrels increased our capacity, and one thing led to another. In the seventies we decided to keep all our grapes, and by the mid-eighties we were producing wine on a commercial scale—two thousand to three thousand cases a year. We now have thirty acres of vines and are producing about five thousand cases of wine a year, half of it Chianti Colli Senesi and half Vino Nobile di Montepulciano."

What Signora de Ferrari didn't, and probably wouldn't, say was that their Vino Nobile had been so lavishly praised by the Italian press that for a time there was a trough of mutual embarrassment between the De Ferraris, as beginners, and neighbors who had been making wine for generations, even centuries, with little public acknowledgment. The family kept a low profile locally—though invited, the De Ferraris did not even join Montepulciano's *consorzio* of growers—and looked for markets away from Tuscany to avoid possible comparison and confrontation. For a time, more than two-thirds of Boscarelli's tiny production was being shipped out of Italy, mostly to the United States and to Germany. The rest went south to Rome or north to Genoa and Milan.

"Neither my husband nor I had had any training for what we were doing," Paola de Ferrari says. "But we managed, and Boscarelli became a passion for us and for our two sons. It so took over our lives that, contrary to what we had intended, we were eventually spending our work weeks in Tuscany and weekends at our home in Genoa just to be away from the constant demands of the vineyard."

* * * * * *

Vino Nobile di Montepulciano is essentially a variant of Chianti. The vineyards that produce it lie within both the commune of Montepulciano and the limits of Chianti Colli Senesi (Chianti of the Hills of Siena), one of the eight zones that make up the Chianti region of Tuscany. Montepulciano has long enjoyed a high reputation for its wine. Many of its well-worn endorsements by popes, poets, and physicians in centuries past might have been prompted by politics or local chauvinism as much as judgment, but that can hardly be said of Thomas Jefferson, who claimed, in 1804, that no wine pleased him more. In a letter of January 14, 1816, to Thomas Appleton, his wine agent in Genoa, Jefferson referred to it as "a very favorite wine"; and the following year, advising the newly elected James Monroe on wines with which to stock the White House cellar, he urged the purchase of Montepulciano. He passed along Appleton's name and said, "I have imported it through him annually ten or twelve years."

It was not until 1932 that a government commission appointed to establish boundaries for Italy's tangled Chianti region recognized the special southeast exposure of Montepulciano's vineyards and confirmed the use of its name as an appellation of wine produced in them. At the time, concepts of legally defined appellations of origin were still hazy, and it was not until 1942 that a *consorzio* of Montepulciano growers was given the formal responsibility for the monitoring their wines' geographic authenticity. Another twenty-five years (and World War II) went by before Italy had a body of law establishing *denominazioni di origine controllata*—often referred to as DOCs—for its wines. Vino Nobile di Montepulciano and Chianti were among the first to be defined and regulated under decrees issued in 1966 and 1967, respectively.

The first regulations—they have since been twice modified—made clear how closely the two appellations were related. Both wines were to be made principally from Sangiovese (called Prugnolo Gentile in Montepulciano, where it exists as a clone specific to the area), the variety that emerged triumphant in Tuscany as part of the nineteenth century's quest for red wines of deep color and solid construction. Canaiolo Nero, the grape that once dominated the region, took a lesser, supportive role, lending suppleness to Sangiovese's tannic rigidity and extending the narrow limits of its aroma and flavor.

A few growers have clung to what has survived of other local black-grape varieties as well. Mammolo, one of the most persistent of these survivors, brings a particularly appealing fragrance to a wine. (The Italian word *mammola*, obviously related, means "violet.") Though the regulations make no specific reference to Mammolo, it can be used in both Chianti and Vino Nobile di Montepulciano as part of a tolerated percentage of "other," optional grape varieties. In addition, a long tradition of mixing a proportion of white grapes with the black to give these wines a silky finish was at first underscored by a regulatory obligation, but at Montepulciano, at least, the practice is now left to each grower's discretion.

* * * * * *

The origin of the expression "Vino Nobile" remains obscure. Some suggest that it came into use as an honorific to distinguish wines from vineyards—usually those with the best exposures—owned by the town's patrician families. Others say it was intended to indicate wines of high quality, those good enough for a nobleman's table.

Curiously, the many early published references to Montepulciano wine never included the words "Vino Nobile." But a passage from Alexander Hamilton's *History of Ancient and Modern Wines* (1824) might shed light on how and why the term came to be used in the nineteenth century:

> In the description of Tuscan wines, much confusion
> has arisen from not attending to their different quali-
> ties. As the press is [used lightly] and the grapes have,

in general ... dried for six or seven weeks within doors
before they are trodden, the first juice ... necessarily
abounds in saccharine matter, and the wine procured
from it will consequently belong to the sweet class.
But when this is drawn off, it is customary to add a
quantity of water to the murk, which, after a short fermentation, yields a very tolerable wine ... In this way,
a great proportion of the ordinary wines of the
country are made; but all the choicest growths ... are
more or less sweet. When a late traveller, therefore,
describes the Montepulciano wine as the most
esteemed in the Tuscan states, and at the same time
compares it to "a weak claret, with little flavour," it
is evident that he cannot be speaking of that "manna
of Montepulciano, which gladdens the heart" ... but
must mean the common wine of the place.

Montepulciano was also celebrated at the time for a sweet red wine
made from Aleatico grapes partially dried before crushing. If Alexander
Hamilton was referring to that wine—his emphasis on sweetness suggests
this—then it is more than likely that the term "Vino Nobile" evolved to
distinguish its first pressing, described by Hamilton, quoting an earlier,
Italian author, as the "manna of Montepulciano." Aleatico has disappeared from many areas, including Montepulciano. It was probably
more than coincidence that the term "Vino Nobile" disappeared from
Montepulciano along with Aleatico late in the nineteenth century.

The term (but not Aleatico vines) reappeared in 1933 when Adamo
Fanetti, owner of the Sant'Agnese estate at Montepulciano, emblazoned
the words "Vino Nobile di Montepulciano" on the labels of his best red
wines—the timing possibly a consequence of the 1932 Chianti commission's recommendation with regard to use of the Montepulciano appellation. Fanetti's wines were made from the usual Chianti varieties, not
from Aleatico, but he could easily have persuaded himself that if any
wines were entitled to be described as "noble," they had to be those he
had just exhibited to great acclaim at a wine fair in Siena. (His pride

was probably justified: One of those Fanetti wines went on to take a gold medal in Paris in 1937.) Where Fanetti led, others followed. By the time the DOC regulations were issued in 1966, Vino Nobile di Montepulciano had already become the wine's accepted name.

The presidential decree establishing the Montepulciano *denominazione* did not, however, usher in an era of glory. If the wines of two or three notable producers are excepted, Vino Nobile di Montepulciano in the sixties and seventies hardly lived up to its grandiose name. All the more reason, then, for general astonishment when, in 1980, the Ministry of Agriculture declared Vino Nobile di Montepulciano raised to the status of a *denominazione di origine controllata e garantita* (DOCG), a new category of appellation introduced that year for Italian wines of the highest quality and prestige, an honor that Vino Nobile di Montepulciano was to share with only Barolo, Barbaresco, and Brunello di Montalcino, three of Italy's most distinguished wines. In the ensuing uproar, the ministry defended its action with references to the antiquity of Vino Nobile di Montepulciano, ignoring, perhaps even ignorant of, Vino Nobile's uncertain genealogy. The Italian wine community was less concerned with viticultural history than with the generally poor quality of most Vino Nobile di Montepulciano, which could attract ridicule and compromise the entire DOCG program. While some improvement had begun at Montepulciano by 1980, there was little yet to show for it. To many the ministry's move seemed at best premature.

· · · · · ·

Fortunately, Montepulciano's growers grabbed their chance. Inspired by neighbors who had been making good and even excellent wine for years—the De Ferraris and the Contuccis eminent among them—and encouraged by the very new and very glossy success of the Falvo brothers at Avignonesi, they took to their vats.

"The competitiveness among us, the obsessive drive to be best, became nothing less than a shared neurosis," Fernando Cattani of La Calonica told me. Neurotic or not, the results soon defused all opposition; each producer not only changed gear—restricting yields in favor of quality, using fruit from only the best sites for Vino Nobile, and allowing the parallel production of Chianti Colli Senesi to absorb the rest—but developed, over the course of the eighties, an individual style largely based on a manipulation of varietal options. In arriving at these separate interpretations of the wine, the growers were prompted not only by differences of temperament but also by what they perceived as the dictates of the variable terrain within the communal boundaries of Montepulciano.

Many growers have chosen to exclude all white grapes from their blends, for example, while others exercise their right to include a small percentage of them. Some use more and some less Canaiolo Nero, as allowed by upper and lower limits set by statute; some do and some don't include a modest proportion of Mammolo. And a few are experimenting with vats made of French oak rather than the milder Slovenian oak traditional to the region.

As a result, each producer's wine is distinct and, on acquaintance, easily recognized. Avignonesi's Vino Nobile, for instance, is particularly lean, even austere, compared to others. Ettore, Leonardo, and Alberto Falvo assumed management of the Avignonesi estate—one of the oldest of Montepulciano—when Ettore Falvo married Adriana Avignonesi. Educated as a classicist, Ettore Falvo claims, tongue only slightly in cheek, to have acquired his knowledge of winemaking from Columella's *Rei Rusticae*, a Latin treatise on agriculture written in the first century. Clearly, he has also been influenced by the new school of Chianti producers who have boosted Sangiovese, thrown out white grapes, and toyed with both Cabernet Sauvignon and French oak barrels. And he seems to have been inspired, too, by Angelo Gaia of Piemonte, an intensely twentieth-century grower whose international reputation for purity of style sets his wines apart. Ettore Falvo dramatizes the structure of his Vino Nobile by using 80 percent Sangiovese (Prugnolo Gentile), well above the minimum set by law and gives it an etched precision by excluding white grapes from the blend. He reinforces both body and color by aging the wine in a battery of vats of new oak—both French and Slovenian—recently installed on Avignonesi's new property, Le Cappezzine.

Since taking control, the Falvo brothers have emphasized the Avignonesi name rather than the Vino Nobile di Montepulciano appellation, extending the range of wines to include varietals such as Il Marzocco (pure Chardonnay) and Desiderio (a blend of Merlot and Cabernet Sauvignon). Matured in French oak barrels (Ettore Falvo goes to France each year to choose the wood personally), these varietal wines are impeccably made to international standards and tastes and are clearly intended to help Avignonesi penetrate the *beau monde* of wine beyond Italy's borders. They are distinguished and follow successfully Gaia's example of stylistic clarity. Nonetheless, perhaps because they are *too* carefully made, they miss some inner warmth. They are, as writer Norman Douglas once said of Tuscan speech, emphatic rather than profound.

Avignonesi's performance has been monitored by others. Both Antinori and Ruffino, two major Chianti producers, recently acquired vineyards within the production zone of Vino Nobile di Montepulciano. The Italian insurance company SAI bought the extensive Fattoria del Cerro in 1978; and the Swiss and Germans, early admirers of the improved Montepulciano who presently buy 75 percent of the appellation's Vino Nobile, have begun to acquire estates there.

SAI's new winery at Fattoria del Cerro, purpose-built in 1986, is a modern, no-nonsense structure; but if Avignonesi's wines can be boldly angular, Fattoria del Cerro's are always round, even floridly rococo at times, with their bouquet of dried fruits and lively flavors long and deep enough to recall many a summer past.

Poliziano's wines, too, are richly flavored, but they are also fleshier, more powerful, lordly—qualities that give them a *grandezza* altogether appropriate for a Vino Nobile, one might think. "I'm not trying to make impressive wines," counters volubly articulate owner and winemaker Federico Carletti. "I just want them to be enjoyable." They are both, and are easily the most broadly appreciated of the appellation. When someone familiar with Vino Nobile di Montepulciano is asked to name three favorite producers, Poliziano is invariably one of them.

· · · · · ·

La Calonica's wines are different again. They are particularly scented—doubtless because Fernando Cattani uses Canaiolo Nero to the permitted limits (and, as he once seemed rather vague in telling me what he thought those limits were, possibly a shade beyond them). I sat with him and his wife, Esther, a few years ago under the giant wisteria that smothers his front porch, comparing La Calonica's 1987 and 1988 Vino Nobile and tasting the 1989 Rosso di Montepulciano. The Rosso, the first vintage possible of this separate new DOC, was made in accordance with regulations that do not require wood aging prior to its early release—recognition that not all wines, sometimes not even an entire vintage, are suitable for aging in wood. Some growers are now selecting lots each year for designation as Rosso di Montepulciano; others, whole sections of their vineyards. Cattani's 1989 Rosso di Montepulciano was particularly aromatic (as his wines always are), but also vigorously fruity and full. Paradoxically, though, La Calonica's perfumed style is seen to greatest advantage in vintages less remarkable than 1989, as was clear from comparing his 1988 and 1987 Vino Nobile di Montepulciano. The former was an excellent example of a successful vintage in Tuscany. The 1987 gave elegant but light wines of moderate quality—some of them, in fact, showing a jagged edge, even a little bitterness. But the aromatic style typical of La Calonica (helped, perhaps, by Cattani's abstemious use of Sangiovese in favor of Canaiolo Nero) gave the estate's 1987 Vino Nobile di Montepulciano Riserva breadth and a semblance of fullness. It's a style that diverts attention from any minor imbalances and leaves an impression of harmony that other 1987s lacked.

◆ ◆ ◆ ◆ ◆ ◆

Harmony should be essential to any wine, of course, but is often rejected for the sake of impact. That cannot be said of the wines of Alamanno Contucci, whose watchwords are balance and discretion—qualities appropriate to his standing both as president of the growers' *consorzio* and as the active director of a family estate now in its eighth century of wine production. Contucci—bespectacled, scholarly, unpretentious, and as good-humored as any well-fed gentleman farmer anywhere—has his cellars beneath the family *palazzo*, built in the sixteenth century on Montepulciano's main square by Sangallo the Elder, one of the architects of Saint Peter's in Rome.

Montepulciano has more than its share of such palaces, and of splendid churches, too. Its Church of the Madonna di San Biago, one of the glories of the Renaissance, was begun by Sangallo on a grassy terrace overlooking vineyards and meadows, still separated from the town by an avenue of cypresses. It is one of the most exquisitely serene buildings in Italy. The magnificence of the town's architecture, out of all proportion to its size and relative commercial importance, is a result of wealth accumulated in the fifteenth and sixteenth centuries through marriages between Montepulciano's leading families and the great banking houses of Florence. They were shrewdly arranged to suit both the interests of the *poliziani* (as inhabitants of Montepulciano are called), who lived in constant fear of Siena, their powerful neighbor, and the interests of the *fiorentini* themselves. The alliance armed Florence with a valuable ally below Siena, its arch-rival, and provided her with a listening post on the border of the dangerously expansionist Papal States. Florence did everything possible to bind the relationship, and the splendor of Montepulciano's few streets and squares still bears witness to the generosity of Florentine fathers-in-law.

Contucci talks freely and knowledgeably about the recent changes in Vino Nobile di Montepulciano and agrees that the 1980 DOCG degree did not coincide with the wine's highest quality mark. "But the new *denominazione* was granted to acknowledge Montepulciano's past and to guarantee its future. It deferred to the historic fame of the wine, not to some temporary phase," he says with the assurance of one whose family has seen both worse and better since the first Contucci planted vines at Montepulciano in the thirteenth century. He welcomes the newcomers. "We don't always do things in the same way," he says diplomatically, "but one learns from dialogue, and the competition is very stimulating. After all, everyone has something to contribute."

Contucci has decided for himself which traditions he will keep and which of the new ideas he will adopt. He adheres to the mingling of white grapes with black—necessary in his view for a classic Vino Nobile. Rather than turning to the more usual Malvasia or Trebbiano of Tuscany, however, he uses the Umbrian Grechetto, or "little Greek," commonly known in Montepulciano as Pulcinculo.

"We crush the white and black grapes and let them ferment together in the same vat. The proportions vary with the vintage," he says, "and in some years the wine is indeed better with no white grapes at all. But in most years, if we use red grapes alone, we risk making a wine that is more like Brunello di Montalcino [the wine made one valley away] than Vino Nobile. The newcomers were all against white grapes. They wanted the regulations rewritten to prohibit their use absolutely. Those already here insisted on tolerance. We told them that if they didn't want to use white grapes, no one would compel them to."

But Contucci is receptive to change, too. "I tried the wine of one of my colleagues who had used oak from the Allier, in central France, rather than the Slovenian oak we usually use, and I thought it had some good qualities. So we are introducing just a few vats of Allier wood, and we shall see."

Under Contucci's presidency the *consorzio* is dynamically active. It now employs two qualified graduates in viticulture and enology, who visit all growers regularly to inspect their vineyards for pruning and treatment practices and their cellars for cleanliness and for timely racking of their wines from the lees. They taste the wines while they are aging and again before they are bottled. "We are as scrupulous as we can be to protect and strengthen the reputation of the wine," Contucci told me.

He seemed proud, too, of the *consorzio*'s contribution to local research conducted under the supervision of the institutes of agriculture and geology of the universities of Siena, Florence, and Trentino. But then, his family has a long tradition of improving the region's agricultural potential. His ancestor Giuseppe di Contucci had the swamps of the Valdichiana drained at the end of the eighteenth century, opening the region up for the cultivation of grains and the raising of cattle. (The Valdichiana breed developed there appears most familiarly off the hoof in the form of the huge *bistecche alla fiorentina* that are a specialty of Tuscany.)

· · · · · ·

The newcomers Contucci referred to were not just the Swiss and the insurance companies but also those from much closer to home, like the Falvo brothers from Cortona, across the valley, and the Dei family of Siena, who acquired its Montepulciano property just below the town in 1970. The Deis sold their grapes to the local cooperative until 1985, and really only hit their stride beginning in 1988 under their former manager, Lorenzo Scian, who studied philosophy and liked to quip about neo-positivism, pragmatism, and analytical empiricism before getting down to serious matters like oak and malolactic fermentation. The Dei family's intensely flavored wines are still aged in big puncheons of new Slovenian oak (Scian was against French oak on the grounds that it could distort his idea of the traditional style of Vino Nobile).

My favorite wines from this appellation are still those of the Boscarelli estate. I don't suggest that Paola de Ferrari and her sons are producing the "best" wine of the region—there is already confusion enough between subjective preference and objective judgment without my adding to it—but their wines reflect the most suitable balance between tradition and evolution. There is no doubt that some of their ideas have changed since they planted their first vines in 1964 (there was a little Cabernet Sauvignon in their glorious 1988). But they have allowed neither their intent nor their vineyard's identity to be blurred by every passing theory. Like Contucci, they usually—though not always—include some white grapes in their blends. Their flawless 1985 was a lesson in all that a Vino Nobile di Montepulciano should be. And although their sales are international they have not tried to make of their Vino Nobile an "international" wine. Its path from vineyard to bottle follows an inherent logic, and I suppose that's why it can be relied on for a consistency of character unfailingly tempered by an engaging grace. It is indeed a Vino Nobile, in every sense. Egidio Corradi, were he still with us, would be both satisfied and vindicated.

PRIORATO:
WINE OF THE ANGELS

THE FIRST STORM OF WINTER HAD DONE ITS WORST JUST DAYS before I arrived in Priorato. In four hours, more rain than is usual during an entire year had washed out dirt roads, hillside terracing, and young vines in this, the poorest and most isolated corner of Catalonia. But the region's winegrowers were in high spirits, buoyed by their first impression of the year's new wine. The rain marked the end of a summer that had taken the vines to the limit of their endurance, and it was already obvious that the resulting wines would be concentrated and powerfully aromatic. The essence, one might say, of Priorato.

Tucked away in hill country west of Tarragona, Priorato was long the butt of local politicians' jokes. So when Joan Clos, the mayor of Barcelona, announced that he wanted to establish, within the city's limits, a municipal vineyard "like the one in Montmartre" and then went on to say, "except that I want ours to produce a great wine. A wine this city can be proud of. A wine like Priorato's Cims de Porrera," it made an impression.

For Sara Perez, who produces that wine, the recognition was gratifying. For Priorato, it was something of a miracle. Though it's not the first time that God's finger has strayed there: In the twelfth century, a local man claimed to have seen a congregation of angels working together on a hillside, each one carrying grapes up and down a great staircase to heaven. An account of the incident so affected Alfonso II of Aragón that, in 1163, he established on that very spot Spain's first Carthusian monastery—called, appropriately, Scala Dei, or "Stairway of God." The monks began planting vines, the first in the region since the Romans had packed up and left centuries before.

Priorato's secret lies in its schist—a crumbly gray-green slate that forces the Grenache and Carignan vines traditionally grown there to send roots down forty feet or more in search of water. The nutrients and minerals they draw from that depth contribute to the intensity of the wine, giving it a strength that throws into relief the rich fruit and ripe, velvety tannins that are Priorato's hallmark.

A mix of Grenache and Carignan is common all around the Mediterranean coasts of Spain and France because the two varieties complement each other. You can see this just by looking at the vines. The Grenache is open, and its oval grapes hang in loose bunches. Its wine, though perfumed and soft, is unstructured and tends to fade quickly. A Carignan vine, on the other hand, is tight and knotty. There are deep indentations in its leaves, and its thick-skinned grapes hang in compact, cylindrical bunches, producing a wine that can seem rigid and even raw when the vines are young but that gains in suppleness as the vines—and the wine—mature. Used together, Grenache and Carignan complete each other, the gentle finish of one braced by the structure of the other.

◆ ◆ ◆ ◆ ◆ ◆

Over a dinner of roast kid and a glass of Cims de Porrera 1998, I talked with Salus Alvarez, the mayor of Porrera, one of the twelve scattered villages that produce Priorato wine. He told me that because of its rich texture and heady mountain flavor, it had been in demand as far back as the sixteenth century. Alvarez likes to browse through old letters and accounts stowed away in his neighbors' attic trunks. "I learn a lot," he said. "For example, I recently found a seventeenth century sheet of instructions for blending wine for the Spanish colonies in South America. Another, prepared a hundred years later, proposed a rule that would have restricted Priorato wine to shipment in bottle to protect its reputation.

"It used to give me a strange feeling," he added, "to be looking at evidence of past prosperity while at the same time watching the decline of our village. The vines were being abandoned, and the people were disappearing with them. A hundred years ago Porrera had a population of more than two thousand. Today it has fewer than three hundred. It has been the same everywhere in Priorato."

Phylloxera ruined Priorato, as it did many other marginal regions with labor-intensive hillside vineyards. They all had difficulty getting started again, and some never did. Priorato's growers made things easier on themselves by changing their varietal emphasis. They planted more Carignan and less Grenache, even though this gave their wine a harsher style. Carignan sets fruit more reliably than Grenache—that tightness carries through—and even in the difficult conditions of Priorato, it will usually yield twice as much fruit as Grenache. The growers sold land to finance the replanting, and gave plots to their workers to supplement what they could afford to pay them in cash. By the 1950s, there were hundreds of tiny holdings—mostly planted with Carignan—and control of local wine production shifted from the estates to the cooperative cellars that sprang up in most of the villages.

The cooperatives were there to make wine, not to market it. But when shipped in bulk for others to blend, even Priorato fetches only a commodity price. The growers tried to cover their expenses by boosting yields. Quality fell, and revenues fell further. But the fundamentals of Priorato's past success remained: schist, exposure to a Mediterranean sun, and altitude. It needed only a spark to set things in motion again. In fact, there were two: José-Luis Perez, Sara Perez's father; and René Barbier. Perez, a wiry biologist now in his sixties, arrived in 1981 as director of the local school of agriculture. He fought for viticulture programs, hoping they would give the young an incentive to stay and a chance to succeed. In 1980, the bearded and heavyset Barbier—grandson of a French *négociant* who had moved to Tarragona from the Rhône Valley at the end of the nineteenth century—bought an abandoned property in the Priorato village of Gratallops. He renamed the steeply pitched vineyard, which came with a ruined house, Clos Mogador.

Though trained in Bordeaux, Barbier knew Priorato well. As a child he had accompanied his father on trips there to buy wine. Friends from Tarragona—writers and painters mostly—spent time with him at Gratallops, helping him salvage old vines and nurse them back into production. Carles and Mariona Pastrana, now owners of Clos de l'Obac, next door, were among them. Others, romantics perhaps, but also excited by the possibilities they saw in these old vines, bought vineyards. At about a hundred dollars an acre at the time, land was cheap enough. They restored, replanted, and extended the vineyards, turning to each other for help and support, and to José-Luis Perez for advice. Having caught their enthusiasm, Perez, too, bought land and, in 1986, planted the vines that would eventually produce his Clos Martinet.

Some, having made a start, got cold feet and pulled back, selling their vines to each other or to newcomers. That's how Alvaro Palacios— son of the Rioja producer with whom Barbier had worked and by then a close friend—came to acquire Finca Dofi in 1989. Strapped for cash, they all thought of themselves as pioneers. (Palacios, too, was on his own. His father, having tried to discourage him from what he saw as a risky venture, refused to finance it. For several years Palacios traveled five days a week as a barrel salesman so that he could support himself and devote his weekends to his vineyard.)

The group shared resources. In fact, their sense of camaraderie was so strong in those days that it seemed perfectly natural that their 1989 vintage—their first—should be made in common as a single *cuvée* in a winery they had jointly set up in a former sheep shed. They continued to share the sheep-shed winery until 1992, but after that first 1989 *cuvée*, they made their wine independently of one another. Or they had René Barbier make it for them. As they labored together in those early years for what had become a common, passionately pursued cause, they did everything themselves. They must have looked to outsiders like an incarnation of the twelfth-century vision.

* * * * * *

In fact, given the limitations of their annual production—at that time it was only in the hundreds of cases—it might have taken years for outsiders even to notice what was going on. But in April 1992, in preparation for the Barcelona Olympic Games, *Gault-Millau* published a guide to Catalonia that included a thumbnail sketch of René Barbier and an account of the revolution he had instigated in Priorato. In giving the 1989 vintages of his Clos Mogador and the Pastranas' Clos de l'Obac appropriately identical ratings of 18/20, the reviewer described their explosive fruit and rich texture. He also warned his readers that the wines, difficult to find, were sold, when available, almost drop by drop. The response was predictable—everyone felt that he or she had to taste it. The new Priorato was launched.

Barbier and his friends had sought out and bought old plantings of Grenache, and in an effort to restore the varietal balance that had been lost decades earlier, they planted yet more of it. Of the one thousand hectares (twenty-four hundred acres) of productive vines in Priorato, well over three hundred are now Grenache, more than twice as many as in 1980. There is still plenty of Carignan, but the vines are mature because little of this variety has been planted. There has been a preference to look to three classic French varieties—Cabernet Sauvignon, Syrah, and Merlot— for the structure Grenache lacks, with an initial enthusiasm for Cabernet Sauvignon gradually shifting to Syrah because of its less imposing varietal character. Clos Mogador, Clos de l'Obac, Finca Dofi, L'Ermita, and Erasmus—estates prominent in the revival— all use, to stunning effect, one or the other (or all three) of these French varieties rather than Carignan. When the proportions are right and the Carignan fruit is from really mature vines, however, traditional combinations of Grenache and Carignan can be equally impressive. In fact, the elegant and distinctive 1998 Cims de Porrera that I'd enjoyed so much on the first evening of my visit (quite possibly the very wine that had inspired Joan Clos) was predominantly Carignan with only one third Grenache and a dash of Cabernet Sauvignon for seasoning.

*　*　*　*　*　*

Success breeds success. Torres, the leading wine producer in neighboring Penedès, has recently bought land in Priorato, and Codorniú has taken a stake in Scala Dei, one of the region's older (and larger) estates. But the most heartening effect has been on small growers. As recently as five years ago, the Priorato cooperatives were distributing forty pesetas (twenty cents) a kilo for grapes to their members. Today, depending on the quality of the fruit, most growers in Priorato can expect to receive from three hundred to six hundred pesetas. In 1990, Alvaro Palacios of Finca Dofi started to buy small lots of grapes from the owners of old vines to make Les Terrasses, a *cuvée* distinct from his own estate wines. His aim was to augment his production in order to justify building a modern winery. The price Palacios was willing to pay for high-quality grapes (Carignan as well as Grenache) put pressure on the cooperatives to rethink their strategies so as to avoid seeing their best fruit simply slip away from them.

In 1991, five small cooperatives formed the Vinicola del Priorato, with a new and well-equipped central winery at Gratallops. Although they had a difficult start—old habits are hard to break—a new management team has, since 1995, introduced a system of paying members for quality rather than volume. "We still sell in bulk any wine that doesn't satisfy us," Jordi Miró, the sales director told me. "But that's now no more than 5 percent of our annual production." Most of the twenty-five thousand cases Vinicola sells each year is Onix, a robust and lively blend based on the fruit from old Grenache and Carignan vines.

*　*　*　*　*　*

Other cooperatives have chosen to form alliances with successful producers to get the technical and marketing skills they need. Through just such an arrangement, the village cooperative in Poboleda now has the help of Joan Maria Riera, a talented young winemaker who worked for a time at Saintsbury in California's Carneros. Its new partners have upgraded the equipment in the cooperative's modest quarters, and although members retained the right to deliver all their grapes there—that was part of the deal—selection is rigorous, and about a quarter of the wine is sold off in bulk.

"We give the growers all the help we can," Riera told me. "And by way of encouragement we routinely pay five hundred pesetas a kilo for impeccable fruit." Riera imposes strict organic cultivation standards on all the cooperative's members. "All our wine is organic," he said, "and the Swiss and German authorities send inspectors here regularly." *All* the reds are traditional blends of Grenache and Carignan, but the best of them, bottled as Mas Igneus, usually contain small proportions of Merlot, Cabernet Sauvignon, or Syrah.

Best known of the cooperative partnerships is Cims de Porrera. The Perez family, with partner Luis Llach, rents the village cooperative's winery, where the huge underground cement tanks in which the wine used to be made have been turned into vaults housing French oak barrels. The fifty-two member growers, who sell their grapes to the winery, cultivate a total of 54 hectares (130 acres) of vines, spread over 150 different plots. "They're all at different altitudes, with different exposures, and often with the Grenache and the Carignan mixed together," Sara Perez told me. "We do our best to pick the two varieties separately anyway," she said, "because they don't ripen at the same time. We judge ripeness by the taste of the skins. When the fruit is ripe, the aroma tells you so. It was nature's way of attracting animals to eat the fruit when the seeds are ready. We follow the same rule, and it seems to work for us, too."

ALBARIÑO:
VINEYARD BY THE SEA

HAS A TOTALLY UNFAMILIAR WHITE WINE EVER GIVEN US SUCH A jolt? Such pleasure? Albariño from Rías Baixas, in northwest Spain, is still no more than an eddy in a puddle compared to the ocean of Chardonnay we consume every year. But in the United States, sales of this seductively aromatic wine have bounded from just two thousand cases in 1992 to more than thirty thousand in 2000. If production could have supported it, sales would have risen even faster.

In Spain, the wines from this small corner of the province of Galicia have won praise on all sides—they are now on the list of every serious restaurant from Seville to San Sebastián—and for at least the past decade, they have had a place at the royal table.

Albariño is actually part of a much larger secret. In summer when northern Europe invades Spain's Mediterranean beaches, the Spanish themselves disappear to Galicia, a private green refuge tucked between Portugal's northern border and the Atlantic. Santiago de Compostela, the region's capital, ranks with Rome and Jerusalem as a place of pilgrimage for the world's Catholics, of course. But for most Americans it's usually just a stop on a wider European tour. Having paid their respects to the cathedral—its altar ablaze with gold and silver—and allowed themselves to be beguiled for a day or two by the medieval charm of narrow, winding streets that open abruptly onto vast plazas of an austere splendor, they are on their way. Rarely do they venture the short distance to the coast, with its countless bays and inlets—the *rías*—or discover, farther inland, the rivers that long ago carved out deep canyons in Galicia's ancient mountains (now mostly protected as natural parks), or walk in woods where paths are banked with creamy rock-roses and clearings edged with beds of tiny scarlet wild strawberries.

Galicia is hardly the Spain of popular imagination: of strumming guitars, stamping heels, and carnations between the teeth. The Moors never established themselves here, so Galicia dances in slippers to the Celtic drum and bagpipe, and its pilgrims walk in sneakers and parkas (but still with cockleshells pinned to their hats) on roads punctuated by tall crucifixes directing them to the tomb of St. James. For curious travelers there are mysterious cave drawings and prehistoric dolmens, feudal castles and Romanesque churches, Roman bridges (still in daily use) and monasteries built near remote passes where pilgrims in centuries past could find a night's shelter and protection from brigands unimpressed by their piety. Elsewhere are sober, seventeenth-century stone *pazos*—manor houses presiding over villages that still live on what they can wrest from a wild land and an even wilder sea. Like Brittany and the west coast of Ireland, Galicia is a place of sudden storms and drowned fishermen, of lighthouses, ghost stories, wee folk, and things that go bump in the night.

Above all, however, it's a place where one eats and drinks well. There are mussel and oyster beds in the *rías*, and every village up and down the coast has its own line of fishing boats. Only Japan consumes more fish per capita than Spain, and in this region, which boasts two of Europe's most important fishing ports—Vigo and La Coruña—meat is rarely more than a footnote on the menu. Even the scruffiest of the bars and taverns that line Santiago's twisting Rua do Franco serve just-caught fish of unimaginable variety cooked with a confidence that would put any restaurant in Paris or New York on the defensive.

No one knows when the vine was introduced to this part of Spain. It can be assumed that the Romans, who settled in the area two thousand years ago to mine the hills near Orense for precious metals, would have provided for themselves somehow. The first reliable record we have that links past to present, however, is of vineyards planted in the twelfth century by Cistercian monks at Armenteira in the Salnés Valley near the fishing port of Cambados. (According to local legend, Albariño is descended from cuttings of Riesling brought from Kloster Eberbach in the Rheingau by some of these Cistercians. It's a pretty story, but recent DNA research has shown beyond a doubt that there is no such connection; the variety's origin is, therefore, still a matter of speculation.)

More vines were planted later on lands granted to the monastery of Santa María de Oia, forty or so miles south within the sharp angle formed by the estuary of the Miño—the river that establishes the frontier with Portugal—and the Atlantic. From these early beginnings evolved the vineyards of Val do Salnés to the north and those of O Rosal and Condado do Tea in the south. (A fourth defined zone roughly midway between them, Soutomaior, was created recently, but it produces such a small quantity of wine that, commercially, it has had no impact as yet.)

There are all kinds of shadings and subtleties to be explored—with wine there always are—but an explanation of the differences between Salnés on the one hand and Rosal and Condado on the other is enough to illustrate most of what one needs to know about Albariño. The vineyards of Salnés form an open bowl facing west to the ocean. From the terrace of the Martín Códax winery on Burgans Hill, above Cambados, there is a limitless view of the bay and the Atlantic beyond. The individual shelves and terraces of vines face this way and that to catch the sun, but all are exposed to whatever blows in from the sea. The vineyards of Rosal and Condado also turn about, to accommodate the rise and fall of a terrain shaped by the streams and rivulets that feed the Miño, but their broad direction is always to the south, to the river. Rosal is affected by the ocean less directly, and Condado—because it is farther upstream—even less. Their vineyards are drier and warmer than those of Salnés; they get less rain and have more hours of sun.

There are other differences, too. Vines in Salnés are on a fairly homogenous granitic sand, while those of Rosal and Condado also contend with crumbled schist, clay, and the rolled pebbles typical of any place where the water's flow has shifted. These differences of soil and prevailing weather do not make any one zone better than the others (though you can be sure that's not the way the growers see it), but they do impose distinct and varied characteristics on their wines. A Salnés Albariño is bolder than one from either Rosal or Condado. It has good acidity, a pungent aroma and flavor (some say of pineapple), and it gives a powerful, fleshy impression. Its focus is intensely varietal. Rosal wines—and to an even greater degree those from Condado—are more graceful and more supple. Their flavor steals across the palate and lingers there. If a Salnés wine tends to express the varietal more than the site, a Rosal or Condado wine does the opposite.

The official revival of Rías Baixas (pronounced REE-as BUY-zhas) had its start in 1980, when the local board of control recognized the distinct qualities of the Albariño wines produced in Galicia with a new *denominación de origen*. The ruling was rewritten by the Spanish legislature in 1988 to conform to European Economic Community standards that required the primary definition of an appellation to be geographic rather than varietal. The redrafted regulations formally established four zones and listed Albariño, Loureiro, Treixadura, and Caíño Blanco as the main vine varieties recommended to be grown within their boundaries.

Any Rías Baixas wine labeled Albariño is made from that variety alone, and a Salnés wine is almost always 100 percent Albariño. The other recommended grape varieties do not grow as well in that valley: Conditions are too extreme. But that isn't the case for either Rosal or Condado, where Loureiro and Treixadura in particular have always contributed to the style of the wines. In fact, regulations require, for example, that a wine labeled Rías Baixas–O Rosal must have at least a little Loureiro to enhance its natural fragrance, and one sold as Rías Baixas–Condado do Tea is understood to have the benefit of Treixadura's finesse and structure. Using other varieties in this way reinforces long-standing distinctions among the zones of Rías Baixas, but Albariño now predominates in more than 90 percent of the vineyards, and most producers offer Rías Baixas only as an Albariño varietal wine.

◆ ◆ ◆ ◆ ◆ ◆

The aroma and bite for which Albariño is celebrated owe much to the cooling proximity of the ocean and to the stress-free growth guaranteed by ample spring rain. In Spain, at least, these are conditions unique to the Rías Baixas. Ground humidity brings potential problems, of course, even though Albariño has a thick skin. As protection from rot, the vines are trained over high, horizontal *pergolas*. The hefty granite pillars used are not the most elegant supports, but they fit in with the local custom of scattering vines about in handkerchief-size plots like untidy afterthoughts. A vineyard is sometimes no more than an arbor attached to the side of a house, an arrangement of granite and wire in an awkward bend of the road, or a backyard shared with a patch of turnips or cabbages. For years, most families in Rías Baixas have had vines to make wine only for their own consumption. It was a crop grown for the household—like peppers, corn, and potatoes—that sometimes provided a surplus that could be sold.

Ironically, it was a crisis in the fishing industry that sparked Albariño's resurgence. New restrictions on fishing in European waters in the mid-1980s hit small ports like Cambados, Bayona, and La Guardia badly. The big factory ships of Vigo and La Coruña could go in search of new fishing grounds; boats from the smaller villages have a limited range, though, so these communities had to find a way to supplement what was earned from the sea. Shopkeepers, schoolteachers, and particularly the fishermen themselves—everyone with a few vines—moved from making wine for their own consumption to expanding their production and selling it. From the five hundred acres of vines existing in Rías Baixas in 1986, the acreage is now close to six thousand.

The Martín Códax winery, one of the first to come onto the scene in Salnés, was founded in 1986, funded by a group of small growers who knew they could achieve more together than if each tried to make and market wine on his own. With modern equipment—good presses, refrigeration for cool fermentation, easy-to-clean stainless-steel tanks— they were able to reveal Albariño's forgotten qualities. "And who is Martín Códax?" I asked Pablo Buján, the firm's sales manager. "The prime mover of the project? The partner with the biggest holding?"

"He was a thirteenth-century Galician poet and troubadour from this very place," Buján replied. "He drank a lot of wine."

The thirsty Códax would doubtless be pleased to know that the winery named for him is probably the most successful in Rías Baixas, producing almost 1.5 million bottles of wine in a normal year. To understand the difficulty of this feat, one must remember that the grapes are grown by more than two hundred partners who together own nearly four hundred acres of vines divided over twelve hundred separate plots.

Over the years, land in Galicia has been divided and divided again through successive inheritance. Vineyard plots on the terraced hillsides got smaller and smaller, and in the end those at a distance from the villages were hardly worth the effort needed to cultivate them. In the 1940s and 1950s, under General Franco, most were given over to stands of eucalyptus trees to provide pulp for a paper mill in Pontevedra. In the rain their drooping leaves and peeling bark lend a wistful melancholy to the landscape. But where the trees have been cleared, the original terracing can still be seen.

"Our natural trees are oak and chestnut. Eucalyptus trees give a poor return and are bad for the soil," says Javier Luca de Tena, director of Granja Fillaboa, with a dismissive wave of the hand. Angel Suárez, manager of the Lagar de Cervera (now owned by the Rioja Alta winery), endured several years of painstaking negotiations with disparate owners to put together enough land to restore a rational, workable vineyard. Often a single row of trees belongs to one family and the next one, to another. Each of four brothers will cling to his clump of half a dozen eucalyptus trees when their entire holding, taken together, makes up a block no bigger than a kitchen garden.

A program encouraging owners to swap land in order to build up the size of individual holdings has not been a great success. Apparently, the smaller the patch, the greater its mystical importance to someone unwilling to part with it. To put together an economically viable vineyard, therefore, takes a great deal of forbearance and much money. (One doesn't buy land in Galicia, one bribes the owner to part with it.)

Another Rioja winery, Bodegas Lan, now owns Santiago Ruiz in O Rosal, a small producer of such prestige in Spain that it could afford to dispense with marketing a varietal Albariño, despite the demand, and concentrate on producing a Rías Baixas–O Rosal, a superb wine in which Albariño's exuberance is tempered by Loureiro to just the right degree. La Val, another producer in Rosal, also makes, along with its particularly delicious varietal Albariño, an exquisite wine made from Loureiro and Albariño—reversing the proportions used by Santiago Ruiz.

I was not surprised when José Luis Méndez, son of the owner of Morgadío, told me that his family was trying to think of a way in which Loureiro could be brought back into the vineyard. The producers' dilemma is that they would all like to offer the more stylish wine that a proportion of Loureiro can give, but they don't want to give up the right to the magic name Albariño on the label. Both in Spain and in the U.S., it gives instant recognition. While in Galicia recently, I lunched with Angel Suárez at a restaurant near the old fishing harbor of La Guardia. We chatted over a bottle of his 1998 Albariño and a dish of assorted fish— hake, turbot, and monkfish—simmered with potatoes and served in a sauce of garlic and *pimentón,* a very small pepper, dried over a slow wood fire and ground to a fine powder. It has a hauntingly smoky, sweet-sharp taste, and no Extremaduran or Galician kitchen is ever without it.

I enjoyed the wine, but Suárez said 1998 had been a difficult year for Rías Baixas. Spring came early: The vines sent out tender shoots in February, but the weather then turned very cold, with a predictable effect. Hailstorms in April did further damage, and rain in June meant that the fruit set poorly. As a result, the crop was barely 40 percent of the previous year's and never did reach the level of quality hoped for.

"A red wine region copes with this kind of difficulty more easily," he continued. "Red wine is usually aged for a year or two, and differences of crop size from one year to another can be blurred, at least, by delaying or bringing forward the release date. Albariño is best when bottled and consumed young. We have no stocks to fall back on. Production is increasing a little every year, but at present, even when the crop is of a good size—almost seventeen million kilos of good quality grapes in 2001 as opposed to half that in 2000—it seems there is never quite enough to meet demand."

He poured the last of the 1998 into my glass, leaving none for himself.

KITCHEN AND CELLAR:
A PERFECT MARRIAGE

WHO CAN FORGET THE FIRST TASTE OF AN UNABASHEDLY SWEET white wine with creamy blue cheese; of aromatic, young Pinot Noir with grilled swordfish; or of impeccably balanced Cabernet Sauvignon with roast rack of lamb? And what about aged Barolo with beef stew, long-simmered with cloves, a few dry-cured olives, and orange zest? When a shared sensibility governs a restaurant's kitchen and cellar to draw food and wine in the same direction, there is ample opportunity for such felicitous combinations.

At a recent seminar on wine service in Paris, Gérard Margeon of the Alain Ducasse Restaurant at the Plaza-Athenée told hotel-school students assembled at Pré Catalan, in the Bois de Boulogne, that a good wine steward must understand food. "He and the chef," Margeon said, "should speak a common language." He went on to complain that the knowledge of wine now considered acceptable, even for professionals, is far too narrow. His criticism was probably intended for the teaching establishments, but it has a wider relevance. "All the emphasis now is on explaining details of viticulture and winemaking," he said. "Wine has been divorced from its natural context of food and the convivial ambiance of the table."

He is, of course, absolutely right. There is too much discussion of wine as an end in itself; too much promotion of wine for reasons that have little to do with pleasure; and, as a consequence, too much wine is served (too young) in order to impress rather than delight.

A wine list is praised and given awards for reasons that have little to do with its real purpose, as if it existed only to be admired passively, like a stamp collection. A wine list is good only when it functions well in tandem with a menu. A restaurant's menu should include, for each wine, at least one dish to show it off, as well as others that will reveal its least suspected qualities. And, for each dish, there should be no less than three or four wines that can accompany it interchangeably, to accommodate different tastes, different interests, and different pockets. It would be helpful if a sommelier could tell us which dish he'd had in mind when he purchased a new wine; or whether a particular dish on the menu was conceived in light of that wine—and possibly some others. Most important of all, any wine offered in a restaurant should have been chosen with a view to the contribution it would make to a happy occasion.

* * * * * *

If food and wine are to work well together, which should be considered first? When I put that question recently to Giancarlo Paterlini and Suzette Gresham-Tognetti, partners in San Francisco's much admired Italian restaurant Acquarello (he buys the wine and runs the front of the house, she cooks), their mutual deference was as clear an answer as anything they actually said: Each shows off the other to advantage. Acquarello is known for its remarkable list of Italian and California wines. "But," Giancarlo told me, "the food always comes first." Suzette, the restaurant's award-winning chef, puts it differently. "I make a conscious effort," she said, "to compose a menu of dishes that lead naturally into Giancarlo's wines."

Giancarlo, a graduate of Italy's National Hotel and Restaurant School, grew up in Bologna and came to San Francisco by way of London's Mirabelle and Café Royal. His calm manner hides a passionate interest in food and wine and a deep knowledge of both.

"At Acquarello we offer a *cucina nobile*," he told me, "but also a *cucina della nonna*—grandmother's cooking, which is hard to do in a restaurant because home-style dishes are slow-cooked; moreover, being simple, they must be perfect. It is a refined art that many Americans misunderstand and think of as less, somehow, rather than more."

Giancarlo illustrated his point by referring to Suzette's menu. Rabbit braised on the bone, a preparation typical of Modena, and pork cooked with prunes that have been macerated in wine or grappa both need wines, he said, that confirm their unpretentious elegance. With the rabbit, he usually recommends the Valpolicella Classico made by Giuseppe Quintarelli. "At present we have his highly concentrated 1990 vintage, just right for a dish that has simmered for hours." For the pork he prefers a young Barbera d'Alba from Cordero di Montezemolo, which he explained provides a suitably vigorous contrast.

"Suzette's menu has a good balance of meat, fish, and pasta dishes with many flavors and textures for me to work with. I prefer to buy our wines from small-volume, high-quality producers, so I read a lot—all the Italian wine and food journals—and go to Italy as often as I can to keep track of them. Sometimes I have had a particular wine brought in for us, but there is such an abundance of good Italian wines available in California that this is rarely necessary."

Suzette takes similar pains. "When I develop a dish for the restaurant," she told me, "I investigate more than its traditional recipe. I need to know the history of the dish: how it came to be, where, and for what reason. Only then can I really understand it, re-create it, and discuss it with Giancarlo to allow him to find the right wine—something appropriate to its background as well as to its composition and taste. He is good at doing that. He doesn't just accumulate an impressive array of wines for the cellar. We understand each other and know what to do to bring our wine and food together."

One of the most popular dishes on Acquarello's menu is *tortiglioni* (ridged pasta) with a sauce of *foie gras* and black truffles, a perfect synthesis of Suzette's French antecedents and her apprenticeship with Italian chefs. Guests almost always ask for a great red wine to accompany it. "But after trying the dish with several of our reds," Giancarlo told me, "I realized that a big white wine—a wine of Roberto Anselmi, for example—was a better choice because the rich, creamy texture of the *foie gras* is balanced by the fullness of such a wine yet moderated by its fresh acidity. It's a surprise to many of our customers when I recommend this, but they always enjoy it."

Giancarlo stays closer to tradition with the wine he recommends for Suzette's parsley-crusted loin of lamb and its sauce based on red wine and roasted garlic. "To my mind, Sangiovese is the best choice with young lamb," he told me. "The supple richness of this variety complements the lamb but never overpowers it. La Gioia di Reicine, a wine made by John Dunkley, a grower in Gaiole-in-Chianti, is exclusively Sangiovese and therefore more focused than a conventional, blended Chianti would be. Presently we have the 1993 vintage; it's a deeply complex wine, and the velvety texture of its soft tannins seems to merge with Suzette's sauce."

. . . . . .

Larry Stone, wine director, and Dennis Leary, executive chef, at Rubicon, in San Francisco's financial district, also maintain a close accord between kitchen and cellar. "I must be flexible," Larry explains, "because our menu changes weekly, and specials are created daily to take advantage of whatever is fresh in the market. So, although Dennis does develop dishes that set off specific wines, I usually buy to suit Dennis' style of cooking in general while trying to anticipate dishes he is most likely to prepare over a coming season. His food works particularly well with intense, fruity California and Oregon Pinot Noirs and red Burgundies, for example, which is why we now have six pages of these wines in our list."

Rubicon's clientele, drawn from the surrounding banks and brokerage firms, is inclined to prefer blue-chip wines in every category, and Larry—a former winner of the Meilleur Sommelier International annual competition organized by the French government's Food and Wines from France bureau—is well qualified to select them. So Rubicon's list is sprinkled with all the right names: Bollinger and Veuve Clicquot; Gaja and J. J. Prüm; Stony Hill and Mount Eden; Domaine Leflaive, Michel Lafarge, and Domaine Dujac, among others. In addition to the focus on

Burgundy, there is a persuasive range of Cabernet Sauvignons from Caymus, Diamond Creek, and Heitz Cellars, and an equally imposing array of Bordeaux classed growths. When a customer familiar with the wine list plans to order a special bottle, Larry and Dennis are happiest when they are told ahead of time so that they can confer and suggest a suitable dish to accompany it. Usually they find what they want on the current menu, but sometimes Dennis will propose a dish for that specific wine and for that particular occasion.

A year or two ago, for someone who called to ask that a bottle of Henri Jayer's 1989 Echézeaux be ready, Scott Newman, Dennis' predecessor as the restaurant's executive chef, devised a *confit* of duck leg—the skin sautéed crisp—with a reduction of duck stock, shallots, and Pinot Noir. Diners who order mature Bordeaux wines are encouraged to drink them with rack of lamb or fillet of beef; but Dennis has some signature meat dishes (as well as others inherited from Scott Newman, with whom he worked closely), including short ribs braised in red wine and loin of venison, that were developed to support Larry's selection of red Rhône wines and old-vine Zinfandels.

"When we create a new dish," Dennis told me, "Larry is one of the first to taste it. Changes he suggests with the idea of making it more wine-friendly are usually an improvement. Sometimes a dish meant to accompany a rare wine for a special dinner finds its way onto the regular menu because the combination worked so well. When a 1966 Chevalier-Montrachet was selected for just such a dinner, Scott proposed red snapper with leeks, potatoes, and *haricots verts* moistened with a mildly herbal fish broth. Larry liked the simplicity of the dish but was afraid that the wine's aromas and flavors—which reminded him of toasted hazelnut and candied citrus peel—would overwhelm it. We tried adding crushed, toasted hazelnuts to echo that element in the wine, but they were out of place in the broth. Instead, we made an emulsion of fish stock and brown butter finished with a dash of lemon juice and a sprinkling of chives. That sauce accepted the crushed hazelnuts very well. The dish gave splendid support to the wine and now often appears on the menu. Larry recommends it to customers who order an aged white Burgundy or an older California Chardonnay. The snapper is especially good when served with the 1983 Stony Hill Chardonnay on our list."

* * * * * *

Some of California's best-selling Chardonnays present problems for a restaurant kitchen. They are often flabby, heavy, and oaky, with a slightly sweet finish that is barely discernible but can wreck the balance of any dish ordered to accompany them. Producers of these wines obviously intend them to be a complete experience in themselves rather than part of one.

At Boulevard, perhaps San Francisco's most eclectic restaurant, sommelier John Lancaster prides himself on selecting well-balanced Chardonnays, and Nancy Oakes, chef and owner, has developed a number of dishes to complement them. "We really worked at it," she told me, "because of California Chardonnay's popularity." The results include Maine lobster with corn cakes and a watercress, radish, and bacon salad; sea scallops and crab salad served with *beurre blanc* on field greens; California sea bass on a bed of sweet white corn; and pan-roasted halibut on fried green tomatoes with heirloom corn, Cherokee tomatoes, blackeyed peas, and roasted lemon vinaigrette.

"Nancy roasts the lemons slowly," John explained to me, "and uses the juice in a vinaigrette made with olive oil, Champagne vinegar, a dash of simple syrup, and thyme. The vinaigrette brings the dish together and at the same time creates a bridge to even a big, citrussy wine."

Nancy Oakes likes to feed people—to nurture them. "The food here is expressive and personal," she says, "and we like our wines to be that way, too. We buy from small growers—both in California and elsewhere—so that the customer knows who cooked the food and who made the wine. Something's missing when food and wine are anonymous. I think people know me better when they eat what I've cooked, and I like to feel that I have learned something about a grower when I've tasted his wine. I'm as committed to our California winegrowers as I am to the small farmers from whom we buy our produce."

That commitment is obvious from the range of California wines offered. The list is not vast, but it's a who's who of the state's growers. John Lancaster likes to find wines with an element of surprise—that's the style of the kitchen, after all—and offers a selection of them by the glass, matched to appropriate dishes. By the bottle, he offers a complete page with thirty-five entries of what he calls "Interesting Whites." They range from a Roussanne made by Qupé in Santa Barbara County to Gaston Huet's semi-dry Vouvray, and they start at eighteen dollars a bottle. ("I don't think anyone should have to float a loan to buy a bottle of good wine in a restaurant," Nancy says.) He has an even greater number of "Interesting Reds," including wines as diverse as a Flora Springs California Sangiovese, Auguste Clape's Cornas, and a special *cuvée* from Vega Sicilia in Ribera del Duero. These supplement a fairly comprehensive list of classic California varietals, Burgundies, Bordeaux, and Ports.

Eclectic, expressive, personal—at first one is overwhelmed by such an embarrassment of riches. But Boulevard pays attention to the harmony of its kitchen and cellar instinctively: The same sensibility rules both. John understands the essence of a dish as well as Nancy herself does, and he knows exactly which wine to propose with it. He urged me, for example, to try a concentrated Russian River Valley Pinot Noir with the restaurant's wood-oven roasted squab. "The dish is richer than you might think," he said, provoking my appetite as he spoke. "The bird is served on a custardy cornbread with grilled figs and baby beets. But the key is a warm sultana-walnut vinaigrette. It adds a lusciousness that makes this dish a perfect match for the Pinot Noir from Dehlinger's Goldridge Vineyard."

John also recommends Pinot Noir to accompany Nancy's roasted Alaskan salmon—but this time the wine's a lighter, more fragrant, and more subtle 1993 Vosne-Romanée from Jean Gros or an Aloxe-Corton of the same year from Tollot-Beaut. With her braised veal cheeks and sauté of sweetbreads on a potato "risotto" he suggests the exuberance of either the 1995 Qupé Syrah or the 1995 Rasteau, a Côtes-du-Rhône-Villages from Domaine de Beaurenard. To those who order oysters he recommends a glass of Didier Dagueneau's Pouilly-Fumé, and for those who prefer to start with scallops and caviar there's a steely but deep-flavored Chablis from Raveneau. When Rhode Island black bass is available, a Puligny-Montrachet from Etienne Sauzet—intense yet elegantly svelte—could have been created with that very dish in mind. And for Nancy's grilled Sonoma rabbit (stuffed with long-roasted garlic and served with a sauce of caramelized onions) the perfect choice of a Ravenswood Wood Road Zinfandel is everything we expect of California.

* * * * * *

Most distinguished restaurants these days have a selection of wines, many of them by the glass, that are offered with their dessert menus. Matching each wine to a specific sweet is not always, however, easy. Creamy pastries can make a wine seem thin, and chocolate is notorious for its distorting effect.

On their dessert menu at Acquarello, Giancarlo Paterlini and Suzette Gresham-Tognetti pair each dish with a glass of wine. "We could see that customers who understood very well the principle of one red wine's being different from another were failing to understand the distinctions among our sweet wines," Giancarlo told me. "They were ordering wines and desserts that wouldn't benefit from each other's company."

A favorite among Acquarello's new combinations is a rich chocolate praline cake on a meringue base served under a cloud of whipped cream—not an easy dessert for wine—and a 1995 Brachetto Passito made by Giancarlo Scaglione at Loazzola in the Piedmont from Brachetto grapes that are partly dried, and therefore concentrated, before being crushed and fermented. Brachetto, an old regional variety once in danger of disappearing but now being revived, has an aroma of roses so affecting that its wines have always been known as *vini da meditazione*—wines that provoke delicious thoughts. "This one is quite delicate," Giancarlo said, "yet it soars above the rich chocolate cake because of its extraordinary aroma. The two are thrilling in combination."

Wine and food should be thrilling; and part of the thrill is the conviviality that comes with sharing them. That, too, was included in

Gérard Margeon's message that day in the Bois de Boulogne, because sharing means choosing a wine for the pleasure it will give to all, a wine in harmony with the occasion and with those present as well as with the food. As Nancy Oakes puts it, "We can sit on chairs in a circle and talk to each other anywhere, anytime. But, when we sit down around a table for food and wine and conversation, we are there to enjoy each other. And that's magic."

THE JUDGMENT OF PARIS

IN THE EARLY 1970S STEVEN SPURRIER, AN ENGLISH WINE merchant, and Patricia Gallagher, his American partner, had a small wine shop in Paris in a cul-de-sac near the Place de la Concorde, where, in an adjacent building, they also gave courses in wine to their enthusiastic customers. Almost inevitably, Spurrier and Gallagher developed a considerable clientele among expatriate Americans. The U.S. Embassy was a block or two away, the substantial offices of IBM were almost next door, and American law firms were scattered all around them. Through word of mouth, their Caves de la Madeleine became a regular stop for California wine producers and others making the rounds of the French wine scene. Often these visitors brought a bottle or two with them, and Spurrier was able to taste what he has described as "some exceptional [California] wines."

At their shop, Spurrier and Gallagher dealt in French wines (except for a few of the most ordinary commercial blends, there were no California wines available in Paris at that time), but they decided to use the excuse of the United States' bicentenary to show a selection of California wines to French journalists and others connected with the wine world. They were sure that they would make a good impression on the French and thought they might even surprise them. They hoped, too, that any stories generated in the press might bring in a new client or two.

With their bicentenary plan in mind, Gallagher visited California in the fall of 1975 and Spurrier followed in the spring of 1976, during which time he picked out six Chardonnays and six Cabernet Sauvignons, all of recent vintages, that he thought would give a fair picture of what was going on in California. He needed two bottles of each, and, knowing he might have difficulty bringing two cases of wine through French customs, he arranged for a group of twelve tennis enthusiasts on the point of leaving for a wine and tennis tour of France to carry two bottles each in their hand baggage.

To give the wines a context and ensure they would be judged without prejudice, he decided to offer them for tasting in unidentified, wrapped bottles and to mix in among them a few white Burgundies and red Bordeaux. He knew he would have to choose among the very best of these or risk the suspicion that he and Gallagher had set up the California wines to score off the French. He knew, too, that because he would be showing the wines blind—that is, unmarked—and asking the tasters to rank their preferences, the credentials of those participating would have to be impeccable; otherwise any approving nods toward California might be dismissed as stemming from a lack of familiarity with the niceties of French wines.

The tasting took place at the Inter-Continental Hotel. The panel members—experienced and of high repute—were all French: Pierre Bréjoux, then chief inspector of the Institut National des Appellations d'Origine; Aubert de Villaine, part-owner of Domaine de la Romanée-Conti; Michel Dovaz, a wine writer and enologist; Claude Dubois-Millot, from *Le Nouveau Guide;* Odette Kahn, editor of the influential *Revue du Vin de France;* Raymond Oliver, the celebrated chef and owner of Le Grand Véfour; Pierre Tari, owner of Château Giscours, a *cru classé* of the Médoc, and secretary-general of the Syndicat des Grands Crus Classés; Christian Vannèque, head sommelier of Tour d'Argent; and Jean-Claude Vrinat, owner of Taillevent.

The Chardonnays brought by Spurrier's tennis players from California bore the labels of Spring Mountain '73, Freemark Abbey '72,

Chalone '74, Veedercrest '72, Château Montelena '73, and David Bruce '73. He added to them four white Burgundies: Meursault-Charmes, Domaine Roulot '73; Beaune Clos des Mouches '73, from Drouhin; Bâtard-Montrachet '73, of Ramonet-Prudhon; and Puligny-Montrachet, Premier Cru Les Pucelles '72, from Domaine Leflaive.

Spurrier's Cabernet Sauvignons were Clos du Val's '72; the '71s of Mayacamas and of Ridge Vineyards' Mountain Range; Freemark Abbey's '69; Stag's Leap Wine Cellars' '73; and Heitz Cellar's Martha's Vineyard '70. I wondered why he had not included wines such as Robert Mondavi's '69 Cabernet Sauvignon or the Georges de Latour Private Reserve '70—both of these wines yardsticks by which other California Cabernet Sauvignons were being measured at the time.

"I simply didn't get to taste them," he told me recently, whereas he had already tasted a number of the wines he did select, and the rest had been chosen based on visits to wineries made on the advice of friends.

Nothing was left to chance in his choice of Bordeaux to put along-side the California reds. They were Château Mouton-Rothschild '70, Château Haut-Brion '70, Château Montrose '70, and Château Léoville-Las-Cases '71. A formidable group of wines.

Members of the jury knew only that some of the wines were French and some from California. Once they had graded the ten white wines—poured from their wrapped bottles—on a scale of twenty points, they did the same with the reds, and a group order of preference was determined. Among the journalists present as spectators was the Paris bureau chief of *Time*, and in the magazine's international edition of June 7 he announced the group's decisions to the world.

Among the white wines, California's Château Montelena headed the list, followed by the Meursault-Charmes, Chalone, Spring Mountain, Beaune Clos des Mouches, Freemark Abbey, Bâtard-Montrachet, Puligny-Montrachet, Veedercrest, and David Bruce. A California wine, the Stag's Leap Wine Cellars '73, was first among the reds, too. It was followed, in order, by the Château Mouton-Rothschild, Château Haut-Brion, Château Montrose, Ridge Mountain Range,

Château Léoville-Las-Cases, Mayacamas, Clos du Val, Heitz Cellar Martha's Vineyard, and Freemark Abbey.

· · · · · ·

In California, growers took the news calmly—"Not bad for kids from the sticks" was the reported response of Château Montelena's owner, Jim Barrett. But in France, and particularly in Bordeaux, there was consternation and, one might say without exaggeration, a degree of shock. It was not that California's success diminished in any way the real quality or value of the French wines—they had been used, after all, as the measure by which the others were judged—but the published results challenged the French in a field where they had assumed their superiority to be unassailable.

The French experts who had participated in the tasting, greatly embarrassed, felt a need to excuse themselves: Sophisticated arguments were put forward to explain away their choices. But, even allowing for every extenuating circumstance and accepting—as Spurrier has since said repeatedly—that another jury, or even the same jury on another day, might have placed the wines in a different order, it was clear that California had arrived. Regardless of the statistical reliability of the point system Spurrier had used to establish the group preferences, serious California wines, tasted seriously by serious judges, had at the very least stood shoulder to shoulder with French wines produced from similar grape varieties.

The tasting gave California a shot of confidence and earned it a respect that was long overdue. But it also gave the French a valuable incentive to review traditions that were sometimes mere accumulations of habit and expediency, and to reexamine convictions that were little more than myths taken on trust.

The French were soon all over California—a place they had until then largely ignored—to see what was going on. In no time at all the first of many of their sons and daughters had enrolled in courses at Davis or begun working a crush in California, just as many young Americans had always done in France. And within the year, Baron Philippe de Rothschild, of Château Mouton-Rothschild, was in deep negotiation with Robert Mondavi to form the joint venture we know today as Opus One.

In an article in the British publication *Decanter* commemorating the twentieth anniversary of the tasting, Steven Spurrier said that the recognition given California was recompense for the state's investment in research and equipment. To some extent he is right. As a consequence of Prohibition, California vineyards had been replanted with coarse shipping varieties, winemaking standards had been seriously compromised, and most wineries had fallen into disrepair. The University of California had had to send its professors on the road to show vintners who had missed traditional father-son instruction how to make clean, flawless wines again. They never claimed to be teaching the art of making fine wine; their task—much more basic—was simply to reestablish the essentials of the craft, to reconnect post-Prohibition wine producers to a heritage that had been lost.

Certain vineyard sites that today are recognized for the quality of the wines they yield may well owe their survival to the professors' tour—but in fact many were first cultivated a century ago. Robert Mondavi's Reserve Cabernet Sauvignon is essentially the product of a vineyard, To-Kalon, originally planted by Hamilton Crabb in the 1880s. Spring Mountain occupied the winery built by Tiburcio Parrott in 1884. (Parrott's house is familiar to viewers of "Falcon Crest"; in the 1890s he produced there an exceptional Cabernet Sauvignon.) And, as our subject is recognition, the Liparita winery on Howell Mountain, now active again, took a gold medal for its Cabernet Sauvignon at the Paris Exposition of 1900—then, too, in competition with French wines.

◆ ◆ ◆ ◆ ◆ ◆

Eventually I got to see the actual scores awarded each wine by individual members of the 1976 Paris jury—as opposed to the final rankings published at the time. I was struck first by the fact that all nine judges had given their highest scores for white wine to California—either to

Château Montelena or to Chalone. That, it seemed to me, was indeed an endorsement—at least for young wines—of California grape maturity, technique, and hygiene.

And yet something about Spurrier's attribution of California's success to equipment—to technology—bothered me. I thought, for example, of Richard Graff's Chalone Vineyard as I had known it in 1974. Graff had always been a maverick among California wine producers. His vineyard, waterless and difficult to reach, was planted with an old clone of Chardonnay that he had cultivated vine by vine. Neither his methods of cultivation nor his winemaking had much to do with modern California technology. Chalone had little equipment to speak of; in 1974 it was still generating its own limited supply of electricity. And most important of all, at a time when California was only beginning to flirt with oak barrels, Graff had spent a year in France researching a treatise on oak and, probably alone in the California of that period, was fermenting his Chardonnay in the barrel and aging it on the lees. Now, more than twenty years later, that practice is commonplace.

Mike Grgich, then winemaker at Château Montelena, was born into a winegrowing family in Croatia and had perfected his craft first with Lee Stewart at the old Souverain winery on Howell Mountain (now the home of Burgess Cellars). A legend in California in the 1950s and 1960s, Stewart, self-taught, was obsessed by the details of winemaking. For him, it was the small things that counted. "I learned from Lee to watch over a wine as I would a baby," Grgich told Richard Paul Hinkle in an anniversary interview for the trade publication *Wines & Vines*. From Stewart, Grgich moved to André Tchelistcheff, the man behind the success of Beaulieu Vineyard's Georges de Latour Private Reserve, "who taught me to look at wine from the vineyard," and then to Robert Mondavi, "who made me aware of temperature control and French oak." When Grgich went to Château Montelena, he applied what he'd learned. "By then I knew how to handle a wine gently," he told me. "To disturb it as little as possible." The grapes for his winning 1973 had, like Graff's, also come from an old Chardonnay clone.

The Stag's Leap Wine Cellars Cabernet Sauvignon was the only California red to place among the first four. Surely it is more than coincidence that Warren Winiarski, the man who made it, should also have been an alumnus first of Lee Stewart, "a fastidious man who applied himself to every aspect of his wine," then of André Tchelistcheff, and, finally, of Robert Mondavi. "André gave us the soaring, the poetic vision. He had the gift of articulating what wine was to be, raising our horizons," Winiarski told Hinkle. "Robert provided the push, the thrust to get things done. Details and vision are nothing without the will to execute them."

It took a while longer for California's new crop of younger winemakers to learn these same lessons: to free themselves from technology; to abandon their expensive high-speed pumps and centrifuges; to reassess what "cellar hygiene" means (it doesn't mean keeping nature at bay with laboratory-prepared yeasts, preventing contact between a wine and its lees, and avoiding malolactic fermentation, the bacterial change that softens a wine and draws its disparate elements together); and to understand that fine wine is indeed made in the vineyard. In fact, it was a traditional, low-tech California that was honored that day in Paris in 1976. What the French recognized in wines they'd never tasted before was not equipment and rampant technology. It was the quality inherent in mature California vines; the skill and artistry of men like Richard Graff, Mike Grgich, and Warren Winiarski; and the vision of those who had gone before them.

THE SILENT REVOLUTION

HOW GOOD ARE ORGANIC WINES? FOR A START, THERE ARE FAR more of them out there than you might suspect. They're not in some fringe niche either: They include, for instance, Château Margaux, the Médoc first growth; the wines of the Domaine Leroy in Burgundy; those of Robert Sinskey Vineyards in Napa Valley; and certain bottlings from the Penfolds vineyards in South Australia's Clare Valley.

The question, then, would seem to answer itself, but there's a catch: Wines like these rarely display the word "organic." Sometimes it's to avoid having the wine perceived as funky, or bought for what the grower believes is the wrong reason. Robert Sinskey says he doesn't want people to think first about the way he cultivates his grapes and then about the quality of the wine. "We want the customer to buy our wine because it's good. The way we nurture the vines is simply part of our efforts to make it that way."

Robert Gross of Cooper Mountain Vineyards in Oregon also insists that quality is the point of the wine and that organic cultivation is simply a technique. Gross does use the words "organically grown" on his label because he knows there are people looking for it. "But it can also be a turnoff," he said. "Some wine drinkers see it and think we're being preachy."

Many producers of wine from organically grown grapes keep mum on the subject to leave their options open in the vineyard. Organizations that certify organic compliance sometimes impose parameters based on philosophically wholesome principles rather than on the practical needs of viticulture. In an extreme emergency, growers might be faced with the choice of spraying, as innocuously as possible, or losing a crop. They argue that it's better not to carry an "organic" statement at all—even when the vineyard is certified—rather than find themselves obliged to explain, in such a situation, why it had to be dropped. And then there are the many grape growers of California who ignored the chemical revolution of the 1950s and continue to do what they have always done. As bemused as Monsieur Jourdain—the character in Molière's *Le Bourgeois Gentilhomme* who discovered he'd been speaking prose all his life—they now learn that they have long been practicing organic viticulture without having once given it a thought. "They just don't make a big deal of it," Bob Blue, winemaker for the Bonterra organic wines of Fetzer Vineyards, told me. "They don't even bother to sell their grapes as 'organically grown.' But that's probably because they'd have to get involved with the maze of certifying organizations and state regulators to do it. And the fees can be heavy for a small producer."

Aside from those who had never grown grapes in any other way, the return to organic practices, both in California and in Europe, began in the early 1980s. I remember my surprise, sometime about then, when I found Ulysses Lolonis of Redwood Valley in Mendocino County dumping buckets of predator ladybugs among the vines in his family's vineyard. He says he started because of concern about the pesticides being proposed to him. "Eventually we found we didn't need them at all," he told me recently. "If we left enough grass between the rows of vines to serve as bug territory, it soon had a mixed population of insects keeping themselves busy devouring each other without bothering us.

"We've come a long way since then. Now, rather than grass, we grow a nitrogen-rich cover crop to feed the soil when we plow it under. The bugs are just as happy, and we can do without pesticides, herbicides, and fertilizers. Do these organic methods enhance the flavor or quality of our wine? Well, they don't seem to take anything away from it." (In fact, Lolonis' Zinfandel is one of the best in California.)

• • • • • •

John Williams of Frog's Leap Winery in Napa Valley is more forthright. He is convinced that organic cultivation does make a difference to wine quality. "The first vineyard we purchased in 1987," he said, "had been farmed by an old-timer on what we would now call organic principles. Wanting to do things right, we retained a firm to test the vines and the soil and make recommendations to us. They found many things wrong, but fortunately were able to supply us with all the chemical supplements they said we needed. The effort was grandly expensive and soon led to a general decline in the vineyard, the quality of its fruit, and the wine we made from it.

"I was urged to talk to an organic-farming consultant. Amigo Bob [Cantisano] certainly looked the part—ponytail, shorts, and tie-dyed T-shirt. What he said made sense, and we decided to give it a try in a couple of test areas. We now have nine growers in Napa Valley producing organically grown grapes for us.

"We found that a soil rich in organic matter absorbs and holds moisture better—so we were able to go back to dry farming, the old way of growing grapes in California, instead of relying on irrigation. We discovered that plants fed by compost and cover crops, rather than chemical fertilizers, draw in nutrients in a measured way that helps control growth. Our vines are therefore strong and healthy and give balanced fruit. We've learned to think about the causes of problems rather than react with a quick fix to each one as it comes up. It's made us better farmers. In doing all this, I'm not trying to save the world. I just want to make good wine."

There are others who farm organically simply because they don't like the idea of using industrial products in the vineyard. Jean-Pierre Margan of Château La Canorgue in the Côtes de Luberon (Peter Mayle country) told me he was taught in his viticulture courses which synthetic fertilizers to use and what and when to spray. "I never liked the idea," he said. "My father and grandfather had made good wine in the traditional way, and when my wife and I started to revive her family's dormant vineyard, I decided to do the same. It wasn't an act of defiance.

"But confronting nature directly means you have to be vigilant. You must look ahead—mistakes are difficult to correct organically. You become more efficient because you have to stay on top of every detail of every vine—and perhaps that's why the wine is better.

"Though the 'organic' aspect of the vineyard is simply the way we work, I put it on the label to allow those who want wine from organically grown grapes to find us. But there should be no need for me to say anything. Organic cultivation is and should be the norm. It's those who use chemicals that should have to identify themselves.

"I'm not alone in the way I work. There has been a tremendous awakening among winegrowers in France. Usually it starts with the growers getting involved with a program of reduced reliance on synthetic sprays and fertilizers and the reintroduction of more benign techniques—but they soon see the difference in their vineyards and move increasingly toward the freedom that organic cultivation allows."

That awakening has been greatly accelerated by the work of Claude Bourguignon, whose highly influential book, *Le sol, la terre et les champs* (The Soil, the Land and the Fields), is now in its third edition. Almost every French winegrower I've talked to in the past several years has at some point introduced Bourguignon's name into our conversation. Now he's one of the leading French experts in soil analysis—his client list includes Domaine de la Romanée-Conti and Château Latour and reads, in fact, like an honor roll of French viticulture. Much of what he has to say comes down to the essential role of microorganic life in the soil. He expresses regret, in the introduction to his book, that the issues involved have become noisily politicized.

In the second edition of his book *Burgundy*, Anthony Hanson describes a visit to Bourguignon's laboratory, north of Dijon. Having collected a random sample of earth from a flower bed, Bourguignon shook it with water, adding a coloring agent, then put it under his microscope for Hanson to look at. "I shall never forget the sight," Hanson writes. "Tiny specks of solid particles (clays and other inanimate matter) were bathed in liquid which teemed with swimming, turning, thrashing, pulsing little organisms—bacteria, yeasts, microbes of all sorts."

In an ounce or two of healthy soil, Bourguignon will tell you, there are billions of such microorganisms. They transform mineral elements in the soil to make them available to plants that could not otherwise assimilate them. They attach iron to acetic acid, for example, forming the iron acetate that a plant can absorb. This symbiotic relationship allows a plant to function properly, to capture the energy in sunlight. That's where the energy-into-matter and matter-into-energy food chain starts. Soil bacteria need no human presence to flourish and do their work. It's sobering to be reminded that our lives depend on them.

* * * * * *

Biodynamic farming takes organic cultivation one step further by paying special attention to soil bacteria and to harnessing the rest of the energy in the cosmos in ways that strengthen the vine. It has developed from theories expounded by Rudolph Steiner, the Austrian social philosopher, in the 1920s. Those who practice it are used to the skepticism, even the mockery, of others—there's an air of both New Age mysticism and Old Age witchcraft about it. But it works.

Robert Sinskey, who is heading toward biodynamic certification for all his vineyards, got interested because of a specific problem with one vineyard in particular. "The soil was as hard as rock," he told me. "It was dead. It was planted with Chardonnay, and the wine from those vines was always green and lean. We put in a cover crop and began using biodynamic sprays to encourage the development of microorganisms in the soil. Gradually we brought that vineyard around, and the wine is now so appealing and distinctive that we will soon be bottling it with a special designation."

Robert Gross, a physician whose interests include alternative medicine, is also moving toward biodynamic certification for his vineyards at

Cooper Mountain. "It brings the vines into harmony with their environment," he told me.

Two of the biodynamic sprays—500, a very dilute solution of cow manure that has been aged in a cow horn placed underground through the winter and then stirred into blood-warm water with a motion calculated to maximize its effect; and 501, a similarly dilute solution of powdered silica—are basic to the system. Other sprays, mostly homeopathic teas of herbs and flowers, are used by some and not by others. Working in accordance with phases of the moon and reserving certain days for spraying, pruning, or planting to take advantage of propitious movements of the planets are ideas that some accept and others reserve judgment on.

Farming with due provision for the gravitational pull of the moon is ancient wisdom. Jim Fetzer—who started the program of wines made from organic grapes at Fetzer and is now owner of the Ceago Vinegarden, a fully accredited biodynamic vineyard estate in Mendocino County—said he never has to explain any of this to his Mexican workers. "They're used to the idea that various aspects of agricultural work should coincide with the phases of the moon," he said. "It makes sense: If the changes in atmospheric pressure associated with the moon's waxing and waning can affect the rise and fall of oceans, you can be sure it affects the position of the sap in the vines." As for the special days, Alan York, Ceago Vinegarden's biodynamics consultant (and consultant to Joseph Phelps and Benziger, among others), put it to me this way: "We don't know why or how the plant responds to the changing positions of the planets. It's like surfing. There's this force and you try to ride it."

There is much more to biodynamics than homeopathy and "root" days. A key element is the systematic introduction of other plants among the principal crop. There is a rich diversity of them growing among the vines at Ceago Vinegarden, including olive trees, lavender, and buckwheat—habitat to tiny wasps that lay their eggs inside the eggs of leafhoppers and stop that problem before it starts. When I was young, I took it for granted that most vines in Italy and France had peach trees and even a line or two of corn planted among them. I thought it was to make full use of the land, but now I know better.

"Biodynamics is neither a recipe nor even a specific technique," says Nicolas Joly, owner of Coulée de Serrant, the white-wine jewel of Loire Valley vineyards. "It can't be applied mechanically. It demands a complete understanding of what is happening in the life cycle of a plant and the formation of its fruit so that the functions can be enhanced."

Joly, an articulate advocate and proselytizer, condemns completely what he sees as the sins of modern viticulture. "Herbicides and pesticides annihilate the microbial life peculiar to any particular soil, and synthetic fertilizers then standardize the vines' nourishment and thus the character of the fruit. What is the point of talking about *terroir* in such circumstances?"

* * * * * *

There is a wide gap between biodynamics and conventional viticulture, and a considerable one even between standard and organic practices. Part of that difference is cost. The abuse of pesticides, herbicides, and synthetic fertilizers can create an imbalance even more expensive to address. But the considerable handwork involved in organic viticulture is also costly—and justified economically only if higher quality attracts a better price for the wine.

In the detailed report on its experiment of organically cultivating roughly 125 acres of vineyard on its Clare Valley estate over the past ten or twenty years, Penfolds (owned by Southcorp Wines) shows that the cost of cultivating those blocks of vines was as much as 50 percent higher than that of cultivating similar neighboring blocks by conventional methods. Australia has high labor costs, which accounts to some extent for this startling difference; but, when expressed as cost per ton because of the smaller yields when compared with conventional viticulture, the cost of Penfolds' organically grown grapes becomes 100 percent higher.

In the face of such numbers, we can't ignore the fact that whatever satisfaction growers may get from the quality of their products and from their stewardship of the land, they accept the risk inherent in growing a crop as fragile as grapes in order to make a fair return.

* * * * * *

In most parts of the winemaking world, particularly in California, there are programs designed and supported by growers' associations to help members wean themselves from dependence on synthetic chemical treatments and to combine organic farming principles with a sound and limited use of environmentally safe products in a cost-effective manner. The program run by the Lodi-Woodbridge Winegrape Commission, financed by an assessment on grape production voted by the growers themselves, includes a step-by-step workbook that encourages growers to meet regularly in small groups for mutual support and the exchange of information and to constantly survey every aspect of their work. They evaluate their progress in sowing cover crops, for example, and installing nesting boxes near their vineyards for predator barn owls. There are similar programs organized by the Central Coast Vineyard Team, and still more are being developed on a smaller scale in Amador and Lake Counties.

These programs encourage growers to check their vines closely and, by thinking ahead, to discover new options for dealing with problems. They lead them to a system of fully sustainable agriculture—or beyond—and at the same time help them steadily improve the quality of their wines.

Paul Pontallier, manager of Château Margaux—where herbicides, pesticides, and synthetic fertilizers are rarely used—commented to me recently that there's much to be said for organic farming and for biodynamic viticulture, whatever the circumstance, so long as the approach is always practical. "The danger comes," he said, "when some particular way of doing things is turned into an ideology."

COULD IT BE CORKED?

TO SOME IT'S A RITUAL, TO OTHERS A TORMENT. A WAITER POURS wine into a glass. His customer sniffs, tastes, and must then tell him whether the wine is acceptable. Sometimes it's too cold (or not cold enough)—a temporary problem. But occasionally the wine has a serious defect. Being "corked" or "corky" is the most common.

A "corked" bottle is one in which the wine has been tainted by the cork. In the glass, a "corked" wine has a musty smell of damp cardboard or old newspapers. Sometimes the smell is of beets or of garden soil.

There *are* marginal cases when even the most expert are unsure; at a certain level the compounds that cause corkiness suppress the wine's own aroma and flavor without immediately revealing their presence more directly. Familiarity with how a particular wine usually tastes is then the only real guide, but anyone should be suspicious when wine of a quality that normally guarantees both aroma and flavor has neither. Very often the corkiness will reveal itself more clearly after a minute or two in the glass.

A few years ago, a German study on the problems of corkiness suggested that as much as 2 percent of all bottled wine—one bottle in fifty—was tainted by off-flavors originating in the cork. Recent estimates in the United States would have us believe that the incidence of corkiness has climbed higher than that, but there is no hard evidence available to support those claims. I open and taste scores of bottles almost every week, and I don't find the proportion of them that are "corked" to be any greater now than I remember it having been a few years ago. Today, as then, I would guess it to be about one half of one percent.

In my view, it's not the scale of the problem that has changed but our awareness of it. That's because winemaking standards have risen almost everywhere in recent years, and what might formerly have passed as one flaw among many is now more conspicuous. Americans are also more sensitive to flawed wines and less tolerant of them. Many who began to drink table wines in the seventies and eighties now know very well what to expect of those they most frequently enjoy. They can tell when something is amiss and have the confidence in their own judgment to say so.

◆ ◆ ◆ ◆ ◆ ◆

Because of the musty smell, it was always assumed that the odor and flavor typical of "corked" wine came from a mold, invisible to the naked eye, that developed within poorly stored corks prior to use. (A cork that crumbles into the wine, incidentally, is a nuisance but is not a sign of a "corked" bottle; and a sticky mold on the top of a cork when the capsule is removed is unlikely to be anything worse than an eyesore.)

Research a few years ago at the University of New South Wales in Australia revealed that the principal cause of corkiness is not mold itself but a substance with a name like a football cheer: 2,4,6-TCA (2,4,6-trichloroanisole to its friends). It is formed by a mold growing in the presence of a compound of phenols and chlorine.

Phenols are abundantly present in wood (and therefore in cork bark) as well as in grape skins (and therefore in red wine). Chlorine is everywhere—there are traces of it in the atmosphere, let alone in our drinking water—and it has commonly been used to bleach and sterilize cork bark after it has been stripped from the tree. Other compounds contribute to corkiness along with TCA, but chlorine is rarely part of their molecular road maps, and to be noticed the compounds must be present at higher concentrations than TCA. One of the most severe aspects of

TCA is that a very little of it goes a long way. The human nose can pick it up at concentrations as low as four parts per trillion, a ratio equivalent to four seconds in thirty-two thousand years.

The cork oak grows all around the western Mediterranean, but most of the world's cork comes from forests in eastern Portugal. Portuguese cork manufacturers, pushed by California winemakers and American wine importers, have made a commitment to rid their corks of TCA, or at least to prevent TCA from contaminating wine. Most manufacturers have already taken the obvious step of using methods other than a chlorine bath to cleanse and bleach the newly stripped cork.

But any change from a tested tradition, whatever benefits one might hope for, also entails risk. Though the desired end of the cleansing process is to disinfect the cork, there is a thin line between disinfecting and corroding. Other possible processes could be too extreme in their effect. And in any case, as the four factors contributing to the formation of TCA (phenols, chlorine, atmospheric moisture, and mold) are present at almost every stage of handling cork—from the tree to the moment the stopper goes into the wine bottle—prevention of TCA at one point might merely delay its formation.

Some treatments—heating corks to a temperature of 140°C, for instance, to vaporize TCA already formed and kill mold spores present—risk damaging the cork cells and losing some of the elasticity that is one of cork's essential qualities as a closure. Others, like radiation, can rid the cork of spores though not of TCA. But research continues. It's possible that strengthening the virtually invisible film of wax intended to lubricate corks on their passage through the bottling system could create a protective barrier between the wine and any TCA within the cork's pores. In the old days, before cork manufacturers were clever enough to apply a film of wax so fine as to be immeasurable, the conventional hot wax treatment given to corks probably *did* act as a barrier, even though that's not what it was there for.

Cork, a plentiful and renewable resource, is ideal as a closure for wine bottles because after being compressed for insertion into a bottle neck it immediately springs back to form a tight, impermeable seal. Except for the TCA problem, it introduces no taste of its own.

· · · · · ·

Both the ancient Greeks and the Romans sealed vessels with cork, but its use was forgotten, along with much else from the ancient world, during the long Dark Ages. We don't know whether the practice completely disappeared, but our earliest references to it in the modern world date from only the sixteenth century. In his plays, Shakespeare made such frequent allusions to cork as a closure that we can be sure it was in general use in England by the end of that century.

It's curious that the revival of cork stoppers was in England, a country in which cork doesn't grow. It was widely employed there as a closure for bottles of cider and beer. In his *Delightes for Ladies,* first published in 1609, Sir Hugh Plat advised waiting until the tumultuous barrel fermentation of beer was complete before bottling it (to avoid "windy and muddy, thundering and smoking upon the opening") and counseled the use of corks "very fit for the bottles [to] stop them close."

Fitting bottles "close" calls for reasonably uniform neck dimensions, and the earliest progress in manufacturing bottles with any kind of uniformity was indeed in England. The first patent for such containers was granted by Parliament to Sir Kenelm Digby in 1662, though his work on the manufacture of glass bottles dates back to 1642, when it had been a diversion for him while languishing in jail as a Royalist prisoner of Cromwell.

Sir Kenelm seemed, however, to favor ground-glass stoppers over cork. (Hugh Johnson reports in *Vintage: The Story of Wine* that glass stoppers, ground with emery powder and oil to ensure a tight fit, were used for some wine bottles until as late as 1825.) John Worlidge, in his *Treatise of Cider,* published in London in 1676, says plainly that glass stoppers were to be preferred because of "much liquor being absolutely spoiled through the only defect of the cork." Clearly TCA was with us long before we had a name for it.

· · · · · ·

There have been attempts to move away from cork as a closure. After all, one rarely hears of bottles closed with aluminum screw-tops reeking with TCA. But the matter is more complex than one might suppose. In the late 1970s and early 1980s two of Australia's largest wineries, Yalumba and Hardy's, decided to drop corks in favor of screw caps, partly to avoid all the potential problems inherent in corks and also to make their wines more accessible to the kind of people who forget to take corkscrews on picnics. Sales had fallen by as much as 40 percent before the two companies decided to reverse themselves. For better or worse, cork stoppers remain indispensable to the image of good wine.

One American company is now producing a synthetic cork, Cellucork, which has many of the properties of cork—it even looks a little like cork—though it is made from a plastic: ethylene vinyl acetate. Its elasticity is not quite that of natural cork; to regain its volume after being compressed in a bottling machine, the Cellucork must stand in an upright bottle for twenty-four hours before packing. But the synthetic stopper is removed with a corkscrew, and those who don't look too closely can easily assume it to be cork of a particularly smooth texture.

After years of testing, including controlled marketing tests in 1992, the St. Francis Winery in Sonoma Valley decided that from 1993 all its wines would be closed with Cellucork rather than natural cork. Other wineries are said to be considering Cellucork, too. Still others are skeptical because they feel that TCA can be generated independently of both cork and Cellucork and could therefore contaminate their surfaces anyway. That's taking a very pessimistic view.

◆ ◆ ◆ ◆ ◆ ◆

Any reduction in corkiness would be a good thing, of course, even if the incidence is already lower than some would have us believe. After all, there is nothing sadder than to open a bottle one has stored for years against the right occasion, having waited for the wine to be truly ready, only to find a cork-tainted liquid inside. The disappointment is compounded by loss because one cannot return a bottle purchased ten years before. On the other hand, wines of a current vintage should always be returned promptly if found to be corky. And one owes it to one's guests—as well as oneself—to reject a corky bottle presented in a restaurant. Both retailer and restaurant will automatically return the bottle to the producer for credit.

Those not sure if they would recognize TCA with certainty and afraid of embarrassing themselves or others can obtain a small phial of it. Send a written request with a check for five dollars to cover costs to the Cork Quality Council at 7305 Bodega Avenue, Sebastopol, CA 95472. Once smelled, TCA is never forgotten. One can then banish all terror and give the waiter the nod (or not) with full confidence.

A small caveat: *Don't* carry the phial around in pocket or purse as a comparison. Its mustiness will quickly permeate everything worn or carried with it. And thirty-two thousand years is an awfully long time to have to wait for the smell to disappear.

MOUNT VEEDER:
VINES AMONG THE REDWOODS

A CORNER OF MY WINE CELLAR THAT IS ESPECIALLY AWKWARD TO reach is reserved for bottles that can be forgotten for a while. I rummage there from time to time and, on occasion, surprise myself. One Christmas I found some 1971 Château Doisy-Védrines, a Sauternes that I must have put there twenty years before. It was delicious. And in the spring I came across a bottle of Mount Veeder Winery's 1979 Cabernet Sauvignon. In the late 1970s, when the superfluous tannins in many California Cabernet Sauvignons were a matter of controversy, Mount Veeder Winery was managing to get it right—the tannins were big but ripe and in balance with the scale of the wine. (This hadn't made Mount Veeder Cabernet Sauvignons any easier to appreciate when they were young, but it does explain why I would have put a bottle of it to one side while not wasting space on many another.) I had lamb shanks braising in the oven with a little garlic, rosemary, and lemon zest. The aroma was compelling, and I wanted something to drink that I would enjoy just as unreservedly. I wasn't disappointed: That 1979 Cabernet Sauvignon was superb. It had a royal color, a sweetly comforting bouquet, and a texture of old velvet.

The red wines of Mount Veeder—the appellation itself, not just the winery—have a reputation for being stubborn when young and idiosyncratic when mature, but I have yet to taste one that was boring. In his book *Making Sense of California Wine*, Matt Kramer writes, "Against more polished but less site-specific Cabernets, [Mount Veeder's] very character sets them uncomfortably apart, like a wild fish in a school of tank-raised trout." Maybe so, but they are mountain wines and they need time. Those who have patience are usually as well rewarded as I was.

Rising to an altitude of almost twenty-seven hundred feet, Mount Veeder is part of the Mayacamas coastal range separating Napa and Sonoma Valleys. The word "mount" suggests a smooth-sided cone—a California Fuji, if you will—but through the merging of school and fire districts many years ago, the area defined as Mount Veeder now includes many contiguous hillsides, valleys, and canyons known collectively until World War II as the Napa Redwoods. Lying on the east side—the Napa side—of the divide, most of this area is still untamed. Madrona, fir, oak, and redwood give cover to deer, coyote, mountain lions, and black bear, while eagles soar above. But scattered through it—sometimes on isolated slopes carefully protected from erosion, more often on even steeper, terraced hillsides, and occasionally on small, flat shelves of land from which one can look down precipitously toward a distant San Francisco Bay—are more than a thousand acres of vineyards significant for the distinctive style and quality of the wine they produce. The wines of Mount Veeder are so characteristic of themselves, in fact, that the region is now an officially defined Viticultural Area within the larger one of Napa Valley.

"The wines up here have always had strong character," says Brother Timothy, winemaster for fifty years at the Christian Brothers' Mont La Salle winery. "They were more concentrated than valley wines. We could always recognize Mount Veeder grapes just by tasting them and comparing them with any others that came into the winery."

Bob Travers of Mayacamas Vineyards, the most venerable winery on the mountain, is himself a producer of quintessential Mount Veeder wines: unyielding in youth, slow to evolve, and imposingly grand in their prime. He describes the mountain's wines as intense but never showy. They have an unruly element: In the fruit of the young red wines there is a reminder of the hedgerow briar rather than the cultivated berry patch.

"Even Chardonnay grown here has depth and character," Travers says. "It takes on, with time, an opulence one wouldn't have expected from tasting it when it was young and angular."

* * * * * *

A Captain Stalham Wing (about whom little is known) planted the first vines on Mount Veeder, in what is now called Wing Canyon, before 1860. The descendants of others who planted vines soon after him, most of them immigrants of German origin, still live on the mountain. And many vineyards established there in the 1880s—a boom time for Napa Valley, as vineyards expanded from three thousand to twenty thousand acres within the decade—flourish still, despite the ravages of phylloxera at the turn of the nineteenth century and the even worse depredations of Prohibition. Some vineyards have come, gone, and come again, however, and all have passed through the hands of several owners. The Hess Collection, for example, which is presently Mount Veeder's largest winery, is really the continuum of a vineyard first planted in 1862. With adjustments to boundaries and buildings, this site has been both the Theodore Gier Winery, one of the most important in California in the years before Prohibition, and the Mont La Salle estate of Christian Brothers. Mayacamas Vineyards started life in the 1880s when John Fisher, doubtless following the Napa trend, built a stone winery, still in use, on the rim of an extinct volcano and planted vines on surrounding land where he had previously grazed sheep.

These vineyards and wineries were no mere adjuncts to mainstream activity in the valley below. At Castle Rock, a winery preserved on Mount Veeder though no longer operating as such, Rudolf Jordan was the first in California to experiment commercially with low-temperature fermentation (he pumped cold water through a coiled pipe plunged into the fermenting juice), using selected (as opposed to indigenous) yeast. In the account of his work submitted to a local publication in 1912, Jordan wrote: "By the addition of pure yeast to start a fermentation, as well as by the cooling of all fermenting musts, a product can be obtained that is superior to that made in the old 'let alone' way." Jordan explained that fermentation at low temperatures preserved the alcohol in the wine, precipitated sharp tartaric acid in crystal form, and checked the formation of volatile acidity, all of which combined to give "wine [that] tastes smoother and more pleasant." He introduced, in fact, controlled fermentation—a turning point for California.

Mount Veeder Winery, which produced the 1979 Cabernet Sauvignon I enjoyed with my braised lamb shank, does not have its roots in an earlier era. In 1964, Michael and Arlene Bernstein bought a small farmhouse on Mount Veeder Road that was attached to a fifteen-acre prune-plum orchard. At the time they had nothing more in mind than to use the house as a weekend retreat, although Michael, a Philadelphia lawyer transplanted to San Francisco, was already a wine enthusiast and knew something of the area's grape-growing history.

"When I first came to California," he told me, "I drank Cabernet Sauvignon and Barbera from Louis Martini's Monte Rosso vineyard up on the Mayacamas ridge. Martini explained on every back label why grapes grown on hillsides give better wine, and the argument stuck in my head. Then in 1960 we answered an advertisement directed at anyone interested in making a small investment in a winery. It turned out to be Mayacamas Vineyards. The estate was being revived by Jack and Mary Taylor, who had bought it in 1941. Encouraged by my bit of learning about the superiority of hillside grapes, we bought twenty shares at ten dollars apiece. This entitled us to attend regular shareholder meetings at which much wine was consumed and even more sold to the shareholders with a 20 percent discount. It certainly stoked my interest in the viticultural possibilities of the Mayacamas."

When the Bernsteins bought the orchard, the farmer—getting on in years and wanting to wind down—showed them what to do with the plum trees. But they soon began putting in a few vines, just for fun.

"By 1968 we were pulling out trees and planting four or five hundred vines a year—hard work because we did it all ourselves on weekends. Then I took a year's leave of absence from the Federal Trade Commission, and we moved up here."

Their idea was to sell the grapes, just as they'd sold fruit to the plum driers. But in 1970 they began to make a little wine for their own consumption and by the following year they were hooked. The Bernsteins raised some cash, put up a simple wood-faced building, and had their first crush in 1973.

"I never did go back to the Federal Trade Commission. We released the 1973 vintage in 1976, having already introduced into the vineyard a little of all the other classic Bordeaux varieties—Merlot, Cabernet Franc, Malbec, and Petit Verdot—to soften the rigor of the Cabernet Sauvignon. We also planted some Zinfandel. But, as we tasted our young wines, we realized that the mountain itself, not the variety, was the determining factor in each of them."

The wines had power and intense flavor as a matter of course, they found, regardless of what the variety was, but their concentrated tannins often obscured all else. The next step was to learn to work with those tannins, and even to modify them, without losing or weakening the qualities that gave the Cabernet Sauvignon, in particular, its personality.

"I did what the French usually do in such circumstances. Starting with the 1976 vintage, I fined the wine with plenty of fresh egg whites to reduce the tannins—they attach themselves to the protein and sink to the bottom of the barrel—while leaving everything else intact and, in fact, more attractively revealed than before."

．　．　．　．　．　．

Up the hill, meanwhile, the Taylors had sold Mayacamas Vineyards to Robert and Elinor Travers. Travers, a man with a tradition of farming on both sides of his family, had decided three years earlier to quit his job with an investment bank and get back to the land. He wanted a vineyard where he could grow grapes and make a wine with character, one distinctive enough to be recognized as the product of a single estate. Mayacamas Vineyards, two thousand feet above the Napa Valley floor, was the first property he looked at, and eventually, after visiting more than a hundred others throughout the world, it was the one he settled on.

"Our vineyards," he told me when I visited him, my interest in Mount Veeder having been stimulated anew by that splendid 1979, "are among the highest on the mountain, from eighteen hundred to twenty four hundred feet—well above the morning fog. In fact, most vines on Mount Veeder have sunlight all day, yet it doesn't get too hot here because of breezes straight off the bay; temperatures rarely go into the nineties. An inversion—our cool air flows down to the valley, their warm air rises here—keeps us temperate at night, too. Because the vines are rarely shut down, whether from heat or cold, our wines have great intensity and concentration when compared with others from Napa."

Travers studied geology—his brother teaches it at Cornell—and he talks confidently of the compressed volcanic ash and pyroclastic rocks on Mount Veeder. Other specialists, too, explain the contribution of volcanic debris to the character of these wines: The shallow depth of topsoil over bedrock, allied to the steep topography, allows no more than negligible reserves of water to accumulate, even though due to a quirk in the way moisture-laden air passes over the Mayacamas range, Mount Veeder has almost double the average annual rainfall of the valley floor. On the lower slopes, there is more clay (which increases the tannic element in a wine), and in some of the valleys—Wing Canyon, for instance—there are pockets of flint and gravelly loam that contribute to the wines' elegance.

This same low level of nutrients can be found in the volcanic debris throughout the area, and that keeps crop levels down.

"We average about a ton and a half of fruit per acre from our Cabernet Sauvignon vines," Bob Travers told me. "And we get half that from our Chardonnay." On the richer soils of the Napa Valley floor, growers commonly get four tons to the acre.

The Bernsteins sold Mount Veeder Winery in 1983, and it is now associated with the Franciscan Winery of Rutherford. Augustin Huneeus, one of the partners there, reiterated the shared wisdom regarding the Mount Veeder appellation: "The wines are much more dense than those produced in the valley; in fact, their concentration is often used to give a boost to blends. Some of Napa Valley's best Cabernet Sauvignons are as successful as they are because of the inclusion of a small proportion of Mount Veeder grapes. The tannins in Mount Veeder wines must, however, be managed judiciously. If you go too far in trying to control them, you will lose the best of what the wines have to offer. You have to find a way of working with the tannins, not against them."

Every grower on the mountain has his own way of doing that. Michael Bernstein gently peeled some of the tannins away with his egg whites. Robert Travers, having made sure that the grape tannins are fully ripe before picking, gives the wine long aging in wood before bottling— eighteen months in thousand-gallon oval oak casks followed by a year in conventional sixty-gallon barrels—to allow the tannins time to resolve before gradually merging, in bottle, into the wine's textured depths.

Bill Jenkins, of Wing Canyon Vineyard (an organic winery—even the energy he uses is generated most of the year only by sun and wind), approaches the problem differently. He ferments his crushed grapes in small, shallow bins—there's room for little more than a barrel of wine in each, if that—allowing for maximum contact between the cap of skins and the juice. When the cap is spread out over the contents of a small container, it's easier to punch down the skins frequently and extract the color and flavor quickly. Jenkins runs the juice off into barrel just before the fermentation has finished, usually after no more than six days.

"That last remnant of unfermented sugar," he told me, "is converted in the barrel and generates a little carbon dioxide to keep the new wine fresh." I don't know what the carbon dioxide does for his wine, but it seems to me that the important effect of his technique is to control the presence and quality of his wines' tannins. Tannins are more easily extracted from grape skins in the presence of alcohol, so if the new wine and the spent skins are separated as soon as the fermentation is complete—or even a little before the maximum level of alcohol is attained— then the tannins in the wine are more efficiently controlled and the harshest tannins, the last to be released into the wine, can be avoided altogether. Bill Jenkins produces wines at Wing Canyon in which he has infused the natural power and distinction of Mount Veeder with an extraordinary grace.

Jenkins manages the cap of skins—the source of tannins and there-fore the key to controlling them—literally with hands on. Randle Johnson, at the Hess Collection, and Tony Sargent, at Rubissow-Sargent, also focus their attention on the cap, but each handles it in a different way. "We have worked at finding a way to extract what we need without overmanipulating the cap," Johnson told me. He has developed a technique that translates Jenkins' palm-of-the-hand in a large bucket to the circumstances of a high-volume winery. "We use gentle air pres-sure to drive an automatic system of punching down the skins," Johnson told me. "Even so, we watch the maturity of the tannins in our grapes before picking so that they will contribute to the texture of the wines and, contrary to what is usually expected of tannins, contribute to their suppleness."

Tony Sargent, a biophysicist by training and experience and the partner at Rubissow-Sargent responsible for fermentation, is eclectic in his cap management. He follows the traditional routine of pumping the fermenting wine from the bottom of the vat over the top of the layer of skins. But, instead of allowing the pumped wine to hit the cap fiercely and break it up, he uses a revolving sprinkler to spread the fermenting wine gently over the cap and seep slowly through it. Having extracted his tannins in this way, he fines the wine at a later stage with two or three egg whites to the barrel—about half what would be used in Bordeaux. "We expect the wines to have some snap to them," he said. "But the place and time to manage what that should be is in the vineyard."

Marketta Fourmeaux, of Château Potelle, also insisted that the real control of tannins takes place in the vineyard. "When the grapes are in balance, we can stand back and interfere minimally in the winemaking. We make picking decisions based on flavor and tannin maturity, trusting our palates more than analysis numbers. Over the years we have learned what to expect from each block of vines. This one might always give a rather luscious result, that one might contribute more austerity.

"The most important decisions are made during picking. That's the time when we shape the wine; every subsequent decision flows from what we decide then."

Madame Fourmeaux takes a fundamentally different tack from all the others. "We give our Cabernet Sauvignon, in particular, a long maceration with the skins—sometimes up to thirty-five days. Inevitably the tannins are both heavy and harsh at first. But, left alone, they polymerize," she said, referring to the way in which tannins, when massively present, often form heavy molecular chains that taste rounder and eventually fall out of the wine with other sediment. "We rack the wines off their lees by gravity, manipulating them as little as possible. All this takes time, but it's necessary if the wine is to be pure pleasure, something to enjoy. Without that, we shall have failed."

The growers on the mountain rarely do fail. Even the Zinfandels of such tiny producers as Lori Olds and Linn Brinner at Sky, and Bill Hawley at Random Ridge, are memorable. Of course, almost any Mount Veeder wine can, on occasion, seem *too* intense, and therefore overly dramatic. But that goes with the territory.

BRAVE NEW MONTEREY

I FIRST VISITED THE SALINAS VALLEY IN MONTEREY COUNTY, CAL-
ifornia, in 1974, when its transformation from salad bowl to wine region
was so recent that no one I knew in San Francisco, barely a hundred
miles in the north, was aware of what had happened there. The establishment of more than thirty thousand acres of vines—half as many
again as in Burgundy's Côte d'Or—had even the valley's farmers confused, and sometimes resentful of the sudden change.

Wente, Mirassou, and Paul Masson, important wine producers
squeezed by urban development around San Francisco Bay, had bought
land and established vineyards in the valley in the mid-1960s. And they
led the way for others—August and William Jekel of Jekel Vineyards,
Douglas Meador of Ventana Vineyards, and Richard and Claudia Smith
of Paraiso Springs, in addition to partnerships set up by businessmen
from California's Central Valley. Land was cheaper in Monterey County
than in Napa, but harder to come by. When, in the 1870s, the railway
reached Soledad, about thirty miles south of Salinas, it brought Italian-
Swiss dairy farmers and milk trains. Descendants of those families still
regard the land as their capital. They sometimes lease plots to outsiders,
but they rarely sell. The vineyards went in regardless.

From its source far south of the county line to its mouth on
Monterey Bay, the Salinas River flows (mostly underground; it is the
largest aquifer in the United States) in a northwesterly direction. Its

valley, a rather gaunt ten miles or so across, is flanked on the east by the Gavilans, a series of rocky uplands along the San Andreas Fault, where the Pacific and Continental plates continue to grind into each other. To the west the valley is protected from the ocean by the Santa Lucia Range, mountains that are a tangle of forest, canyon, and untamed woodland— a refuge for deer, mountain lions, and, it is said, an occasional black bear.

Wente, Mirassou, and Paul Masson's decisions to plant vines there were not arbitrary. To ease the work of replanting California's vineyards in the 1930s, when Prohibition ended, professors Albert Winkler and Maynard Amerine of the University of California at Davis identified the state's potential grape-growing regions and classified them broadly according to average daily temperatures during the growing season. But within the Salinas Valley they had identified three distinct zones, not one. By two o'clock on summer afternoons, high temperatures at the head of the valley in neighboring San Luis Obispo County pull from the ocean a strong, persistent wind. As a result, the fifty miles or so from King City down to Salinas, a distance covered most mornings by sea fog that rolls in from the bay, are a cool-climate area—like Carneros or Anderson Valley—as those who planted Cabernet Sauvignon and Merlot there in that first rush to establish vineyards soon found out.

Initially, most of the vines in the valley were planted in tracts that stretched to the horizon. Walking the mile-long rows was out of the question. Vineyard managers made their inspections on motorized tricycles fitted with small, tractor-style wheels. Equipped with hard hats and walkie-talkies, they skimmed over sandy clay at dare-devil speeds, taking bearings on the irrigation system's network of pumping stations: massive pipes, painted orange and bright blue, rearing up from the ground at regular intervals like the looped contortions of Fernand Léger's industrial fantasies. Daily reports from weather stations and soil-humidity gauges were fed into field office computers. Familiar only with the pocket-sized, virtually hand-hoed vineyards of Europe, I found this mixture of vast scale and high technology exotic and at times quite heady. There were days on that first visit when I felt I had strayed into Aldous

Huxley's *Brave New World* rather than the setting for John Steinbeck's *East of Eden.*

Far stranger to me, however, was the fact that, on the large, professionally managed estates owned by absent partners and financed by banks and insurance companies, grape varieties had been selected based on surveys of consumer preferences and sales trends. And so Johannisberg Riesling was planted alongside Cabernet Sauvignon; Sauvignon Blanc next to Pinot Noir; and Gewürztraminer shared space with Petite Sirah. No one seemed concerned that each of these varieties needs disparate conditions to give of its best. To be fair, ignoring those conditions was a common attitude in California at the time (though elsewhere in the state it had been at least tempered by experience of what would and would not ripen where). Few growers showed concern for matching variety to soil, exposure, and microclimate. As far as most of California was concerned, *terroir* was something that existed only in Frenchmen's heads.

* * * * * *

For anyone interested during this period, a model of vine varieties successfully matched to *terroir* in the conventional European way did in fact exist only a few miles above Soledad in the Gavilans. Early in the 1920s—long before Winkler and Amerine came on the scene—the Silvear brothers purchased the property now known as Chalone Vineyard, and they planted about twenty acres of Thompson Seedless vines. When Will Silvear bought his three brothers' shares, he replanted the vineyard with Pinot Noir, Pinot Blanc, Chardonnay, and Chenin Blanc. He probably knew that the mix of limestone and granitic sand, formed by the meshing of ocean floor and volcanic debris, was not dissimilar to Burgundy's soils. André Tchelistcheff, who arrived from France in 1938 to take over winemaking at Beaulieu Vineyard in Napa Valley, described Will Silvear as "a Francophile [who] admired Burgundies more than anything else."

During Prohibition, Will Silvear had sold his grapes not only to Beaulieu but also to Wente in Livermore (both had been licensed to make sacramental wine). Silvear shipped to them, and later to others, even when Prohibition was over and he was free to make wine himself. His widow, Agnes, said that her husband never had enough money to build a winery of his own. She sold the property in 1957, two years after Will died in a fall from a redwood tree. The new owners sold their first crop to Mirassou and then set about making wine themselves, though they did so in primitive conditions—a rickety barn with little equipment and neither water nor electricity.

From then until the mid-1960s, when the late Richard Graff became involved with the property, changes in ownership brought a succession of winemakers—including Philip Togni and Rodney Strong, who later distinguished themselves elsewhere in California—and in all that time no one questioned the wisdom of Will Silvear's pronounced preference for Burgundian varieties. The quality of the fruit was obvious. Many of the vines he planted continue to yield grapes for Chalone's reserve wines.

When I visited Chalone in 1974, I was deeply impressed by the austerity of the place—still without water or electricity—and by the grandiose landscape, with the Pinnacles looming in the near distance. Given what I then knew about by-the-book winemaking in California, I was surprised by the heretical nonchalance with which the wines were made and aged. Everyone does it now, but at the time Chalone was probably the only winery in the state to allow its Chardonnay to rest for months on the lees in the fermenting barrel. Above all, I was struck by the grace of the Chalone wines. They were luminous, as the Gavilans are luminous, and had a directness of fragrance and flavor that conveyed the essence of the vineyard.

Reaction to wines from some of the new vineyards was mixed and led to the first of many changes. There were basic corrections—red-wine varieties planted where they ripened with difficulty were grafted to white, and a few vineyards were removed altogether. But, as the 1970s progressed into the 1980s, vines migrated within the valley from inappropriate sites to places where each variety would have the conditions it needed. In short, each variety was matched to a suitable *terroir*, though no one, of course, ever used that word. Despite the disappearance of

some varieties and the arrival of others never considered a quarter century ago, the acreage of vines in Monterey County has not changed. But
it is more sensitively (and more sensibly) distributed.

• • • • • •

The insurance companies have disappeared from Salinas Valley, while
more of the state's leading wineries have been attracted to it. Robert
Mondavi, Estancia, Kendall-Jackson, and Caymus are among those that
have bought or leased land there. A high proportion of it is planted with
Chardonnay—inevitable, one might think, given the demand. But here
there is a perfect fit between vineyard, variety, and market. Charles
Thomas, senior vice-president for winegrowing at Jackson Family Farms,
praises the Salinas Valley's Chardonnay for its structure, acidity, and texture. "This Chardonnay brings much to a blend," he said, "but it can stand
alone superbly. Beginning with the 1995 vintage, we now release each year
a Monterey wine made exclusively from grapes harvested on our Paradise
Vineyard." Caymus already offers a site-designated Chardonnay from its
Mer Soleil vineyard, and Jekel one from Gravelstone in Arroyo Seco.

I was back in Monterey County in 1997, tasting Chardonnays at the
Morgan Winery, in Salinas. We made an early-morning start with the
flamboyantly generous 1995 and the brighter, more intense 1994
Reserve. The flavor of that 1994 expanded dramatically in the few sec-
onds between sip and swallow, evolving from one mouthful to the next.
It was quite a wake-up call.

I'd enjoyed Morgan wines for years but hadn't before met Dan Lee,
the man responsible for them. He explained that the intensity of the 1994
was the result of a growing season that had been particularly cool, even
for the northern Salinas Valley. In 1995, poor weather arrived while the
vines were in flower, interfering with the fruit-set and reducing the size of
the crop. The year produced generous wines, however, because the vines,
less burdened, were able to bring their smaller, sparser clusters to perfect
maturity.

"I opened the winery in 1982, while I was still winemaker at Jekel
Vineyards, about thirty miles south of here," Lee told me. "Morgan was

my mother's family name. I sold my car and in that first year, with my father's blessing (and the bank manager's), made about two thousand cases of Chardonnay in a warehouse in Salinas. I bought Monterey County grapes from vineyards I knew. About half of them came from Cobblestone Vineyard in Arroyo Seco and the rest from Hillside, a vineyard on an even cooler site in the Santa Lucia Highlands—the west side of the valley—opposite Gonzales. I sold the wine to fish restaurants in Monterey, Santa Cruz, and San Francisco. And they liked it.

"There had been mistakes made when the first red-wine varieties were planted here, so I was tentative in approaching them. It wasn't until 1986 that I bought some Pinot Noir grapes from Sleepy Hollow, a vineyard not far from Hillside, and also a small lot from Paraiso Springs, at the southern end of the Highlands. I bought some grapes in Carneros, too, but fermented them separately. The Monterey wine was earthy and spicy. I blended the two, being careful to preserve the Carneros structure; but it was the Monterey character that gave the wine interest.

"We made the first of our unblended Reserve Pinot Noirs in 1990," Lee continued. "We made two, and, when given the choice, our customers preferred—by two to one—the Monterey Pinot Noir over the one we made from the fruit I'd bought in Carneros."

Today the core of what Morgan offers is Chardonnay and Pinot Noir made mostly from Monterey County grapes. Dan Lee buys Sauvignon Blanc from Alexander Valley and makes a small amount of Zinfandel from fruit grown in Dry Creek Valley. "But now I'm committed to Monterey and so to Chardonnay and Pinot Noir, the varieties I think best express its character," he declares. "I've bought sixty-five acres in the Santa Lucia Highlands and hope to build a winery there."

From 1986 to 1991, however, Lee did make some Cabernet Sauvignon, with grapes bought in Carmel Valley, another of the county's American Viticultural Areas. The vineyards are tucked away at Cachagua, near the valley's upper limit. Cachagua—the Native American name is a corruption of the Spanish for "hidden water"—is a wide basin, a suntrap, a thousand feet up in the Santa Lucias. The road there twists and turns up the valley from Carmel to a point so narrow that ocean influence is barely felt beyond it. Cachagua, well above the fog line, is sunnier and warmer than Salinas Valley, and so Cabernet Sauvignon and other Bordeaux varieties that present problems when planted near Salinas do very well there.

* * * * * *

As it happened, I was expected that same day for lunch at Bernardus, a new winery in Carmel Valley. I'd been intrigued by its first releases and was particularly interested in its Marinus Vineyard, established in 1990 on one of the area's best sites for Bordeaux varieties. I visited Marinus with Todd Kenyon, the vineyard manager, who told me he had come to vines after training in horticulture. "That background teaches you to focus on the individual plant," he said. "And that's what Dan Blackburn, our first winemaker, wanted." Blackburn, who has since left the winery, planned the vineyard's layout himself. A forestry graduate of the University of Montana as well as a viticulture and enology *diplômé* of the University of Montpelier in France, he worked at some of the most distinguished wine properties in Burgundy and Bordeaux (including Château Cheval Blanc) before coming to California.

"I was sent to France as an exchange student to learn French," Blackburn told me, "and found myself living in the house of Jean Mongeard-Mugneret in Vosne-Romanée." Mongeard-Mugneret, one of Burgundy's leading growers, is president of the Association des Viticulteurs de la Côte d'Or. "I was soon in the cellar, and in no time had enrolled at the École de Viticulture in Beaune. That is how my involvement in wine began."

Before drawing up his plan for the vineyard, he walked the site repeatedly, noting every variation of soil, every change in the grade of a slope, the direction of every tilt. The varieties—predominantly Cabernet Sauvignon, with Merlot, Cabernet Franc, and Petit Verdot in supporting roles—are arranged in patterns of small blocks that correspond to changes of soil and exposure.

"We're adapting French methods, not adopting them," Blackburn said. "The Marinus site would not be planted with Cabernet Sauvignon if it were in France. There is too much clay, and the French prefer to plant Cabernet Sauvignon in gravel. In clay, which is colder than gravel because it doesn't drain as easily, they would plant Merlot. We do have some Merlot, but this site has a good slope—some of it has a grade of fifteen degrees—and it faces full south. So, although the clay might be cooler than we would like, the vine itself will get more sun and be warmer than it would be anywhere in Bordeaux.

"Still, to make all this work we had to watch carefully how we mixed the varieties and where we placed them. We set our rows to allow wind to blow along them, not against them. We varied the density of the vines and the severity of the pruning according to the potential of each plot. The quality of our wine depends on getting the best from every vine—from every bunch—so we assign each block to a particular worker to encourage personal involvement. But eventually everything must come together as a reflection of the vineyard. I'm using Bordeaux varieties, but I am not making a Bordeaux wine. And I'm not trying to make a California varietal either. I'm using Bordeaux varieties because they alone express the character of this site. I'm making Marinus."

It's a distinction we'll appreciate to the full only as the vines, and the wines they give, mature. But the potential character of the vineyard was already obvious from the recently bottled 1994 Marinus we drank with a few slices of cold stuffed squab at lunch. Its color was deep, its aroma seductively rich, and on the palate it was long and seamlessly complete. These are qualities impossible to create in the fermenting vat. They are the serendipitous consequence of cultivating the right vines, in the right way, in the right place. To achieve that kind of harmony means taking a long view, and requires both patience and courage. Brave new world? Perhaps not. But brave new Monterey? I think so.

SONOMA CHARDONNAY

EVEN WHEN DISGUISED BY AN OVERLAY OF OAK AND RESIDUAL sugar, it's difficult to hide completely the elegantly lean structure of a Carneros Chardonnay, the suave power of Chardonnay from the Westside Road area of the Russian River Valley, or the fruity exuberance of one from the Alexander Valley. The acreage of Chardonnay in Sonoma County was surpassed by that in Monterey three years ago, but no other California area is producing wines from this grape with anything like the same diversity and distinction. Incursions of the ocean in ages past, volcanic eruptions, and a massive tremor that probably diverted the course of the Russian River left Sonoma with an abrupt topography, a tangle of soils, and a shifting marine influence that affect its wines in ways that growers are only now beginning to appreciate and master.

Sonoma is where winegrowing in northern California began, but Chardonnay has a short history there. Until the 1980s, this was still predominantly red-wine country. One could say the turning point was in 1976, the year in which Château St. Jean released its first single-vineyard bottling of the 1975 Robert Young Vineyard Chardonnay. The county had little more than nine hundred acres of the variety actually bearing fruit in 1975; by 2000 there were well over fifteen thousand. Chardonnay is now as emblematic of Sonoma County as Cabernet Sauvignon is of Napa.

An early impetus for Chardonnay's ascension in the region came in 1953, when James D. Zellerbach, a former U.S. ambassador to Italy and an ardent admirer of the wines of Burgundy, established a vineyard and winery—Hanzell—on the south flank of the Mayacamas Mountains just a few miles from the Sonoma town plaza. He wanted to produce wines that could be poured without embarrassment alongside the great growths, red and white, of the Côte d'Or.

Zellerbach had deep pockets, and though his winery was modest in scale, it was expensively equipped. Its Burgundian demeanor extended to a cellar filled with French oak barrels. Everyone uses French oak now, but at that time California winemakers used cooperage made of redwood, and, to a lesser extent, of American oak. The locals thought the imported barrels an unwarranted extravagance. But Zellerbach was a man who understood that perfection in all things, and especially in wine, depends on taking pains over details.

His first vines, both Chardonnay and Pinot Noir, were washed away in a storm. The first crop of those planted to replace them was harvested in 1957, and when the Chardonnay began to trickle out a couple of years later the response was sheer astonishment. For the first time, it seemed, California had produced a wine with characteristics reminiscent of the white wines of the Côte de Beaune. The role of those French oak barrels became a matter of much speculation. Eventually, as we all know, Zellerbach's innovation was widely emulated, and the result was a sea change in our perception of Chardonnay in California.

Zellerbach died in 1963, just as the winery was hitting its stride. But his achievements encouraged others. Throughout the sixties, the University of California's county farm advisor, Bob Sisson, urged growers in northern Sonoma to plant Chardonnay. Robert Young was growing prunes in the Alexander Valley when Sisson persuaded him to turn a hayfield into a vineyard. "I got my first grapes from it in 1966," he told me in 1994. "Two tons to the acre—very good for a first crop. You get that much fruit from prune trees only when they're mature, and at the time both grapes and prunes were selling for $300 to $350 a ton. Then when we started to have some problems with the aging prune trees on the valley floor, I didn't hesitate. I pulled them out, and in 1967 I planted Chardonnay in their place."

It was from those vines that Richard Arrowood, then winemaker at Chateau St. Jean, produced that 1975, a wine so voluptuous it turned the world on its ear. "Our 1974 Alexander Valley had been made from a blend of Robert Young grapes and grapes grown at Belle Terre, a vineyard about a mile and half down the valley toward Healdsburg," he told me. "Belle Terre had been planted with cuttings taken from Robert Young's vines, so they were genetically similar if not identical. They were cultivated in the same fashion and at the winery there was no difference in the way we handled their fruit. Yet the wines we produced from these two vineyards had characteristics that made them totally distinct. In particular, there was a remarkably lush quality about the fruit in the Robert Young wine. When the French have vineyards with unique qualities like that, they protect them. They wouldn't blend Meursault-Charmes with Chevalier-Montrachet. That's why we decided to make a single vineyard bottling."

The impact of the Robert Young wine, and, doubtless, the success of Château Montelena in Paris at about the same time, led to the release of other single-vineyard Sonoma Chardonnays. The status of the variety went up. And so did the prices, providing a greater incentive for growers to plant more of it.

I made a series of visits to different segments of Sonoma to see if I could get past winemakers' styles and find the essential differences between, say, Chardonnay grown in Green Valley, close to the ocean and one of the county's coolest areas, and that grown in the upper Dry Creek Valley, one of the warmest. I hoped to get a better grip on characteristics imposed by red volcanic clay on the Sonoma Valley hillsides, sandy loam on the Santa Rosa plain, gravel beds in the Alexander Valley, and white volcanic ash—it's not chalk at all—on Chalk Hill.

I began at lunch with Jim Bundschu of the Gundlach-Bundschu winery. Sea bass on a bed of black beans and braised collard greens was delicious with Gundlach-Bundschu's 1990 Sonoma Valley Rhinefarm Chardonnay. Though some would argue for 1994, 1990 was probably the best vintage for Chardonnay in the county in the last decade, and the

Rhinefarm wine was both soft and refreshingly lively, a discreet acidity giving it a lift while reinforcing its long, mature flavor.

Gundlach-Bundschu's Chardonnay vineyard was planted thirty years ago and lies right up against a boundary that separates Sonoma Valley from Carneros. Not far from the Rhinefarm, the Sonoma and Carneros AVAs (American Viticultural Areas) actually overlap. Several growers inside the area included in both appellations have the right to choose either or both of them for their wines—a rather clear indication that no one is sure exactly where the division between them should be. Soils rarely change abruptly; they merge. And the microclimates that affect vine growth and grape flavor are seldom in exact step with soil changes anyway.

Jim Bundschu, however, knows where he stands on the issue. "We simply don't belong in Carneros," he told me. "Instead of their clay hard-pan, we have clay loam here mixed with limestone scree carried down from the Mayacamas. It's soil with a light texture that drains well and warms up early in the spring. The vineyard can be breezy, but it's sheltered from the kind of winds that blow across Carneros every afternoon. That's why our Chardonnay, though just as delicate, is different from theirs. It's low-key when young and we're careful to do as little as possible to it at that stage beyond seeing it safely through fermentation. But it ages well. These days, that's not what's expected. Most Chardonnay is made to be consumer-friendly as soon as it's bottled, rather than consumer-interesting later. As a result, you get a wine that's put together in the winery rather than produced in the vineyard."

· · · · · ·

David Noyes, the winemaker at Kunde Estate Winery, farther up Sonoma Valley, had arranged an extensive tasting to show me how Kunde shifts emphasis from style to character as it moves from its estate wines to its single-vineyard selections. "We try to preserve character in all our wines," he told me. "But in the estate wines we introduce more of those elements of style—oak, malolactic fermentation, and so on—that many consumers like. In the single-vineyard wines we take a more purist approach. There wouldn't otherwise be much point in taking the trouble to bottle a wine from a unique site. But even then, we introduce, with discretion, some malolactic fermentation [a secondary fermentation that softens the wine and reduces its acidity]. We're lucky in this valley: We have good acidity and we always have full fruit flavor. So we can afford to temper our wines with malolactic to some degree and make them more subtle, more mysterious."

Kunde's wines also have good structure, though they are always soft and approachable. The vineyards in this part of the valley are warmer than those closer to Carneros. The wines have impeccable balance: They are silky, harmonious, and complete.

Sonoma-Cutrer, a winery that produces only Sonoma Chardonnay, has one of its two most distinguished vineyards in the lower part of the valley. Les Pierres is on the lowest part of the slope of Sonoma Mountain, just across the valley from Gundlach-Bundschu. The other important vineyard, The Cutrer, surrounds the winery west of Santa Rosa in the Russian River Valley.

"The vines at Les Pierres are planted on a rocky, gravelly mix that drains well and allows the roots to go down," Brice Cutrer Jones, Sonoma-Cutrer's former president, told me. "Weather arrives there from the Pacific through gaps in the Sonoma Mountains. The Cutrer vineyard, in the way of that same flow of marine air but less protected from the fog, is cooler."

Both of these vineyards give wines that are—like those of Gundlach-Bundschu—rather reserved when young. When I tasted a series of them with Sonoma-Cutrer's winemaker, Terry Adams, they had me thinking of stones rather than fruits and flowers. Les Pierres presents itself immediately: It's all about structure and balance—very much Sonoma Valley characteristics. The Cutrer wines have more depth and more power, but less refinement. Tasting several lots from the two sites, I saw how choice of clone—subvarieties of Chardonnay—age of vines, and date of picking also affect the wine, sometimes to so great an extent that it was difficult to believe that all the lots from a single vineyard had indeed originated in the same place.

"Fog flows up the Russian River Valley just as it spreads over the water of San Francisco Bay," Jones said, "and burns off quickly in June and July. But it hangs around longer each day as the equinox approaches and the sun recedes to the south. It's a marine layer that stays close to the ground and never rises above eight hundred feet. That's why we made that contour the limit of the Sonoma Coast AVA, an appellation that exists parallel to and encompassing others in the county. It's intended to define the zone within which fog keeps us cool at night, whatever the day's temperatures might have been."

Sonoma's marine fog begins to make an impact in August at about the time the grapes turn color. That's also when the crucial phase of ripening begins. The grapes accumulate sugar, flavor develops in the skins, and the vine breaks down acids, using them as a source of energy. At low temperatures—usually below fifty degrees Fahrenheit—the vine functions minimally, so sites with low night temperatures tend to retain high acidity. Warm days combined with cool nights therefore usually give fruit with ripe flavors, high sugar, and a refreshing acidity. It's what every winegrower hopes for. Cool days and cold nights give low sugars, pinched flavor, and high acidity—the typical result of a poor vintage. Warm days and warm nights, on the other hand, give high sugars, a generous flavor, and low acidity; a prescription for forward, even seductive, wines that do not usually age very well.

◆　◆　◆　◆　◆　◆

Marcello Monticelli, director of winemaking at Gallo of Sonoma, set up a tasting that began with a range of 1998 Sonoma Chardonnays to illustrate some of the basic differences among them. First there was the lean structure and low profile of a 1998 Carneros, followed, in sharp contrast, by the big aroma and creamy—almost viscous—texture of a blend from the warm upper sections of the Dry Creek and Alexander Valleys. Next we tasted a Dry Creek Chardonnay that had been fermented in an old and well-used barrel. Though not nearly as full-blown as the blend had been, it had a ripe flavor and displayed an edge of good, clean acidity. Then came a sample of the same wine fermented in new oak. What a surprise that was. The wood itself was no more in evidence than that of the old barrel, but everything else about the wine was both intensified and integrated. The flavor was enhanced and the character of the wine was buttressed. Neither was overwhelmed.

Like Sonoma-Cutrer, Gallo of Sonoma has two Chardonnay vineyards of particular distinction: Laguna Ranch, in a cool area of the Russian River Valley ("In a site like that," I was told, "we're farming sunlight. Everything depends on getting the trellising right, the canopy in balance"), and Stefani, in the much warmer upper Dry Creek Valley. The Stefani Chardonnay makes a big impression but leaves little to remember. The Laguna Ranch (the best of which goes into the Estate Chardonnay), on the other hand, is brighter and fresher and leaves a typically Russian River impression of power and elegance.

Chalk Hill Estates' vineyard is in a section of the Russian River Valley as distinct for its soils as it is for its climate. It was thereabouts that some mighty cataclysm turned the region topsy-turvy, creating hills and canyons that marine fog rarely penetrates. So, though cooler than the Alexander Valley, it's warmer than the rest of the Russian River Valley and the wines have a character all their own.

Bill Knuttel, Chalk Hill's winemaker, and Mark Lingenfelder, the vineyard manager, offered me a vertical selection of the winery's Chardonnays from the years 1990 to 1997 so that I could see how the vineyard—the area—comes through no matter the weather. Recent vintages in California have presented winemakers with extremes: It was cold in 1995; there was rain on the bloom in 1996, followed by heat spikes late in the season; and rain just before harvest in 1997.

Brice Jones had said to me earlier that Chardonnay is particularly responsive to a winemaker's technique. "It's easy to overwhelm the wine's character with your own style," he said. "The winemaker's contribution should be no more than a personal thumbprint."

Knuttel went further. "There's pressure on a winemaker to let style take precedence over both character and vintage," he said. "Certain styles will make a quick impression, grab the ratings, and get the sales. The wine could have come from anywhere." Which is why many

Chardonnays are so predictable, of course. But the imprint of vintage and the particular character of Chalk Hill—plump and smooth, a hint of lime, an effusiveness—came through in every one of Knuttel's wines.

That same effusiveness and creamy texture mark the Chalk Hill wines of Rodney Strong. "Lemon-cream" is the way winemaker Rick Sayre described it. Sayre put together a horizontal tasting of 1998s with samples that ranged from the winery's vineyards on Chalk Hill and on both sides of the Russian River to wines made from grapes from one of the Murphy Ranch vineyards in the Alexander Valley.

The way in which acidity dropped as one went east from the lower sections of the Russian River Valley to Chalk Hill and on to the Alexander Valley was obvious. But other factors also affected the differences among those wines, some originating in the vineyards (again, the selection of clones had a noticeable effect) and some in the cellar (particularly the age of the barrels and the use of malolactic fermentation).

The question of clones—and of density of planting, management of leaf canopy, and yield—came up again when I tasted with Marimar Torres the 1996 and 1997 Chardonnays from her Don Miguel vineyard in Green Valley. The wines had all the delicacy one would expect from the vineyard's cool proximity to the Pacific, but they were also impressively intense. "It's all a matter of the clones you plant, the arrangement of the vineyard, how you prune, when you pick," Torres said. "More than half of what's in a glass of wine is viticulture.

"Theories and formulas don't count for much: You must constantly respond to the vine and the conditions of the growing season. In the cellar everything must be done with moderation. If you can actually taste oak, or malolactic, or anything else, it's too much. Winemaking is like cooking: You must enhance the raw materials, not overwhelm them."

I asked her to define for me the *character* of her wine, as opposed to its style and its quality. That, after all, was the basis of my quest. She paused for a moment. "First," she said thoughtfully, "you'll have to tell me exactly where you think one ends and the others begin."

BEAULIEU VINEYARD'S GEORGES DE LATOUR
PRIVATE RESERVE

ABOUT TEN YEARS AGO, A GROUP OF FRENCH MEN AND WOMEN—
professionals in wine, marketing, and law—met in Chinon in the Loire
Valley to ask themselves which was preferable: adapting classic wines
when necessary to meet fluctuations in consumer preferences or using
marketing skills to persuade consumers to accept and appreciate such
wines as they are. A classic wine in Europe is usually identified by the
name of the place from which it comes. Its production is controlled by
statutes based on established local traditions of winemaking. Not surprisingly, the consensus of those present in Chinon seemed to be that,
though even a wine with a controlled appellation evolves over time, a
deliberate change in style or quality could be achieved only by breaking
this tie between origin and winemaking tradition. No matter how delicious the wine that took its place, the classic wine itself would then
cease to be.

Such questions—is a wine created for consumers, or are consumers
created for a wine?—would have been irrelevant to Georges de Latour, a
Frenchman turned United States citizen, when he was again allowed to
sell wine freely from his vineyard in Napa Valley after the repeal of
Prohibition in 1933. Fourteen years of restriction had reduced the wine
industry to tatters. If there had once been a classic California wine of
determined style and quality for Georges de Latour to protect and promote, the Volstead Act would have swept it away. On the other hand,

consumers denied access to wine by Prohibition (which began in many states earlier than 1919) and deflected from its use by ceaseless propaganda long before it was banned had little understanding of wine and no preferences to be gauged and met.

Born in Bordeaux and raised in Périgord, de Latour studied chemistry in Paris and then came to California in 1884 to seek his fortune in the gold mines. He soon decided there was greater opportunity in collecting and processing the cream of tartar going to waste as a by-product of the burgeoning California wine industry. Establishing himself first in San Jose (in those days Santa Clara was a more important wine county than Napa) and later in Healdsburg, in Sonoma County, his business flourished.

By the end of the century he had married and bought a small farm— 120 acres, mostly wheat and orchards—in Rutherford, Napa Valley. His wife gave it the name Beaulieu. (No matter how the French pronounce it, in California the word is *boh-lyoo*. Nor is that particularly odd. After all, the English call the Beaulieu in Hampshire, England, *byoolee* and will feign not to understand if a visitor says it any other way.) Vineyards were planted, and a former grain store on the property was converted into a small winery. De Latour's daughter, Hélène, the Marquise de Pins, remembered in a 1966 memoir that from his first crop of what she called "ordinary grapes" her father made five barrels of wine.

✦ ✦ ✦ ✦ ✦ ✦

In 1908 de Latour brought back from a trip to France a selection of varietal cuttings which he then planted on a property, adjoining his own, that he'd bought for the purpose. They included a fair quantity of Cabernet Sauvignon and other Bordeaux varieties. It was about then that he hired Joseph Ponti, a newly arrived Italian immigrant, as his right-hand man in both the winery and the expanding vineyard.

At about that time, too, San Francisco's Archbishop Riordan, a close family friend, asked de Latour to begin making altar wines for him. Initially a small matter, the altar wine business, together with that of "wines prescribed for medicinal purposes," had grown and had saved Beaulieu by allowing the winery to continue in production throughout Prohibition. While others pulled out their vines and sold their land, de Latour acquired and planted more. In 1923, he moved into the former Seneca Ewer winery on the Rutherford highway opposite his home vineyard and pulled down the old grain store that had served him until then. The handsome Ewer building—today a venerable pile of ivy-covered brick and stone—had gone up in 1895, and it is still Beaulieu's winery.

The vines de Latour had planted in the home vineyard, the one known today as BV No. 1, were fully mature by the time Prohibition ended and were giving fruit of high quality and intense flavor. The wine he made from this fruit in 1936 took the Gold Medal award at the 1939 World's Fair on Treasure Island in San Francisco Bay. Though it had been made mostly from Cabernet Sauvignon grapes, it had to be presented—and was acclaimed—as Beaulieu Burgundy. To post-Prohibition consumers, red wine was Burgundy, and that was that.

In her 1966 memoir, Hélène de Pins described the scene in which her father first opened a bottle of this particular wine in the dining room of the family's home in San Francisco: "I recall as though it were yesterday—it was a wine of such splendor that it totally filled the room with its perfume."

It was not until the spring of 1940 (after Georges de Latour's death), when this award-winning wine was ready for sale, that his widow decided to accept the suggestion of the winery's general manager, Nino Fabbrini, and rename it in honor of her husband. That is how, more than sixty years ago, Beaulieu Vineyard's first Georges de Latour Cabernet Sauvignon came into existence.

The grapes had been harvested and the wine made by Joseph Ponti, counseled by Leon Bonnet, a Frenchman and a professor of enology at the University of California. Bonnet retired in 1937, and there arrived at Beaulieu to take his place in time for the 1938 vintage a Russian-born research assistant from the National Institute of Agronomic Research in Paris named André Tchelistcheff. In his book *The Wines of America*, Leon

Adams said that, in bringing Tchelistcheff to California, Georges de Latour did as much for the state's winemaking as a whole as he did for the wines of Beaulieu.

Tchelistcheff's role at Beaulieu seems to have been at first ill-defined. An article in the *American Wine and Liquor Journal* of May 1941 describes Joseph Ponti as winemaker and André Tchelistcheff as chemist; but in 1942, Joseph Ponti was described in a *Country Life* article as supervisor of the vineyards and winery, and André Tchelistcheff as enologist. When Tchelistcheff retired in 1973, his title was technical director and vice-president. But regardless of the confusion of titles, Tchelistcheff was effectively responsible for the wines of Beaulieu Vineyard for more than thirty years.

In a conversation with me a few years before he died Tchelistcheff referred to the first release of Georges de Latour Private Reserve '36. "It was an elegant wine," he said, "aged in French oak. We had even bottled it in secondhand Bordeaux bottles. But the style was different from what the Private Reserve later became. We decided to make a bigger style of wine, using nothing but Cabernet Sauvignon aged in American oak barrels. I thought American oak would bring to the wine a richer and more distinctive character." Actually, in 1940, Tchelistcheff had little choice but to use American oak if he wanted to age a red wine in barrel: France was at war and might even have already fallen by the time this was being considered. He had more latitude in the matter of grapes, though, had he wished to use it.

Beaulieu lacked only Cabernet Franc in the 1940s; all the other Bordeaux blending varieties—Merlot, Malbec, and Petit Verdot—were available to him. Robert Gorman, in his 1975 book, *California Premium Wines* (an elegantly written, incomprehensibly neglected masterpiece, a snapshot of the California wine industry at an important moment of change), said that Tchelistcheff found Beaulieu's Malbec too neutral, contributing nothing to the wine; that the Petit Verdot failed to ripen to his satisfaction, a problem most years in Bordeaux, too; and that the Merlot provoked a maturing of the wine too rapid to allow adequate development. Tchelistcheff, in using only Cabernet Sauvignon, departed from the Bordeaux tradition of blending.

In the design of the Private Reserve no one, not even Tchelistcheff himself, could later say for certain how much was judgment, how much was the constraint of circumstances, and how much was plain good luck. But that marriage of American oak barrels with Cabernet Sauvignon from mature vines nurtured in a uniquely favored vineyard in Napa Valley gave Beaulieu a wine that became in every sense a classic ("of the highest class being a model of its kind; excellent..." begins the definition of that word in my *Webster's*). The Private Reserve meets the expectations of such a wine anywhere in the world: Like the French wines considered in Chinon, the consistency of style and quality in a Georges de Latour Private Reserve is imposed by its Rutherford origin and by the spirit in which it has come to be made.

• • • • • •

In 1936 there were perhaps two hundred acres of Cabernet Sauvignon vines in California. By the year 2000 there were almost seventy thousand. The Georges de Latour Private Reserve remains an important stylistic benchmark, a definition of what we mean by Cabernet Sauvignon in California, even though it now takes its place among many others that were encouraged—indeed, inspired—by its success.

What is that definition, that stylistic benchmark? If asked to give in a few words an impression of the Private Reserve style, I would certainly put "opulent" among them. There is also a robust vigor about the wines that make them almost a metaphor for California itself. Others have described the wines as huge, dense, and concentrated. There have been references to their overwhelming bouquet (a quality mentioned by Hélène de Pins in her memoir), to their power, and to their intense black-currant flavor. In one vintage or another I have been able to find all of these characteristics, but not necessarily all in the same wine at the same time. Being that most of these words give an impression of heft, let me say that though the most successful vintages of Georges de Latour are indeed rich and full, the balance of every one is impeccable, the proportion elegant, the total effect harmonious. A mature bottle of any particularly successful vintage of the Georges de Latour Private Reserve is, to me, one of the most cogent arguments for drinking wine at all.

Given the unique status of the wine, there was considerable concern when the family sold the Beaulieu winery, together with most of the vineyards (but not BV No. 1) and the rights to its brand name, to Heublein in 1969. Lamentations were premature: No one now disputes the superiority of the 1970 over both the 1964 and the 1966, for example. The 1970 vintage, made after the winery had been acquired by Heublein, stands as one of the best Private Reserves ever made. Later it was whispered that all would be over after Tchelistcheff retired; yet everyone now accepts that the 1976, the 1982, and the 1985, all made by his successors, are great vintages and in perfect concord with the wine's traditional style and quality.

Tchelistcheff had favorites among the thirty-odd vintages for which he was responsible. "Of the forties' vintages, I liked 1940, 1942, and 1948," he once told me. "1958 was my favorite of the fifties—1951 was rather alcoholic—and, although 1964 was very elegant, 1968 was my favorite among vintages of the sixties."

I, too, have favorites. One of them, the 1970, had just been released when I came to California in 1974. Back then I wasn't able to get my hands on any from under the counters of San Francisco. But I could find it on trips back to New York City, where in those days California wine still lacked cachet and Georges de Latours were available to anyone with the sense to buy them. I would lug them by the case back to the West Coast.

Of vintages in the fifties and sixties, my favorites in some instances differ from those of Tchelistcheff. For example, I preferred the 1951 to the 1958. I first tasted the 1951 only in 1978, when it was one of four Napa Valley Cabernet Sauvignons of the forties and fifties served at a dinner in San Francisco. I described it then as "richly preserving all those characteristics associated with Rutherford, with Cabernet Sauvignon, and with American oak that André Tchelistcheff combined into one of the most particular and consistent wines made anywhere."

I could have said much the same thing about the 1951 when I tasted it again ten years later. The bouquet had what we call "tar," because it seems precious to write of an amalgam of roasted coffee, charcoal, prunes—and old wine. Though drying a little, it was still both smooth as silk and splendidly vigorous. I tasted the 1958 only once, a few years ago. It was in perfect condition but lacked the intensity of the 1951. I doubt that the extra years of aging alone had made the 1951 so much more memorable.

On the other hand, I agree with Tchelistcheff about the 1968, even though it is drying a little now. Its flavor has always been distinctly exotic: fruiter, spicier, more lush than that of other great years of the Private Reserve but lacking none of the vibrant richness. I also enjoyed the 1966 on both occasions when I tasted it; but either the two bottles had matured in different ways—not as unusual as one might think—or the wine of this vintage had changed dramatically between 1984, when I first tasted it, and 1989. In 1984 the bouquet was fresh and the wine was lively, but the bottle I tasted in 1989 had the evocatively sad-sweet smell of dried moss and faded flowers. The wine was still fairly full on the palate, but the flavor was as romantically melancholy as the bouquet—damp woods, dried apricots, a hint of past glory. I was in the right nostalgic mood for the wine and found it delicious.

◆　◆　◆　◆　◆　◆

It is said that a Georges de Latour Private Reserve defines the style of its vintage in Napa Valley. The wine itself is basically so consistent that variations in it from year to year point up the local weather's diversity. The 1976 Private Reserve, for example, is richly charged, a product of the first of the seventies' drought years in California. Many less successful Napa Valley Cabernet Sauvignons were heavy that year: condensed, tannic, even tough.

The 1982 crop in the valley had the advantage of a long, cool growing season but was then almost washed out by heavy rains in September. Fortunately, an Indian summer in October raised sugar levels in the Cabernet Sauvignon. Flavors were already intense thanks to the drawn-out ripening. That year, almost a write-off for many whites, was successful for late-picked reds. They were bigger than expected, with intense, tight flavors—much in the style of the 1982 Private Reserve.

The 1985 Private Reserve is perfectly and elegantly balanced. The growing season was slow and long, like that of 1982, with moderate temperatures helping to intensify flavors. There were no surprises, no downpours, no dramatic heat waves. Indeed, after a summer such as growers pray for, the vintage is one of the best of the decade for Cabernet Sauvignon in Napa Valley.

In 1990, Beaulieu Vineyard released the 1986 Georges de Latour Private Reserve and although strictly speaking, it was the wine's fifty-first vintage, it marked the fiftieth anniversary of the release of the first of these extraordinary wines back in 1940. It was an appropriate time to be reminded that Beaulieu's tradition has always been a progressive one. The BV No. 1 vineyard, for example, owned by Georges de Latour's granddaughter but managed by Beaulieu, was first replanted in the 1940s and has since been replanted twice, in the 1960s and in the 1980s. The success of the Private Reserve encouraged the winery to use for the most recent replanting essentially the same clone of Cabernet Sauvignon that has been so successful there for the last fifty years. However, there have been increases in the proportions of two other clones: one because it was found to add more color and a greater intensity of flavor, and the other because it gives fruit with a richer, more definitely black-currant taste and contributes a more supple, more elegant, more forward quality.

Beaulieu has also been experimenting with American oak barrels specially made for them in a variant of the French manner and, indeed, with a proportion of French oak. (Put very simply, the main difference between French and American oak barrels, apart from the variety of oak, is that French barrel staves are hand-split, air-dried, and then made pliable over a fire that toasts them as the barrel is made; whereas American barrels are usually machine-cut, oven-dried, and then made pliable in steam tunnels. It is thought that much, though not all, of the difference between the way American and French barrels affect the taste of wine has less to do with the oak itself than with the way it is handled.) The oak barrels used for Beaulieu's Private Reserve are always two or three years old. They are always first used for the Beaulieu Vineyard Rutherford Cabernet Sauvignon before graduating to hold the Private Reserve. The winery feels that this wine should not be exposed to the shock of raw new wood. American oak barrels assembled from air-dried and lightly toasted oak staves have been used at Beaulieu for some time now, starting with the 1986 vintage. The number of French oak barrels, first introduced by way of experiment with the 1989 vintage, was increased substantially from 1990 and represented roughly half the wood used for aging the 1998 wine."

These changes—strengthening some characteristics in the vineyard and modifying others in the barrel—are intended to intensify the familiar style of the Private Reserve while allowing the wine more grace. In both the 1986 and the 1998, the greater influence was the unusual weather of those years. The 1986, the equal of the 1985, was a classic that no one had to be persuaded to buy. The same is sure to hold true for the 1998.

CALIFORNIA SYRAH

MANY OF US FIRST MEET THE SYRAH GRAPE INCOGNITO. IT MAY cross our path as Shiraz, the name by which it is known in Australia. Or we taste it in a wine from the Rhône Valley identified only geographically—Côte-Rôtie, Hermitage, Saint-Joseph, Cornas, and so on—with no reference to the Syrah from which it was made. That's because the variety is understood: Syrah is indigenous to that section of the Rhône between Vienne and Tain l'Hermitage, and local *appellation* laws require that it be the only black grape used.

There is now an increasing production of Syrah—labeled as such—in California. The acreage planted has increased from a mere eighty-seven acres in 1982, when Syrah was lifted from the anonymity of "Other Reds," to almost thirteen thousand acres in 2000. And because those acres of vineyards are scattered from Mendocino County to San Diego and up into the Sierra foothills, there is a diverse selection from which to choose.

Wineries like Bonny Doon of Santa Cruz, Edmunds St. John and Terre Rouge of Amador County, Qupé and Zaca Mesa of Santa Barbara County, Eberle of Paso Robles, and Joseph Phelps and Sean Thackrey of Napa Valley were among the first to get involved with Rhône Valley varieties (a few years back they were described, in a rash of articles, as

California's Rhône Rangers). They are still among the leading producers of Syrah, but others continue to join them. In fact, Syrah seems, at last, to be fully in the varietal mainstream, and as vines mature we can expect them to give wines as expressive of California as any other.

Perhaps because of the name Shiraz (used only in Australia) and the legends that surround the hill of Hermitage, there are all kinds of myths about the origins of Syrah—that it came from Shiraz in Persia, from Syracuse in Sicily, or from Syria, in the saddlebag of a returning crusader. The subject was given considerable attention at a symposium held in 1992 at which some of the leading lights of the French academic viticultural world brought a privileged few of us up to date on all aspects of their research into the variety—including its early history.

As far as that went, there was general support for a paper published by Jacques André and Louis Levadoux in 1964. Put shortly, André and Levadoux maintained that Syrah and Mondeuse, a related variety from this area where sub-Alpine Savoie meets the Rhône valley, are both descended from a grape they referred to as "proto-Mondeuse" and that they believe to have been the "Vitis Allobrogica" so dear to Martial, Columella, Plutarch, Pliny the Elder, and a host of other first-century Romans. All of them were captivated by the extraordinary red wine made from a grape variety peculiar to this stretch of the Rhône Valley near Vienne and known as "Vinum Picatum"—pitch wine—because of its tarry aroma.

There appear to be parallels between Vitis Allobrogica and its wine as described in the ancient texts, and Syrah and the wines made from it today. André and Levadoux pointed out that, except for plantings known to have originated with cuttings carried from the Rhône Valley—such as those taken to Australia in 1832 by James Busby—the variety exists in no other place; certainly not in Shiraz in Iran, nor in Syracuse, nor in Syria. Furthermore, the profusion of clones and subtypes now found in the Rhône Valley suggested to them that the variety has long existed there. The multiple names—Syrah, Syra, Sirah, Syrac, Sérène, all of them a source of much speculation—are rooted, they explained, in the Indo-

Aryan word *ser*, which had associations of long duration. The grapes do indeed ripen late, and the wine keeps well. DNA research undertaken since then in the laboratory of Professor Carole Meredith of the University of California, Davis, shows that André and Levadoux were at least right in claiming a local origin for the vine: It appears to have come to us as a cross between Mondeuse Blanche and Dureza, two varieties indigenous to the nothern Rhône, though neither much in evidence there today.

Of all the classic grape varieties of France, one could argue that Syrah is particularly adaptable to some of California's quirkier sites. (The Rhône Valley near Vienne, with its difficult terrain and unpredictable weather patterns shaped by pressure differentials between the Alps and the Mediterranean, is not the easiest area in which to grow grapes.) But the use of Syrah in California was held back for years by the controversy over varietal identification in the state—and that of Petite Sirah in particular. Yet Syrah had been one of the first French varieties brought into California. In his 1994 book *Napa Wine—A History,* Charles L. Sullivan says that the variety was established in the Drummond vineyard near Glen Ellen in Sonoma Valley in the year 1878; other references suggest it could have arrived at different vineyards even earlier.

By 1884, at any rate, there was already enough Syrah planted in California for Eugene Hilgard, Professor of Agriculture at the newly founded University of California's College of Agriculture, and Frederic Bioletti, his associate, to be reporting regularly on their work with what they referred to variously as Syrah, Sirah, and Petite Sirah, using all three names for the same variety, as well as their work with Serine—thought, in California, to be a related but separate variety.

According to reports in the University archives, Serine at first found greater favor because its yield was more consistent and its sugar concentrations higher. But in a paper published in 1892, Louis Paparelli, a University instructor responsible for viticulture, set the record straight. "It has been stated several times," he wrote, "that Sirah and Serine were two distinct varieties, for their growth, their crops, and their products have been found somewhat different. Such differences are simply due to the nature of the soil and the selection of the cuttings, for this variety degenerates easily, so as to make it seem that there are two different varieties, while in reality they are identical." Perhaps it was because of this finding that multiple references to the variety in California were gradually reduced to one—*Petite Sirah.*

• • • • • •

Meanwhile, Charles McIver, one of several growers who allowed parts of their vineyards to be monitored by Hilgard and Bioletti in the course of their research, brought into California from the northern Rhône Valley in 1994 a variety newly developed by a Dr. Durif, who is said to have raised it from the seed of Peloursin, a rustic vine native to the Isère, a tributary of the Rhône. (For exact replication, vines must be propagated from cuttings, so Dr. Durif's effort was decidedly experimental.) The vine he produced, named for him, gave wine of quite ordinary quality, but was relatively resistant to mildew—an important advantage in Europe. It was also a prolific bearer, a virtue of even greater interest in California, where cuttings of this new variety were soon introduced into vineyards planted with Petite Sirah—still the true Syrah, remember—to boost yields there as well as to heighten the color and reinforce the keeping qualities of the wine.

Planted together in this way, Petite Sirah and Durif were often mixed with yet other varieties, including Mondeuse, Carignane, and even Zinfandel, but when a mass of cuttings was taken for further propagation elsewhere, it was usually referred to simply as Petite Sirah. At that time, California wines were not sold under varietal names, and growers, who didn't share the academic concerns of Hilgard and Bioletti, weren't too particular about what they called their vinewood. It's easy enough to understand, then, how Durif and Petite Sirah could have merged their separate identities under the Petite Sirah name.

But though that hypothesis is credible, it's unlikely that Durif vines, even while taking over vineyards still described as Petite Sirah, would have replaced Petite Sirah completely. For that to have happened, every grower would have had to make a deliberate effort to avoid cutting Syrah/Sirah/Petite Sirah when he took wood from his vines for new plantings. In fact, I suspect that many of the wines made today on a small scale by winemakers who buy the crops of two- and three-acre family plots of mixed vines planted long before Prohibition are as good as they are not because the vines are old and the yields low but because many of the vines in those plots described as Petite Sirah and assumed to be Durif are indeed Petite Sirah—or Syrah, as we would say today.

That would explain why DNA tests recently applied to six different strains of Petite Sirah at the University of California, Davis, revealed that while four of them were, as expected, Durif (and one, inexplicably, Pinot Noir), the sixth was Syrah—the true Petite Sirah. It wouldn't surprise me to learn that the older a vineyard, the greater the proportion of Syrah to Durif among vines described as Petite Sirah.

Given the confusion—then and now—it is ironic to read Professor Hilgard's remarks in an 1886 report:

> Among the urgent needs of viticulture in California is
> the "straightening out" of the nomenclature of the
> numerous vine varieties now in cultivation, which are
> being constantly increased by new importations. Even the
> latter serve to increase the confusion already existing,
> since in Europe, as well as here, one and the same
> variety often passes under numerous different local
> names, and different varieties under the same name.
> These names are imported with the cuttings to this
> country, where the confusion is further increased by
> intermixture of cuttings and grafts.... Then, under the
> difficulties of identification, there arise new local
> designations, under which, again, old varieties are
> propagated under new names....

Hilgard couldn't have been more right. Because of the jumbling of Durif with Petite Sirah, it was assumed for years that true Syrah simply did not exist in California. We now know that an entire vineyard of it, planted in

1919, is still yielding fruit in McDowell Valley in Mendocino County; and there is at least one other unmixed block, in Napa Valley, planted at about the same time.

The variety made a formal reentry into California in 1936, when Professor Harold Olmo brought to the University of California, Davis, cuttings from the vineyard at the University of Montpellier in the south of France. Growers showed little interest in using it, however, and eventually Olmo asked the Christian brothers, of Napa Valley, to establish a small vineyard of it. They agreed, and planted seven acres in 1959.

Professor Olmo was probably able to draw useful information from these vines, but Christian Brothers seemed unenthusiastic. They never marketed a varietal Syrah, and it has always been assumed that the grapes went into one or another of their blends. In 1974, Christian Brothers gave cuttings from those vines to their neighbors at the Joseph Phelps Winery, who used them to develop a vineyard on a slope just below the winery. The new vines gave their first crop in 1976, the same year Christian Brothers tore out the Syrah vines they had planted to oblige Professor Olmo.

Craig Williams, the winemaker at Joseph Phelps, says that the 1976 and 1979 wines he made from the Montpellier clone vines were the only ones that gave any satisfaction. Eventually the vines were removed, and Phelps developed other Syrah vineyards using cuttings from a source that had not been available earlier on. There seems to have been no other vineyard based on the Montpellier clone, which has therefore disappeared from California except, perhaps, for any specimen kept in the University's archival plant collection.

Almost by chance, I tasted the 1976 Joseph Phelps Syrah—the first wine actually bottled from the Montpellier vines—just a few years ago. In looking for references to Syrah in my files, I came across this note in my tasting records:

12.23.94
Jos Phelps Napa Valley Syrah '76. I'm not sure how I
acquired this bottle: It must have been given to me years

ago. Decanted and served with cheese after a 1970
Léoville-Las Cases. There was a film of crusty deposit
down one side of the bottle. Good color, mature nose,
balanced. The tannins were integrated, but the wine
didn't have the silky flow of the Léoville, and it needed
more substance. But perhaps that's expecting too much
from what must have been very young Syrah vines.

As indeed they were.

There was considerable interest in Syrah in the 1970s: Joseph Phelps
was one among several anxious to plant the variety. The University
brought in from Australia a clone of Syrah propagated and released as
the "Shiraz clone." Another clone, imported from France in 1974, was
not released because of a viral flaw affecting the bark but was eventually
made available because of a fear that withholding it when demand for a
French clone was so strong could lead to illegal importations that might
present greater threats.

Indeed, another French clone of Syrah, with little recorded history,
did make its appearance in California in the mid-seventies. One of the
first plantings of it was on the Estrella River bench near Paso Robles.
Cuttings from those vines, known as the "Estrella River clone," were
widely distributed in California. As far as I can tell, most Syrah presently
produced in the state is from vines either of the Shiraz clone or of the
Estrella River clone.

• • • • • •

The best Syrahs combine elegance with a fruity vigor; the tarry quality so
admired by the ancient Romans is still there, but it comes across as a
foundation, a background flavor. Some winemakers are still finding the
right approach to what is, after all, a variety new to many of them. The
balance of a wine is sometimes askew, or it has a bitter finish because
just too much was extracted from the skins. My favorite among them all
is now a Syrah, loosely speaking, only by association. Sean Thackrey's

Orion was made for years from a small block of very old Syrah vines he discovered on the hill behind Mustards Grill in Napa Valley. The 1991 vintage was his last: The vineyard was then purchased from the elderly owner by Clarke Swanson, whose winemaker continues to make superb wines from the grapes—which is something of a consolation.

Thackrey, meanwhile, found the Rossi vineyard, opposite Spottswoode in Napa Valley—a patch of old vines of unknown identity; one of those indeterminate mixtures I described earlier—and is making from it powerful wines of exceptional brilliance. Thackrey laughs when I tell him that their aroma, as consistent from vintage to vintage as is, say, Heitz's Martha's Vineyard, reminds me of crushed basil leaves.

Each of Thackrey's wines from the Rossi vineyard (1992 was the first) has been as gorgeous as the wine I imagine to have been served in bejeweled cups to Byzantine emperors wearing cloth of gold. Lucky them.

RUSSIAN RIVER VALLEY

SONOMA COUNTY'S RUSSIAN RIVER VALLEY, ABOUT SEVENTY MILES north of San Francisco, was declared an American Viticultural Area in 1983. A rough fourteen-mile square between Healdsburg and Guerneville with some of California's most sturdily handsome country, its western boundary coincides with the coastal range of hills that constrict the river's flow to the ocean. To some extent they also moderate the incoming influence of the ocean, yet Russian River Valley remains more affected by maritime incursions than any other wine region in California. Morning fog rolls along the valley floor with dependable regularity, and a gusting afternoon wind off the ocean is drawn through the Petaluma gap southwest of Santa Rosa whenever temperatures rise uncomfortably.

The effect of the Pacific makes Russian River Valley much cooler than Alexander Valley—the stretch of the river above Healdsburg—and ensures conditions in which Chardonnay and Pinot Noir, varieties which easily lose flavor and acidity in warm climates, can flourish. Temperatures are lowest in the extreme west of the region—Green Valley, a separate appellation within Russian River Valley and adjacent to the coastal hills, is one of California's coolest grapegrowing districts. That's where Iron Horse, Chateau St. Jean, and Jordan's "J" sparkling wines have their vineyards. Warren Dutton grows Chardonnay there for Kistler and Sonoma-Cutrer for its Russian River Ranches Chardonnay label. Marimar Torres and Dan Goldfield (winemaker at Dutton-Goldfield) are hoping, in those same marginal conditions, to extend the boundaries of what we can expect of California Pinot Noir.

Though early settlers in the valley had to clear their land of red-woods, progress was rapid: An agricultural bulletin of 1876 refers to seven thousand acres of vineyards in Russian River Valley, almost as much as today's ten thousand acres. Between those two figures, however, vines were ripped out and vineyards converted to hop fields and prune orchards in the wake of Prohibition. Many wineries of that early era disappeared, but the Korbel winery, established near Guerneville in 1882, is still going strong, though under different owners; the Foppiano family recently celebrated the centenary of its winery south of Healdsburg; the descendants of Giuseppe and Louisa Martinelli still care for the vineyard their great-grandparents planted in 1905 on Jackass Hill; and the Martini family, of Martini & Prati, are still busy at the winery founded by Rafaelo Martini in 1881.

* * * * * *

Viticulture began to recover more generally in the valley in the 1960s and 1970s, thanks, mostly, to outsiders like choreographer Rodney Strong, airline pilot Joseph Swan, firefighter Cecil De Loach, journalist Davis Bynum, and visionary Brice Jones of Sonoma-Cutrer. The newcomers, attracted by the valley's cool climate (Joe Swan made no secret of his hope that it would allow him to make great Pinot Noir), were also drawn by the reasonable cost of Russian River Valley vineyard land in those days. Cecil De Loach told me he paid $60,000 for some acreage in 1970—"We wanted some place in the country, and this was the cheapest land in the Bay Area"—and just accepted that he got a vineyard of Zinfandel planted in 1905 as part of the deal. "We enjoyed wine," he said, "but we'd never thought of having a winery. Then a frost that same year wrought havoc in Napa Valley and our Zinfandel was needed desperately for blending. I got $35,000 for the 1971 crop and went straight out to buy more land. We were in the wine business." Land in Russian River Valley is no longer the bargain it was, but, with forty-five wineries active there, grapegrowers are optimistic.

It was February when I last spent a few days in the valley. Following a week or more of rainstorms so severe they would have had Noah scurrying to find his lathe and level (some vineyards were still under water when I arrived, and a crucial bridge was out of commission because of a flooded approach road), the sun had reappeared and the mimosa—known as acacia in California—was in full bloom. Huge yellow sprays of it hung over the narrow winding roads, adding to the confusion of madrone, willow, oak, and California myrtle. Behind the trees, and beyond the neat, wooden houses, dormant brown vines climbed the hillsides to clumps of redwood and Douglas fir massed above them. As wine regions go, Russian River Valley has a splendor all its own.

I'd decided to concentrate on the heart of the area southwest of Healdsburg, where vineyards on a series of slopes and terraces facing southeast across the river are producing some of California's best Pinot Noir and Chardonnay. My route led me first to grower Charles Bacigalupi, and within minutes I realized that I had started in the right place: Bacigalupi, who bought his land in 1956 from a family that had farmed it for more than ninety years, was among the earliest of those who led the valley's revival. He himself already had roots in the county: Grandparents on both sides planted vineyards there, and he had known the Russian River Valley—and its vines—since childhood.

"There was a typical old-time vineyard on the property when I bought it," he told me. "The vines were mostly Zinfandel mixed with Malvasia, Alicante, and Petite Sirah as well as half a dozen other varieties I didn't recognize. They were yielding a ton and a half of grapes to the acre. We sold the fruit for $55 a ton.

"Prices started to improve in the 1960s. That was when Bob Sisson, the University of California farm advisor, urged me to plant Chardonnay and Pinot Noir. I'd never heard of either of them and had a hard time remembering the names when I went to Karl Wente looking for budwood. My Chardonnay was his old Wente clone. The Pinot Noir he gave me was originally from Martini. I planted six or seven acres of each in 1964.

"White wines were already on a roll in those days, but in the beginning it wasn't easy to sell my Pinot Noir grapes. Everyone seemed to be down on the variety. The winewriters bad-mouthed it constantly. Yet, when California's sparkling wines took off in the seventies, there was suddenly a big demand for the high-yielding Pinot Noir planted on the valley bottom. That helped clear up some of the confusion. It became easier to distinguish and appreciate the difference between the fruit grown there and the grapes we were growing on the benchland.

"Rodney Strong was one of the first to buy my grapes. I sold them out of the county, too. I don't want to claim more than my due, but the 1973 Chardonnay that brought top honors to Napa Valley's Chateau Montelena in Paris in 1976 [the tasting that many feel put California on the international map] included fruit from this vineyard. Mike Grgich, Chateau Montelena's winemaker at the time, sent me a copy of the results of that tasting with a note so that I would know my grapes had contributed to his wine's success. I was very pleased."

• • • • • •

The Rodney Strong Vineyard and Winery is still an important client for Bacigalupi, and we drove over there to talk to Rick Sayre, the winemaker. Sayre had prepared a tasting of several wines made from a single load of Bacigalupi's Chardonnay grapes, along with a wine from a neighboring Westside Road vineyard planted with a different Chardonnay clone and with wines made from grapes grown in other Russian River Valley vineyards, all of the same vintage. Some of these wines had been through malolactic fermentation to lessen their bite (by transforming green malic into milder lactic acid), and some had not. Some of the wines had been fermented in French oak, and some in American. Of the ten wines Sayre had assembled, none was identified with anything more than a code reference. The one I liked best turned out to be from Bacigalupi's grapes. It had been made in used French oak barrels and undergone malolactic fermentation. The wine was deliciously subtle and elegant: well proportioned, perfectly integrated, silky. It was exactly what we think of as a typical Russian River Valley Chardonnay.

Sayre explained what made each of the others different. A wine I thought thin and one-dimensional had been produced, he said, from the same Bacigalupi grapes but had not been through malolactic fermentation. Another, also from the same grapes, had been fermented in American oak. It was heavy and seemed almost sweet. A wine that tasted of pineapple had been made from the Spring Mountain Chardonnay clone—known to give highly aromatic wine.

Sayre was making a point: good Russian River Valley Chardonnay was the result of more than the marriage of a variety and a viticultural area. I saw how the Spring Mountain clone had so dominated a wine that its geographic origin was irrelevant; how the essential delicacy of Bacigalupi's grapes meant that American oak, so often a positive factor—for red wines particularly—could also be overwhelming and out of place, and how the lack of malolactic fermentation had left a potentially elegant wine with its bones poking through. In short, Sayre was demonstrating that a wine, if it is to be an expression of a vineyard, must be made in an appropriate fashion and from the right clone of the right variety.

◆ ◆ ◆ ◆ ◆ ◆

A painted sign farther down Westside Road marks the entrance to George Davis' Porter Creek Vineyard. Behind the house, a vineyard follows the steep contours of a natural amphitheater. Davis, formerly a boat builder, bought his thirty-five-acre property twenty-five years ago and planted Chardonnay and Pinot Noir. It was his interest in Pinot Noir that brought him here. "But the bank was hardly encouraging," he said. "The manager told me I should be in Carneros if I wanted to grow Pinot Noir. Yet, Russian River Valley Pinot Noir has a cult following now. It has become one of the most site-specific varietals in California."

Davis' Pinot Noir vineyard is planted with a mix of Martini (or, rather, the University of California's version of it—clone 13) and Wädenswil, a clone developed at the Swiss viticultural research station on Lake Zurich. The Wädenswil clone brings fragrance and long, delicate flavor to a wine when the growing conditions are right. And they seem to be right at Porter Creek. Davis' Creekside Pinot Noir was seductively aromatic; and the Chardonnay I drank with him at lunch, though more intensely flavored than the wine Rick Sayre had made from Bacigalupi's grapes, was just as silky and equally elegant.

Davis' grapes are known for their delicacy, but probably the most prized, and certainly the best known, red wines from Russian River's Westside Road are made from Pinot Noir vines in the Rochioli vineyard, a mile or two away. Tom Rochioli's grandfather, Joe, bought the land in 1938, when it was still planted mostly in hops. In 1959, Tom's father began growing Cabernet Sauvignon because he saw a market developing for quality grapes. But in the late 1960s, on the advice of Bob Sisson, he planted the Chardonnay and Pinot Noir his vineyard really needed. For Pinot Noir he used the same Martini clone as Charles Bacigalupi. This variety seemed to find, in the west block of Rochioli's vineyard, a perfect environment. The grapes there, together with Pinot Noir from the adjacent Allen Vineyard—which the Rochiolis planted and manage for businessman Howard Allen—have made the reputations of Davis Bynum, Gary Farrell, and Williams Selyem (the three producers on Westside Road with whom Tom Rochioli shares his Pinot Noir), as well as the reputation of the J. Rochioli Vineyard itself.

I spent a pleasant hour tasting with Tom Rochioli. He makes sumptuous wines: His Chardonnays are both rich and delicate, like intricate gold filigree, and his Pinot Noirs have such concentration and power that they seem to be almost viscous. We finished with a 1991 Estate Pinot Noir that was just at the stage when the aromas and flavor take on a nostalgic woodsy patina but none of the varietal fragrance is lost. "As the vines get older, and as I get older," he said, "the wines get better."

Davis Bynum, a home winemaker who turned highly professional, was, in the beginning, Rochioli's only customer for Pinot Noir grapes. Gary Farrell, his former winemaker (and still his part-time consultant) now makes highly structured and stylishly elegant wines under his own label. "In winemaking there's always an element of intuition," he told me. "And that's especially true of Pinot Noir. I'm often asked by an assistant to explain why I do something, and I'm hard put to answer. I've made errors over the years and then found they were completely justified. With Pinot Noir, some special sensitivity, a sixth sense, is at work.

"You must start with good fruit—and, as far as Pinot Noir is concerned, there's not much of it. The site must be right, the clones must be right, and the vineyard practices must be right. I watch our growers' crop levels. I see some people trying to maximize yields by introducing all kinds of trellising systems. It doesn't work. There are just so many bunches you can take from a Pinot Noir vine if you want quality."

The Pinot Noir Farrell makes from Allen Vineyard fruit has clean lines and an intense, brightly enticing flavor. The wine from the Rochioli West Block has more depth and body, but it, too, is recognizably Farrell's work—deftly structured and gracefully defined. All his wines are restrained. I got the impression that Farrell took from his grapes exactly what he needed—and no more.

· · · · · ·

Burt Williams and Ed Selyem—the winery they founded is Williams Selyem—also make Pinot Noir from Rochioli's West Block and Allen Vineyard grapes, but their wines are as different from Gary Farrell's as the two men themselves are from him. Farrell, a political science major before he turned to winemaking, is trim, concise, and cautious. Williams, who was a typesetter for a San Francisco daily paper when he and Ed Selyem started making wine together, wears a plaid shirt and red suspenders and hides behind a slightly gruff image (in fact, he's nothing of the kind) as he works long hours alone at the winery with yesteryear's rock music blasting from a speaker somewhere near the roof. Selyem, the extrovert, formerly the wine buyer for a local market, looks after sales.

"Ed and I are from this area, and we knew there were great grapes here," Williams told me over a glass of his Russian River Valley Pinot Noir. "The growers were selling them to big producers who just tipped them into their blends. We started to buy some to make a little wine for ourselves. Then we made some for friends. And then we got carried away. The Alcohol and Tobacco people warned us that we'd better get bonded, so we did and then went commercial on a shoestring. We both kept our regular jobs. When we were making wine, I'd stop by at five in the morning on my way to work and punch the skins down. Ed would do the same at noon, and I'd punch down again at six on my way home.

"In 1988, Howard Allen—we buy grapes from his vineyard—offered to build us the winery we really needed on a corner of his land and lease it to us. Since then we've been able to increase our production a little. We still have Rochioli grapes as well as grapes from the Allen Vineyard, but we now buy from a dozen other growers, too.

"We are always thinking about body and texture. There has to be some 'fat' in the grape. Of course, we like tremendous aroma; yet the wonderful thing about Pinot Noir is the feel of it in your mouth. We find a potentially different style in every lot. Even the Rochioli and Allen grapes give different wines, and they are from the same clone in vineyards with just a road between them. But then everyone knows Pinot Noir is an expressive variety. When you taste a Pinot Noir grape, you can, if you pay attention, tell where it comes from, what the growing season was like, and how the vineyard was managed. If the wine's made right you should be able to drink it—and enjoy it—straight from the barrel. Although we reckon our wines are at their best four to six years after the vintage date—like this one." He waved his glass at me.

Though Williams Selyem now makes about five thousand cases of Pinot Noir a year, it's as difficult as it ever was for anyone not on the mailing list to find a bottle. And there's a waiting list to get on the mailing list. The wines have an exuberance rare in California Pinot Noir. Their aroma is thrilling; the flavor vibrates; the wines are irrepressible. What was Williams' secret? "We do what others do," was all he said.

It was dark outside after the tasting, and Williams left the door open so that I could see my way to the car. As I drove away I suddenly heard from that strategically positioned speaker the unmistakable sound of Peter Townshend's synthesizer and the crash of Keith Moon's drums as they led into one of the The Who's great hits. The sound swept me down the driveway. Then something clicked. Max Lake, the Australian surgeon-vintner, once told me he played Bach tapes to his Cabernet Sauvignon to get them into a perfectly balanced, structured mode. I'd sensed that something about Burt Williams didn't add up. Suddenly I saw what it was. Plaid shirts and heavy rock don't go together. In a flash, I understood what he was up to. All that Russian River Valley Pinot Noir, maturing in new French oak barrels, was being deliberately exposed to the vibrations, the exuberance, the passion of Pete Townshend and Keith Moon. The idea was fantastic. But thrilling. And irrepressible. Shabam. Wham. Wah.

ARMAGNAC:
THE ELIXIR OF D'ARTAGNAN

TUCKED AWAY IN SOUTHWESTERN FRANCE BETWEEN THE CURVE of the Garonne River and the pine forests of the Landes, the Armagnac region, though hardly more than an hour from Toulouse, is reassuringly bucolic in a way that farm country today rarely is. Bright red poppies line the roadsides in summer, and hedgerows strewn with wild roses divide scattered vineyards from wheat fields and patches of sunflowers. There are no vast tracts of anything. Corn and eggplant flourish alongside pumpkins and plum trees; herds of *blondes de Gascogne* cattle graze contentedly; and in the busy jumble of farmyards, geese and ducks and chickens keep up a lively banter.

The region's past is on display, too. Roman mosaics, somnolent abbeys, and once-impregnable castles dot the landscape between one thirteenth-century bastide and another. On weekly market days in these half-timbered village strongholds, farmers who come to sell their fruits and vegetables, butter and cheese, eggs and *foie gras* take a break to gossip over coffee or a glass of wine at tables set out under the medieval arcades. Doubtless wary after generations of protecting themselves from government tax collectors, they protest that they have no money. "Our wealth," they say, "is in our cellars and on our tables."

Visitors tend to agree once they've tried a lentil terrine studded with *foie gras* and *confit* of duck; a plain roast squab with *haricots verts*; sweetbreads *à l'ancienne*; sauté of suckling lamb with fresh-shelled beans;

grilled *magret* with layered potato and leek; or a soufflé of *pruneaux d'Agen* in Armagnac—a specialty of the southwest. It isn't by chance that some of the most renowned chefs of France were born and learned to cook in this region.

And there are some delicious wines that locals are happy to keep mostly for themselves—Côtes de Gascogne, Pacherenc du Vic-Bilh; Gaillac; both dry and sweet Jurançon; and the red wines from Buzet, Cahors, Côtes du Frontonnais, Madiran, and Irouléguy. Best of all, in even the simplest restaurant, there's always a glass of old Armagnac to linger over after dinner.

Armagnac has the longest history of any brandy in France. The know-how of distilling came from the Arab world (at that time, just beyond the Pyrenees) early in the thirteenth century and was used at the University of Montpellier's school of medicine to extract essences from herbs and flowers. A medical treatise published around 1310 by Vital Dufour, an Armagnac man educated at Montpellier, reveals that less than a century later this new skill was already being used to produce *aygue ardent*—brandy—from wine. Dufour describes forty ways in which brandy helps maintain good health and inspires a sense of well-being. They include the relief of toothache, an end to mental anguish, the restoration of paralyzed limbs, and the gift of courage.

Produced on a very small scale, Armagnac continued to be used mostly as medicine ("Strengthens the memory, preserves youth," claims a document of 1441) until demand for it exploded dramatically in the seventeenth century. An important part of that demand originated in the Netherlands. The Dutch, masters of the largest merchant fleet of the time, sent three or four thousand ships to France every fall to buy the season's new wine. They themselves consumed about a third of what they brought back; the rest was blended, sweetened, and fortified before being shipped out the following spring to clients in other ports of the North and Baltic seas.

Unlike the wine growers of Bordeaux, Armagnac's growers did not have easy access to the Dutch ships; they would have had to haul barrels of their wine on oxcarts to the nearest navigable rivers and the cost would have been prohibitively high. Brandy was another matter. By distilling their wine, the growers reduced its volume and increased its value, making the cost of transport less of an issue. Their production of brandy increased, and so did its use. Large armies on the move during the seventeenth century's protracted wars discovered a need for it. No doubt D'Artagnan, a native of Armagnac, and his three musketeers took their share. And so did the swelling populations of the cities. The reason was simple. There were no cork-sealed bottles then, and as wine was drawn from steadily depleted barrels, what remained was soon spoiled. When dosed with brandy, the Dutch had discovered, wine kept better and longer. And then many came to realize that brandy just by itself could be a comfort and a pleasure.

* * * * * *

As a young man I was told I'd find it easier to understand the essential difference between Cognac and Armagnac if I'd think of the former as fine, industrially produced worsted cloth and of the latter as homespun, handwoven Harris Tweed. The contrast intended—smooth Cognac against rugged Armagnac—is now less obvious than it once was. Both brandies have evolved over the years, but Armagnac is by its very nature both idiosyncratic and diverse. It finds its champions among those who prefer the unexpected and distinctive to the prosaic and conventional.

On the face of it, Armagnac owes its diversity to the common (but by no means universal) practice of bottling each batch—sometimes each barrel—unblended, to preserve the character that develops as it ages. But that character depends on the factors that make each batch, each barrel, different to begin with. First, there is the miscellany of Armagnac soils, ranging from black sand in the extreme west to sandy clay and, eventually, to chalky clay in the east.

A decree of 1909 attempted to define these differences by dividing the region into three segments: Bas-Armagnac in the west, Haut-Armagnac in the east, and Ténarèze between them. All three have since become official sub-appellations of Armagnac. Bas-Armagnac is credited with producing the most elegant and traditional Armagnac; Haut-Armagnac produces, in certain limited areas, small quantities that are highly aromatic and sometimes quite powerful; and Ténarèze holds the middle ground. Though the most productive of the three appellations, one rarely sees the name Ténarèze on a bottle, because the umbrella appellation, Armagnac, is thought to be more acceptable commercially.

The second factor affecting diversity is the grape variety—or varieties—used for the wine from which the Armagnac is distilled. In the last century, Armagnac (and Cognac) was produced almost exclusively from Folle Blanche, a white grape found elsewhere in France under other names. It's a fragrant grape but risky to grow because it leafs early and is therefore particularly vulnerable to spring frost, a constant danger in a region that lies so close to mountains. But whether used alone or as the dominant element of a blend, Folle Blanche can be relied on to give a smooth, delicately perfumed brandy. Today it is used mostly to add grace to Ugni Blanc, the most widely planted variety in the region. Ugni Blanc brings structure to a blend, but it can be austere. For balance it needs the addition of either Colombard (a grape also used in the southwest for table wine) or Baco (an important hybrid that has Folle Blanche and native American vines among its antecedents). Baco was introduced into the region in the confusion that came with phylloxera at the end of the nineteenth century and has been the foundation of some of the most extraordinary brandies produced in the Bas-Armagnac in the last fifty years. Unfortunately, the wine regulators in Paris are determined to eliminate all hybrids from France, and Baco will be banned after the year 2010. Those who rely on it are unhappy (as we all should be) but are already experimenting with other varieties permitted by the appellation regulations but not presently cultivated in the area.

Armagnac growers turned massively to Baco rather than return to Folle Blanche when they replanted after phylloxera—for a time it was the principal variety planted there—while in Cognac, the growers preferred Ugni Blanc. The differences established by robust Baco and trim Ugni Blanc probably led to those worsted and tweed analogies of years ago.

But Armagnac's reputation for sturdy idiosyncrasy is based largely on the curious method of a continuous single distillation—known as *chauffe simple*—developed in and for the region in the early nineteenth century. The words "continuous distillation" bring to mind the towering columns that keep the thousands-of-necks-per-hour bottling lines of the giant spirits industry running. In fact, the Armagnacais still is no larger than an ordinary pot still: It just works differently—its process retaining aromatics that a pot still discards. The mobile version of the continuous still, *l'alambic ambulant*—an ungainly contraption wheeled into the barns of small farmers who produce too little to invest in one of their own—clanks, gurgles, and hisses day and night until the job is finished. Those who watch over it keep up their strength with food grilled in the embers of its wood-burning stove. (One of the jolliest lunches I've ever had in Armagnac was duck legs and potatoes cooked in the heat of the *alambic ambulant* and shared with the crew as they coaxed from the still the last of the new *eau-de-vie*, not to be Armagnac, by law, until aged in wood for a minimum of two years.)

Chauffe double—double distillation—was once standard practice in Armagnac, as it is to this day in Cognac. It was reintroduced into the Armagnac region in the 1970s after Cognac firms began to take an interest in the area and now accounts for about 10 percent of the region's production. The large merchant-blenders, especially, often use both double and single *chauffe*, but the estates generally stick to what is now, after almost two centuries, the traditional method of the continuous still.

Claude Posternak, for example, a small distiller at the Château de Neguebouc near Préchac, is one of the majority who rely on *chauffe simple*. A newcomer (having abandoned his work as head of an advertising firm in Paris nine years ago to bring his young family to a greener life), he bought a neighboring vineyard to get himself started while he replanted one that had long been abandoned on his own property. *Chauffe double* would make his brandies smoother faster and allow him to get his revenues flowing sooner, but he wants the aromatic power that, in the long term, only *chauffe simple* can give. So he sells about a fifth of his production as unaged white *eau-de-vie* from single varieties to get his income kick-started each year. Sitting in his sunny yellow kitchen a few years ago I could easily distinguish in the three colorless liquids in front of me the intense fragrance of Folle Blanche, the elegant severity of Ugni Blanc, and the fat, rich, weighty flavor of Colombard.

"Armagnac distilled by the *chauffe simple* is usually more aromatic," says François Heron, production director of Janneau, a *négociant* where more than half the brandy is now produced from pot stills. "It can be rough when young, but it ages well; it develops for far longer and to greater effect."

He, too, showed me three single grape varieties, but these had been double distilled, and, since then, had been aged in wood. The Ugni Blanc was still rather angular in a way that seemed to relate to the impression I'd had of this variety at Posternak's house. The Colombard was round and moderately full. Its aroma, less rich than that of Posternak's white *eau-de-vie*, was nonetheless delicately nuanced. The third sample was of Baco, and I could make no comparison except with the other two. Against those it was fatter and had a low-key, flowery delicacy.

Jean-Pierre Gimet, a small distiller at Cazeneuve in Ténarèze, also uses both double and single *chauffe*, but he thinks that the result of either depends largely on the distiller's experience and intent. "He has to have a sixth sense. Everything to do with a still, including the ambient atmospheric pressure, is shifting continually and must be monitored closely. It's crucial to catch any possible error before it happens because there's no way to correct it later. Well, one can distill out a fault, I suppose, but that means losing the character of the brandy as well."

At the Château de Laubade in the Bas-Armagnac, one of the largest estate distilleries in the region, they distill entirely by *chauffe simple*. "Our vineyard is half Ugni Blanc and a quarter Baco," says production director Michel Bachoc. "The rest is evenly divided between Colombard and Folle Blanche. We handle each variety separately, from picking to aging. We get the new wines to the still as quickly as possible because they're fragile, and in any case it is an appellation regulation that we distill the wines before the fine particles of fermentation have settled out. Those fine lees, suspended in the wine, make a significant contribution to the aroma of the *eau-de-vie*. And there you have the heart of the matter. Armagnac is, essentially, a rich and complex perfume.

"And that's why we use traditional single distillation only. The vaporization is very slow—contrary to what anyone might imagine from that word 'continuous.' It preserves the wine's more elusive esters. They give the young spirit a rougher cast, but they also ensure a long and worthwhile development in wood. Distillation by *chauffe double* eliminates many of them. That's why brandies distilled by the *chauffe double* can be used in blends after three years. You must wait a minimum of five before using brandy distilled by *chauffe simple*." For many, that represents an important cost difference.

As I talked with Bachoc we tasted his VSOP blend, made from Ugni Blanc and Folle Blanche. It was supple and elegant. The XO was suavely delicate, too. Lastly, we tried a 1978 vintage Armagnac, every bit as smooth as the others, but richer—weightier—in aroma and flavor. I murmured my appreciation. "What you're tasting there is the effect of Baco in a well-aged *chauffe simple* from Bas-Armagnac," he said.

If Baco makes such an important contribution, it's easy to see why producers resent its banishment for reasons that seem ideological rather than practical. Yet it has no place on the Domaine Boignères, the estate thought by many to represent the peak of Armagnac quality. In proportions at odds with most other growers, the Lafitte family have more than half of their fifty-three acres planted in Folle Blanche, the ancient mainstay of Armagnac now reduced elsewhere to a supporting role. On the rest of the property there is slightly more Ugni Blanc than Colombard.

Martine Lafitte, who has run the estate since her father died a few years ago, explains: "In 1997, frost took most of our Folle Blanche, but when we have it, it gives a good result. We pick early to get good acidity— that's what carries fruit to the spirit—and press the grapes as if we were making a delicate table wine. We ferment in stainless steel or cement tanks and make our *cuvée* of the different varieties just before distilling. That way the varieties marry as they age. We make one *cuvée* of pure Folle Blanche. That is Armagnac as it was before phylloxera."

Every barrel at Domaine Boignères remains as it comes from the still, and although two or three of them are blended from time to time to make the domaine's five-year-old Armagnac, each is bottled separately, by hand, when it is needed. I tasted a 1995 pure Folle Blanche from the wood. Though young, it was like perfumed silk. Lafitte drew a sample of the *cuvée* of 1995 so that I could see the assertive, angular difference the other varieties make. We went on to taste the 1990 Folle Blanche, and then the 1985; the first showing just hints of amber and the second already deepening in color. The 1990 was less suave than the 1995, but the 1985 was the most gentle. "For the first few years, the new spirit develops flavor and depth," she said. "Then it smooths out and acquires finesse and delicacy."

Michel Bachoc had told me that as an Armagnac ages the wood plays an increasingly imposing role. "When an Armagnac is young—six years old, say—it owes perhaps 30 percent of its effect to the wine, 30 percent to the method of distillation, and 40 percent to the wood. By the time an Armagnac is twenty-five years old, the wood will have determined its style to an extent that overwhelms—though never entirely eliminates—the other two."

So I understood when Lafitte explained her insistence on using only the white oak from a nearby forest for her barrels—"the trees and the vines have grown together"—and why she is scrupulously careful in her choice of the staves from which they are made.

Marc Darroze, who now directs the business founded near Villeneuve-de-Marsan by his father, Francis, in 1973, also insists on aging his Armagnac in barrels made from the local white oak. Francis Darroze had already spent a lifetime buying from small producers in the Bas-Armagnac for his family's restaurant at Villeneuve-de-Marsan when he decided to set up as a trader in single vineyard, single vintage Armagnac of the finest quality. The stocks he acquired for aging, augmented by the continuing purchases of his son, now constitute an unequaled resource for top restaurants and retailers all over France.

The collection is a national treasure, boasting Armagnac from most years back to the 1940s, and some even older. There are often as many as a dozen vintages from the stills of small producers who have long since disappeared. Among them are many made purely or predominantly from

Baco, including some of venerable age produced from vines planted in the early years of the century and torn out decades ago. Entire vineyards exist now only in the captivating and heady aroma of the Armagnac that was produced from them. With its suggestions of walnuts, dried fruits, and honey, and insistent reminder of sun on ripe figs, it's an aroma that is, near enough, a distillation of the region itself.

THE SPIRIT OF CALIFORNIA

JÖRG RUPF CAME TO CALIFORNIA IN 1978 AT THE BEHEST OF THE
Bavarian State government to do postdoctoral research at the University
of California, Berkeley, on the connection between government and the
arts—of which he himself was a walking example. He had combined his
duties as an administrative judge in Munich with professional engage-
ments as a violinist. He enjoyed his time in California so much that he
returned to Berkeley in 1979 and there married a professional pianist.

At this point I should say they made beautiful music together and
lived happily ever after. What they actually did was send for one of the
small copper stills crafted by Arnold Holstein in Markdorf, a village on
the German side of Lake Constance, and set up a cottage fruit distillery
in a cramped and rather precarious shed in Emeryville—a light industrial no-man's-land between Berkeley and Oakland that would have
dumbfounded Gertrude Stein.

The shores of Lake Constance and the banks of the Rhine, as it flows
from the lake to divide first Switzerland from Germany and then Germany
from France, are strewn with gingerbread villages liberally punctuated
with flower-filled window boxes under carved wooden eaves. Already
blessed with seductively aromatic wines and a quality of cooking that
combines richly promising ingredients with the traditional virtues of the
domestic hearth, the residents of this part of Europe illuminate their

tables with tarts made from a bewildering variety of wild and cultivated fruits garnered from hedgerows, orchards, and woods that smother the surrounding hillsides. The essence of that same cornucopia is captured in an array of *eaux-de-vie*, or white fruit brandies, that are the pride and pleasure of those who distill them. Regardless of the international borders among these villages, and of the different dialects heard on their streets, all who live in them—collectively they refer to their corner of the world as the *regio*—take for granted their common gastronomic treasure. Though it is safe, in Europe, to assume that wherever there is fruit someone will be ready to distill it, the *regio* has long been the world's unchallenged center for the production of the finest white fruit brandy.

Rupf, born in Alsace of a German mother and a father of Swiss descent, has, on the face of it, all the necessary genes to make a good fruit distiller. His mother's family had been brewers in the old university town of Freiburg, between the Rhine and the Black Forest. They made *eaux-de-vie*, too, and, while training both as a lawyer and as a violinist, Rupf worked at their still, acquiring the family's inherited skills.

Fruit *eaux-de-vie* are not to be confused with cordials or sweetened fruit liqueurs. An *eau-de-vie* presents the essential flavor of a fruit so intensely that a few drops in a compote of fresh fruit will perfume the bowl, if not the entire room. The aroma can cling for hours to an empty glass that had held no more than a spoonful.

European fruit distillers who produce *eaux-de-vie* are dedicated artisans. They work only with perfect fruit, distilling it whole as a fermented mash of pulp and liquid together. The flavor that distinguishes each fruit, that makes a raspberry taste different from a strawberry, is based on particular patterns of acids and alcohols present. Each distiller has his own way of coaxing and capturing the complete range of these elusive trace compounds—they volatilize at different temperatures—in order to re-create a fruit's flavor faithfully in an intensified and stabilized form. Success calls for patience and intuition as well as mastery of a craft; the *eau-de-vie* distiller's *métier* is an art based on temperament as much as it is a skill based on experience.

Europeans work with small stills of individual and sometimes idiosyncratic design (the best of them from Arnold Holstein) based on the principle of a *bain-marie:* Unlike the pot still used to make Cognac, a fruit still has a double pot with steam in its cavity, allowing solids in the interior that would scorch over direct heat. (Rupf says that much of a fruit's flavor is in the pulp and skin: "If you distill only the pressed liquid you waste the better half of the potential.") Peering at dials through hissing steam; teasing the right response from rumbling tubes and stainless-steel spigots; fiddling with gauges, funnels, jars, and buckets—a distiller at work with a Holstein is a picture of Rube Goldberg himself in search of the Elixir of Life.

* * * * * *

Emeryville bears little resemblance to the Hansel and Gretel villages of the Black Forest. A few miles away, Alameda (best known for its naval air station), where Rupf is now installed with greater working space in part of a hangar once used to house ships under construction, is hardly an improvement. But Rupf, oblivious to his surroundings, simply concentrates on reducing every thirty pounds of perfect fruit to one exquisite bottle.

"When I first came here," Rupf says, "I was astonished to find that with all the interest in wine and food, and despite the abundance of wonderful California fruit, there was no *eau-de-vie* to be had. My original idea had been to work as a violinist, but what I like about the Bay Area is the way people just set up businesses in things that interest them.

"I hadn't been actively engaged in distilling for a while, and I needed to get up-to-date. So I asked two graduates of the Swiss Wädenswil distillery school near Zurich—the Julliard of fruit distilling—to come over to help me set up. Each then worked here for a year. Hans Tanner, a professor at Wädenswil, the best in his field in Europe—his book is the fruit distillers' bible—has been both friend and mentor, and we follow his advice.

"It took a while to find the right fruit. I'm not after size, shippability, or even sugar. It is flavor alone that concerns me. I first found good pears in Placerville, in the Sierra foothills; and now, after trying a supply from Oregon, I have settled on orchards back in California in Lake County. For my purpose, the best raspberries are from the Pacific Northwest— both Oregon and Washington. Finding the right growers is my highest priority, because nothing works without good fruit. I look for unirrigated orchards with old trees.

"It's obvious that each fruit needs to be handled differently. But beyond that, I find that every batch must be given individual and undivided attention. No two are the same. They continue to be different after distillation. Most people believe that all fruit brandies, being crystal clear, are bottled straight from the still. But after distillation, fruit *eaux-de-vie* need time for their edges to become smooth and for the complexity of esters to synthesize. Pitted fruits take longer than others. Kirsch—from cherries—can take up to ten years.

"When I started I was entranced by exotic possibilities not available to distillers in Switzerland and France. I tried working with everything—even mangoes and papayas. But now I concentrate on the tried classics—especially Williams' pears—they are called Bartletts here—raspberries, and quinces. An *eau-de-vie* should be easy to identify from its smell and taste, though some fruits bring their original flavor through fermentation more cleanly than others. Those fruits with a clear, dominant flavor do best, as one might imagine.

"Those are the ones consumers try first. But then they often find themselves appreciating fruits with more complex flavors, or those *eaux-de-vie* in which there has been a subtle change of flavor in the course of capturing it.

"I distill grapes, too, as any other fruit—as if I were making an *eau-de-vie* from them. I don't distill their fermented juice alone, as a Cognac distiller would, nor do I distill the re-fermented skins and lees, as a marc distiller would. I use everything: the fermented juice, the lees, and the skins—just like any other fruit mash. That's why my marc made from Gewürztraminer grapes tastes like a fruit *eau-de-vie* made from Gewürztraminer grapes. I have to label it marc, though, because the labeling requirements of the Bureau of Alcohol, Tobacco, and Firearms are so rigid. Officials there will not recognize grapes as a fruit: only as the raw material for making brandy or marc."

The space at Alameda permits Rupf to bring in more fruit now and allows him to house bigger and more efficient fermenting tanks. "I ferment at low temperature—I have learned a great deal from the wineries around me. Cold fermentation helps preserve the fruits' volatile elements. It also inhibits bacterial changes that might otherwise modify fruit flavors undesirably. I like to distill as soon as the fermentation is finished, organizing my fruit deliveries to match the tempo of distilling. I have two Holsteins now, and each takes from two to two and a half hours to distill sixty-five gallons of fruit mash."

Rupf's *eaux-de-vie*, grappas, and liqueurs (a raspberry liqueur is made from an infusion of fresh raspberries in raspberry *eau-de-vie*; Williams' pear liqueur is a blend of pear juice and pear *eau-de-vie*) are available in several states under his brand name of St. George Spirits. Most of his clientele, though, have discovered him, rather than the other way round. ("I have never learned how to be a salesman," Rupf admits, with no apparent regret.) His customers include some of the most distinguished restaurants from coast to coast, from New York's Jean Georges and Four Seasons—where Paul Kovi was from the first especially taken by Rupf's *eau-de-vie* of quince—to San Francisco's Postrio and Masa's.

Soon Rupf began making shipments to Europe, and his *eaux-de-vie*, on sale in the *regio* itself, brought an enthusiastic response from the local press. "Imagine yourself in a raspberry field," wrote Wolfhard Geile, a gastronomic correspondent, in an issue of *Regio*, "or think of a slice of sun-warmed pear melting on your tongue. I need say no more of what distinguishes these *eaux-de-vie* from California."

· · · · · ·

Despite his progress, Rupf has felt himself at times to be a lonely prophet. To get others interested in fine distilled spirits and to broaden the range of those available on the market, he began working with wineries that wanted him to distill their pressed grape skins ("pomace" in wine jargon) into marc for aging. He distilled a marc of Pinot Noir for Saintsbury, the Carneros winery, in 1985 and again in 1986 and 1987.

"He made a barrel of it for us each year," Richard Ward of Saintsbury told me. "It wasn't much, but we bottled it in half bottles after giving it some time in barrel and shared it around as best we could. We enjoyed doing it, but, when Jörg couldn't make it in 1988 because he was moving or in 1989 because he was distilling to capacity, we let it drop."

A pity: The aroma of that first Saintsbury marc of Pinot Noir had taken me back to the haystacks I climbed in as a boy, and its flavor recalled the few drops of marc we would drink after lunch from our emptied coffee cups when I was sent, later on, to Burgundy as a wine-trade student.

In 1987, Rupf had also distilled marc for Randall Grahm of Bonny Doon Vineyard, using the pomace of each of the three varieties Grahm uses to compose his successful Rhône-style blend Le Cigare Volant. Grahm, a man known for his passionate enthusiasms, was so taken by the results that he asked Rupf's help in getting a Holstein still for himself and in learning how to operate it.

"The still arrived in 1988," Grahm told me, "and I immediately set to, distilling the same marc from Syrah, Mourvèdre, and Grenache pomace. But then I thought: Why stop at that? There's a universe of fruits. For a time I distilled everything from apricots to New York *labrusca* grapes. We made some mistakes—using dried figs was one I'd rather not talk about—but I planted a small orchard near Santa Cruz with *mirabelle* and damson plums, cherries, nectarines, pears, and apple specifically to allow me to experiment with perfect fruit. I am aging both apple and pear *eaux-de-vie* in wood for eventual blending, and I have ordered from Italy small barrels of wild cherry wood for aging a distillate of those sharp little Montmorency cherries.

"I am looking at other grapes, too—and not just the usual California varietals. When I learned that Isabella, a *labrusca* vine of the New York Finger Lakes, was being used in Italy under the name Fragola to make a distinctive type of grappa, I had the idea of asking a Finger Lakes winery to crush, ferment, and ship some Isabella to me as a fruit mash for distillation. That led me to distill a mash of Niagara, too, and then a Muscat. They are all brandies, really—true grappa is fermented from pomace only—but the BATF won't allow us to use grapes' varietal names if we call them brandies. But we are allowed to name the varietals if we call them grappas. It's not worth trying to understand bureaucratic logic; one must just bend with it."

In 1987, a little before bringing in a Holstein still for Grahm, Rupf had arranged to have one shipped for Don Johnson of Creekside Vineyards near California's Suisun Valley, a peaceful fruit growing area with some of the rural charm of the *regio* in a New World translation. Johnson, after twenty-five years as an executive with a large retailing organization in the San Francisco Bay Area, had bought his Creekside property in 1977 for the sake of its twenty acres of vines. Though famous for its cherries, peaches, and pears, Suisun Valley—tight against the Napa County border—is included in California's North Coast Viticultural Area. Johnson had soon expanded the twenty acres of vineyard to four hundred; and though he was selling all his grapes without difficulty to coastal wineries, he felt he needed a way to use some of them himself, if only as a buffer against future market fluctuations.

Johnson didn't want to join the already swollen ranks of small, unknown wineries, and so he decided to distill, inspired by classes he had taken in extension courses of the University of California's Department of Viticulture and Enology. He thought there would be a niche in the market for skillfully made distilled brandies from sound, quality fruit. Johnson was encouraged not only by Rupf's *eaux-de-vie* but by the efforts of Rémy-Martin to launch a pot-still brandy distillery in Napa and by start-up efforts in Mendocino of a Frenchman from an old Cognac family, and his American partner.

Johnson began by distilling a fermented grape mash from some of his own grapes for a cask-aged grape brandy. Soon he went on to make an apple brandy, using the sound but undersized or excess fruit from a grower at Sebastopol in Sonoma County and aging it for two years in old French oak barrels. Johnson's Holstein still, with its *bain-marie* steam bath, gave him an advantage over those who distill Calvados apple brandy in Normandy. They use traditional pot stills, for which they must first separate juice from solids, whereas he distills an apple mash—juice and solids together—intensifying the aroma and lengthening the flavor of the brandy. Creekside barrel-aged apple brandy (Johnson uses barrels previously used to age California Chardonnay) has been an instant success.

· · · · · ·

Don Johnson—who has since sold his interest in Creekside to the Kautz family of Iron Stone Vineyards in the Sierra foothills—had taken a keen interest in the Mendocino distillery being set up by Hubert Germain-Robin and Ansley Coale, Jr. They were using the traditional pot still of Cognac (not a Holstein) to double distill a brandy they intended to blend and age to a quality to rival Cognac itself.

By the time Germain-Robin had finished his apprenticeship as a distiller, working with a series of small, independent producers, his family firm had been gradually ceded to Martell. In 1981, he decided to look around North and South America and, by chance, when he was doing just that, he hitched a ride from Ansley Coale.

Coale, a former teacher of ancient history at the University of California, Berkeley, and his wife, Cynthia, had purchased in 1973 a remote Mendocino ranch—some two thousand acres of redwoods, pines, and pasture hidden in a tangle of hills and dirt roads. The Coales were renting out the pastureland to local sheep farmers, but they wanted some activity that would allow them to live on the ranch year round. The Coales and Germain-Robin agreed among themselves to set up a distillery there, drawing on Mendocino grapes as the base for a fine brandy.

Germain-Robin went back to France and found an old hammered-copper three-hundred-gallon pot still: a size once standard, but abandoned when stills of double that capacity were installed throughout the Cognac region in the 1960s. He had it fully restored, brought it to Mendocino, and built a small, kitchen-neat distillery to house it. Germain-Robin was ready to go in time for the 1983 vintage.

In addition to French Colombard (one of the traditional grape varieties used in France for Cognac but now, in fact, largely replaced there by the more prolific Ugni Blanc), Germain-Robin used Chenin Blanc and Gamay-Beaujolais. The grapes were crushed and fermented for him at neighboring wineries.

The first lot of 125 cases of aged brandy was released in 1987. By 2000 the annual release had been stepped up to 4,000 cases. They are still building inventory for their ten to fifteen year old special bottlings (one of which is reserved for the White House), and their Anno Domini, a high-priced seventeen-year-old brandy, has received lavish praise.

Germain-Robin has experimented with a number of varieties, including Semillon and Pinot Noir, always separating each batch according to variety and vineyard. Though it is unlikely that he would have known it, he is using an approach that has a precedent in California. Henry Naglee, a West Point graduate who first came to San Francisco in the late 1840s at the time of the separation from Mexico, settled on a vineyard near San Jose after the Civil War. He visited Cognac, perhaps on more than one occasion, before setting up a still on his property and experimenting, as Germain-Robin was later to do, with a range of whatever varietal grapes were available. In the end, it is said, he preferred to use Pinot Noir (Germain-Robin prefers Semillon), but he had good results from Riesling, too. He, too, aged his brandies in small oak barrels. At a tasting in December 1878, members of a wine-judging panel, assembled under the chairmanship of Professor Eugene Hilgard of the University of California for San Francisco's thirteenth Industrial Exhibition, praised Naglee's brandy as the best in the state. His Pinot Noir brandy was even given a perfect score of a hundred points according to Ruth Teiser and Catherine Harroun in their historical account of winemaking in California. In a second judging, a few days after the first, his brandy again rated a perfect score as compared with a mature French brandy that received only a sixty-seven.

In the course of following where such varietal grapes seemed to lead him, Germain-Robin has changed many of his own ideas since he started.

For example, like Naglee before him, no doubt, he has found that his distillates, thanks to the grape varieties used, have a richer, more complex flavor than many Cognacs; so he does not need to rely as heavily on a dominant note of Limousin oak. To carry this through logically, he looks for grapes from old vines wherever possible.

"Mendocino offers innumerable small batches of grapes from plots of vines planted years ago by families that settled in the county," he told me. "The grapes used to be sold as mixed whites or mixed reds to Guild or Gallo or some other large winery where their quality was lost in the tanks. Ansley and I now spend a lot of time coaxing the grandchildren of those early growers not to pull out their old Charbono to plant Chardonnay."

Ansley Coale, responsible for the marketing, has found that building a name for a brand of fine brandy is a slower process than that of building recognition for a fine wine. For a start the production process (including aging) takes much longer. And sales are slower. A waiter's recommendation of a wine sells a bottle straight off; his recommendation of Germain-Robin brandy sells one glass at a time.

"But we are moving ahead well," said Coale. "We are now selling about a thousand cases a year in California, and there aren't many Cognacs of our quality that can say as much. It takes work. We have to be out and around talking about the brandy, doing the missionary work. But when all is said and done, it is the brandy itself that makes the sale for us. Consumers can tell good from not-so-good, let alone good from bad. When they taste Germain-Robin brandy, they like it. They are ready for it."

* * * * * *

There are two other Cognac-style copper pot stills active in Mendocino, each with a capacity of more than six hundred gallons, more than double that of the old Germain-Robin still.

Jepson Vineyards, near Ukiah, is making mostly Chardonnay and Sauvignon Blanc estate-bottled varietal wines, together with a small annual release of Champagne-method sparkling wines. But when purchased by a former owner, William Baccala, the property included eleven acres of very old French Colombard vines, which Baccala had been reluctant to root out. He decided to install a pot still and to use the French Colombard grapes for a fine brandy. Jepson released the first lot, a blend of 1983 and 1984, in 1989. Its style is broader than that of the Germain-Robin brandy, its flavor more robust. (Hubert Germain-Robin has said he wants his brandy to be in the style of Delamain's Cognac: fine and delicate, fruity rather than oaky.)

The Jepson still had been installed there by Miles Karakasevic, a Napa Valley producer whose family have been growers and distillers in Yugoslavia since the eighteenth century. Karakasevic, a large man with a flamboyant mustache and the warm exuberance of Zorba the Greek, has his own six-hundred-gallon pot still in a disarmingly mundane warehouse on the edge of Ukiah, where he, too, has been distilling brandies since 1983. As yet he has released none of them.

Meanwhile he has been using some of the brandy in a dessert wine he has named Charbay, a blend of a sweetened brandy liqueur and Chardonnay, and some of it to produce a liqueur called Nostalgie, a maceration of walnuts, vanilla, and spices. "It is something one of my uncles at home used to make for the family," he says.

Karakasevic, like Rupf, had contacts with wineries interested in distillation. One was Quady Winery in California's Madera County, where Andrew Quady has built a reputation on California Ports and on two dessert wines: Essensia, from Orange Muscat grapes, and Elysium, from Black Muscat. Karakasevic tried to persuade Quady to use for fortification brandies distilled from the same grape varieties as those used in the wines' production. (Ports and dessert wines are made by adding brandy part way through fermentation to preserve the grapes' natural sweetness.)

Quady had come to no decision on that, but he had thought of adding a third dessert wine: one made in the style of the rich Malvasia from Italy's Lipari Islands.

"I wasn't happy with the result," Quady told me, "and asked Miles if he would distill it for me. The result was a white spirit with the delicate flavor of Malvasia but without the harshness there might have been had

I distilled a Malvasia pomace for grappa. I decided to bottle it and sell it as Spirit of Malvasia. Because it is made from grapes, and not some other fruit, I have to call it "Immature Brandy." That wouldn't be the case if I had used plums, but the BATF regulations for grapes are rather byzantine.

"Anyhow, the quality off the Spirit of Malvasia encouraged me to ask Miles to distill some of my Black Muscat wine, Elysium. I wanted to see if he could capture the rose aroma that consumers like in this variety. It came through only faintly, but it makes quite a delicate white spirit." They were both one-off experiments, but Quady is thinking of producing another batch of the Spirit of Malvasia.

With the growing number of *eaux-de-vie* and brandies on the market, Jörg Rupf feels less isolated; but he too has been pushing his boundaries. The last time I heard from him he sent me a sample of something new: a single malt, carefully described on its label as "Pure Barley Spirit" rather than whisky (no doubt to avoid any potential tangle with the Bureau). But that gaunt statement gave no hint of the pale gold liquid in the bottle, an *eau-du-vie* of grains distilled in the Holstein as if they had been some exotic fruit. There was no smoky peat or sherry butt aroma to mask the pure aroma of freshly toasted barley. I was so impressed I began to wonder if perhaps he was about to abandon his violin for the bagpipes.

LODI:
A CALIFORNIA RENAISSANCE

WE ARE DRINKING MORE CALIFORNIA MERLOT IN THE UNITED States. More California Zinfandel, Pinot Noir, and Cabernet Sauvignon as well. And, of course, more Chardonnay. Sales of all California wines, in fact, are moving ahead even though the grape crop in some parts of the state fell behind because of the replanting made necessary by the ravages of phylloxera. Yet, overall, there seems to be no shortage of good California varietal wines at reasonable prices. If that seems contrary to economic law, perhaps it's because factor x is helping to balance the equation—x being Lodi, a town in California's Mokelumne Valley, about midway between Sacramento and Stockton. Lodi, the brunt of a Creedence Clearwater Revival rock ballad of the late 1960s ("But those guys only ever stopped here once, for gas," the town still complains), now produces almost 27 percent of the key varietal grapes grown in California.

There have been vineyards around Lodi for more than a century. But changes in the last decade or so have been dramatic. The area under vines has increased substantially and, more significantly, the growers have pulled out Carignane, Grenache, Alicante-Bouschet, and Palomino—reminders of a time when the region had been pushed into growing grapes for jug wines—and have planted in their place Chardonnay, Cabernet Sauvignon, Merlot, Syrah, and Sauvignon Blanc. The acreage of Zinfandel has doubled. Most important of all, Lodi growers are leading

California farmers in the direction of allowing nature itself to control the pests and weeds that threaten their crops.

* * * * * *

Though it's barely an hour and a half from San Francisco, the Mokelumne (pronounced m'*kahl*-amee) Valley has never lost its rural vocation— probably because it has never been the easiest place to get to. Originating as a stream in the high Sierra Nevada, the Mokelumne River empties into a skein of channels formed by the Sacramento and San Joaquin rivers as they merge in an island-choked delta behind the Carquinez Straits, their narrow exit to San Francisco Bay. Crossing the delta in any direction has always been difficult, so the main routes east from San Francisco run to the north of the valley, through Sacramento, or to the south, through Stockton. For this reason the Mokelumne Valley escaped suburban sprawl. Recent signs of wine-country gentrification—here a house slightly showier than customary for these parts, there a flowery bed-and-breakfast, and, lately, a talented chef at the Wine and Roses Country Inn—could be portents of what is to come. But perhaps not. Lodi doesn't really go in for lifestyle.

The Lodi region is both in and separate from the Central Valley, lying as it does in the direct path of the cool air stream drawn from the Pacific across the delta whenever Central Valley temperatures rise. It has the advantages, too, of good alluvial soil brought down from the Sierra Nevada and of Mokelumne water, organized since the 1920s through a locally managed irrigation scheme. This has long been serious farming country.

The town itself began in 1869 as Mokelumne Station, a halt on the Central Pacific Railroad. By 1880, according to Christi Kennedy's *Lodi: A Vintage Valley Town*, the new railroad was shipping from its Lodi depot 3.4 million bushels of locally grown wheat a year. But as the Great Plains—served by the same railroad—became progressively the nation's granary, Mokelumne farmers looked to other crops. After a short spell as the "Watermelon Capital of the World," Lodi turned to grapes, which became, before 1900, the town's principal economic resource.

* * * * * *

Lodi was then renowned for its Flame Tokay, a fleshy, thick-skinned table grape grown on vines as sturdy, and almost as big, as small trees. Lodi's warm days and cool nights—thanks to those breezes through the Golden Gate—gave its Flame Tokay a particularly juicy flavor and a bright flame-red color not matched by grapes of this variety grown elsewhere. Flame Tokay and Lodi became synonymous, with 95 percent of the world's tonnage of the variety produced within a five-mile radius of town. Yet, in spite of its popularity and the ease with which it sustained handling, packing and shipping, demand for Flame Tokay as a dessert grape fell abruptly once the sweeter, seedless grapes grown farther south in the San Joaquin Valley could be shipped east for table use. Though more fragile, they also transported well, thanks to newly introduced refrigerated rail cars.

Flame Tokay was reprieved by the onset of Prohibition, its tough skin making the grape as practical for shipping for home winemaking as it had been for table use. The table-grape packing sheds at Lodi, close to the railroad, made the town a natural center for the dispatch of all Central Valley grapes. Many of the mature Zinfandel vineyards for which Lodi is now particularly distinguished were planted during Prohibition to meet the ever-growing demand from the shippers.

When Prohibition ended, Lodi's Flame Tokay crop was turned to good use as a base for sparkling wine and brandy. Zinfandel, which ripened well in Lodi, giving wine with good color and rich flavor, was diverted to Port production; and Palomino, a popular shipping variety planted during Prohibition, gave local wineries the idea of making Sherry, the wine for which this grape is used in Spain. These wines were well received, and such was local pride in their success that Lodi's growers petitioned for—and Washington, in 1956, granted—recognition of Lodi as a "district of origin," for use on its wine labels. This special status—the first of its kind in California and a precursor of the American Viticultural Area program introduced in the 1980s—brought the town to a high pitch of expectation. "As a result of the new definition," a smiling John Hoggatt of the Lodi District Chamber of Commerce told a press conference in the town, "this area will soon be known throughout the world as America's Sherryland."

Unfortunately, he was right. Through hard work and vigorous self-promotion, Lodi bound its reputation to fortified wines just when consumer interest in California's table wines was reviving: The focus of wine production shifted to Napa and Sonoma and the other coastal counties, and the market for fortified wines collapsed. In the 1960s and 1970s Lodi's wineries failed, to be taken over as satellite production facilities, or closed.

The vineyards were replanted with the usual Central Valley jug-wine varieties—Carignane, Grenache, and Alicante-Bouschet among others. A reconversion to quality varieties began, very slowly, only in the late 1970s. But as wineries throughout California recognized the potential of fruit coming from Lodi's new vineyards, change accelerated. By the year 2000, the area producing Flame Tokay grapes had shrunk from twenty thousand acres to barely a tenth of that. Ironically, there is now something of a conservationist ardor about protecting those that remain. Flame Tokay, it's reasoned, is part of Lodi history, and the huge, gaunt vines across the Lodi landscape are a signature as defining as Tuscany's olive trees. Lodi now has some eighteen thousand acres of Zinfandel, sixteen thousand acres of Chardonnay, fifteen thousand acres of Cabernet Sauvignon, and ten thousand of Merlot. (According to published statistics, it is still possible to find there twenty-two acres of Palomino, the pride of America's Sherryland. But I suspect one would need to know where to look.)

* * * * * *

Change of this magnitude is usually a response to the market. Interest in wines from old Zinfandel vines—Lodi probably has more mature Zinfandel vineyards than any other California region—had already drawn the attention of serious wine producers by the 1980s. Then the shift from jug wines to moderately priced "fighting" varietals persuaded producers to press their area contract growers to graft vines to meet that demand. Few were prepared for the consistent quality Lodi would provide. But once Robert Mondavi installed himself in 1978 in an old area winery and began to promote a series of table wines under the Woodbridge name, Lodi was brought into the mainstream.

Mondavi brought to this Lodi enterprise policies that had worked for him in Napa Valley, one of which was to use small-winery techniques, no matter how big the winery. This practice made possible a program that changed the way Lodi growers saw themselves and their crops. For years Lodi growers had delivered their grapes to cooperatives or to large-production wineries, where they were quickly lost in the mass. Except by reading the degree of sugar concentration, a key factor in the payment they received, growers had no way of knowing whether their grapes were better or worse than their neighbors'. At Woodbridge, however, the presses are just large enough to take the volume of grapes necessary to fill one fermenting tank. The wine made from that—and every—lot there keeps its individual identity until final blending. By keeping separate the wines made from each category of grape received from each grower, Mondavi's Woodbridge winery was able to establish a wine archive in which the growers had discrete sections. Having samples of every lot allowed both the winery and the grower to keep track of the wines' development and what each lot contributed as it matured. Checking on the wines in this way gave the winery an opportunity to assess over time the potential of individual growers and the cultivation techniques that seemed to work (and didn't). It also enabled managers to identify sections of the Lodi area that seemed best suited for the style and quality they wanted in specific varieties.

When the Mondavi winery began bringing growers together to compare wines, their perspectives were soon raised beyond questions of healthy and unhealthy, economic and uneconomic, sugar bonus or no sugar bonus to consideration of why one wine had more flavor, another more intense color, or yet another better balance. Such changed attitudes were important to Mondavi because the firm's approach is based on conserving and emphasizing varietal fruit and vineyard personality—characteristics that must be intrinsic to the grapes themselves. They can't be invented in the winery.

"We work with two hundred growers in Lodi," Bradley Alderson, the winery's general manager, told me. "We've tried hard to show them that grapes are not a commodity, that the distinctiveness—the quality of the fruit they grow—makes it more or less useful, more or less desirable, more or less valuable to us.

"We've demonstrated that balanced grapes give wine better flavor and better color. I don't want to be obliged to adjust the acidity of a wine. We shouldn't have to adjust anything at all in the winery. If something isn't right, it must be corrected in the vineyard. Every wine is made in the vineyard—not just Château Lafite, but every wine. If one grower is able to give us exactly the fruit we want, why, we have to ask, is another having a problem? That's what we try to discover so that we can help resolve it."

Alderson arranges seminars for his growers and fosters their deepening knowledge by taking them on trips to other regions, even other countries. Brothers Brad and Randy Lange are among a small group of Mondavi growers who belong to a red wine circle. They meet regularly at the Mondavi winery to taste and compare and discuss the wines made from their respective grapes. Brad told me how these tastings, backed up by explanations of the practical application of recent research at the University of California, Davis, can help them. "By tasting how the measure of water a vine got during different phases of its growth cycle affects a wine, we've learned how and when to adjust irrigation in order to leave the vine in slight stress just after the fruit sets. Who would have thought that stress just at that moment would have the effect it does on flavor and color? Until I got involved with this, I was just a grape grower. Now I'm a winegrower."

Alex Delu and his son, Kevin, grow mostly Merlot. "We used to grow grapes for jug wine," the Delus told me. "And our chief concern was operating cost. That's all changed. We now spend twice as much money and time cultivating each acre, because positioning shoots, thinning the crop, and pulling leaves are expensive, labor-intensive activities. But it's work that has to be done. Everyone here is serious about quality, and there's tremendous pressure to keep up."

· · · · · ·

Pressure to "keep up" is to be expected in a region where families have farmed together for three or more generations. Relationships are constructive. After the growers and wineries of the state of California voted against a wine commission to be funded by an industry-wide levy, the growers of the Lodi Viticultural Area (the "district of origin" status was converted, with slight adjustments to its borders, into an American Viticultural Area in 1986) voted, in 1991, for a wine-grape commission of their own, to work on problems of common concern. Along with a determination to raise and maintain quality levels, high among those concerns was an integrated system of sustainable agriculture—using, in other words, natural means to reduce and even eliminate reliance on sprays for pest and weed management.

Growers in California have for some time used natural predators to rid themselves of harmful pests, but programs are difficult to control when a farmer is surrounded by people who use other methods or when the predators are not part of a naturally modified environment. In Lodi, the commission's own entomologist supervises strategies effective throughout the area. *Everyone* participates. Most vineyards, for example, are now bordered with French prune trees to provide the habitat for wasps that destroy the grape leafhopper, and throughout the area there are hundreds of nesting boxes for barn owls and kestrels. I'm told that a "to let" sign on a newly erected box will be noted and acted upon within hours. A pair of barn owls raising their young will consume as many as a thousand gophers or voles in a year.

The barn owls' role is essential because growers now use native California grasses as a cover crop between rows, both to harbor insect life and to keep weeds down (under the vines they spread chopped-up vine cuttings to accomplish the same thing). As well as providing a haven for friendly predators (friendly to the growers, that is), the cover crop contributes nutrients and conserves soil; it reduces dust in summer—and hence mites—and in winter, when the soil is normally wet and muddy, it improves access to the vineyards.

The programs initiated by Lodi growers through their elected Lodi-Woodbridge Winegrape Commission have provoked such interest throughout California that its meetings and seminars now attract growers from all over the state. And the results have been so effective that the commission has received grants from California's Department of Pesticide Regulation and the U.S. Environmental Protection Agency to allow two vineyards—a 30-acre plot of Zinfandel and a 120-acre block of Cabernet Sauvignon—to serve as classroom sites for growers who want to learn how to apply Lodi techniques on their own farms.

"Conventional farmers were looking for a shining example of a district-wide program that demonstrates how it's done," Mark Chandler, the commission's executive director, said. "We hope to be that example."

· · · · · · ·

With appropriate justice, Lodi grapes are now in demand. "They give wines with ripe, varietal expression," said Mary Sullivan, a winemaker at Sebastiani when it was involved in several brand programs based on Lodi grapes. "Lodi grapes offer a lot of quality for the dollar," Frank Cabral, the buyer at Sutter Home, told me. "The climate there gives grapes with better balance than you'll find elsewhere in the Central Valley. The growers are enthusiastic about what Mother Nature provides. They've been willing to adapt. It's thanks to Lodi fruit that we can sell good wine at a good price."

The irony is that very few California wines show a Lodi identity on the label, despite the important role the region now plays. That's partly because Lodi lost its own wineries in the 1960s and 1970s: Those since installed in the region buy grapes from elsewhere to use with Lodi fruit. Wineries in other areas buy Lodi fruit to supplement their local grapes. In all these cases the concern is to build brand identities rather than geographic appellations. But as the grower relations manager for one large winery says: "The Lodi Viticultural Area might get little recognition from the consumer, but it gets a lot of respect from the industry." In a competitive world, it's their winning x factor.

VINTAGE YEARS:
THANKS FOR THE MEMORIES

I DISCOVERED BIRTHDAYS ONLY WHEN I WAS GROWN, AND THE older I get the more I relish them. A favorite celebration, back in the 1970s, was a dinner at Berkeley's Chez Panisse when it was still a neighborhood restaurant rather than a national institution. Alice Waters, knowing why I'd reserved a larger table than usual, created for that evening a menu of dishes she knew I liked. There's a *prix-fixe* formula at Chez Panisse, so everyone else in the restaurant also sat down to a *tabbouleh* salad (I enjoy Lebanese food), poached halibut, roast leg of lamb with *flageolets,* and a plum tart. I hope it was as great a pleasure for them as it was for me. I can't now remember the Champagne we drank, but I know we had a red Bandol from Domaine Tempier with the lamb.

For my fiftieth birthday, friends arranged a dinner, cooked by Jeremiah Tower at the Santa Fe Bar & Grill (it was before he opened Stars), which was every bit the surprise intended. The friend delegated to fetch me—I'd been led to believe that he and I were to have dinner together—got very impatient with me as I insisted on rooting around in my cellar to find just the right bottle for us to drink. "I'm sure there'll be plenty of wine at the restaurant," he said, which made me just as impatient with him, of course. He knew *exactly* what was waiting for us— Dom Pérignon Rosé '69, a fresh 1981 Fleurie, a magnum of Joseph Phelps 1974 Cabernet Sauvignon, and Château d'Yquem '67, which we sipped with figs poached in Sauternes with rose petals.

I had a yet bigger surprise when Barbara Tropp, of San Francisco's China Moon Café fame, conspired with my sons another year to give me a Chinese birthday dinner—a "Longevity Feast"—which meant keeping me out of the house for most of the day so that two carloads of equipment and ingredients could be smuggled into the kitchen. With high-heat woks plugged in everywhere, the power failed before every course, giving us more time to drink and talk by candlelight as we waited for each dish. The evening finally ended, abruptly but in great style, with the entire apartment building being plunged into darkness.

The menu, decorated with flower petals, was as long as a novel. I remember particularly the fire-dried walnuts we ate with Pommery '70; the chicken with gingered apricot sauce; steamed salmon with ginger threads and black beans; and pressed duck with toasted almonds. Some of the dishes had magical names: flower rolls, carrot coins, honeyed cassia blossoms. We drank a Mount Veeder 1975 Chardonnay with some of the early courses, but the thrill of the evening was having both the 1959 and 1961 vintages of Château Lynch-Bages (thanks to my sons, who were presenting me with wines I'd laid down for each of them when they were born). When the lights went out for the last time we were sipping—with fresh litchis and almond-cookie cake—a lusciously golden 1974 Caluso Passito, a rarely seen dessert wine made north of Turin from a local grape called Erbaluce. It was as exotic an experience as all that had gone before.

For my sixtieth birthday my friend Narsai David and his son, Daniel, cooked dinner for me at their house in Berkeley. From fresh water chestnuts and local smoked salmon we went on to a *mezzaluna* of roast duck—like a giant raviolo—in broth; whisky-marinated squab with stir-fried pea shoots and pilaf made with Dom Sia rice (a particularly aromatic, long-grain variety best when it has been stored, as this had been, for several years before use); and *panna cotta*. Narsai had managed to find Butler, Nephew Vintage Port of my birth year—an amazing feat, as 1932 was such a poor vintage everywhere that I'd never before tasted a wine of my own age. As an encouragement to me to put my clock back, he produced—along with a splendid selection of early California red wines, mostly from Louis Martini—a 1942 Meursault Charmes and a 1942 Meursault Perrières, both originally from the cellar of Comtes Lafon and both wearing their years well.

To be born or to launch a venture in a year of good vintage repute is not essential for success, but it helps. It's not that anyone is actually admired or condemned because of the quality of wine he or she was born with, so to speak; or that a new enterprise is primed or tainted by vintage chart ratings. But there are those with reserves of old wines, and at some time or another a vintage of significance to the guest of honor will be brought up from the cellar. If the guest's birth, marriage, or business foundation coincided with a vintage of less than star quality, he or she will hardly win the hearts of fellow guests who had had the good sense to make their own moves in years more likely to raise smiles all around. It feels even worse the second time it happens.

Elin McCoy and John Frederick Walker, in their book *Thinking About Wine,* remind hosts of the risks they take, particularly when matching bottles and birth years. They point out that great years for people are not necessarily great years for wine, and they end with the caution: "If you do serve a wine from a guest's birth year, don't make the mistake of dramatizing how old the wine is and how amazing it is that it's still alive . . . ."

I usually find it more agreeable, anyway, to see a colleague honored (preferably one born, say, in 1929 or even 1945) or to celebrate the anniversary of a friend's marriage or career (especially if either began in 1953 or 1961) than to be honored myself. But that's because I was born in 1932, a year when the wine crop everywhere was so unspeakably bad that, mercifully, no one thought to keep any of it.

Unfortunately, the lack of wine from abysmal vintages is not in itself a guarantee that something better will appear. A host who feels challenged by his inability to match a significant year with the significant wine often reacts unpredictably. In my experience he is as likely to make amends by offering a fabulously ancient bottle of obscure origin and great rarity, its exhausted genie within sacrificed to no purpose, as he is to serve one of those undemandingly delicious wines he supposes his guests are encountering every week in just about any house well stocked with such banalities as Cheval Blanc '47 or Château Margaux '53. I am not alone, I'm sure, in finding that those who seek to please often underestimate the human capacity to be thrilled by the obvious.

So I empathize with fellow guests who show signs of anxiety when they see me or some other born in a low-caste year ushered to the privileged chair, especially if the occasion is one when it would be appropriate to expect a few special bottles. They know only too well what can happen.

Sometimes the responsibility for what we do unto others weighs so heavily that a little fudging is understandable, and even excusable. Had I been born in 1930 or 1933 I would have been tempted, for the most selfless of reasons of course, to ease myself into a 1929 or 1934. I laid down 1959 Bordeaux for my elder son, though he was born in 1958, because I saw no reason to penalize him for my having been hasty. But weaving a tangled web is not without risk. I cannot forget the anguished face of a colleague who, as I sat in his office on his birthday in 1971, received a call from a winegrower friend in Germany wishing to congratulate him on reaching his half century. "But I'm only forty-nine," he had blurted out, almost indignantly, before remembering that for years an accommodation of dates had allowed him to enjoy at his friend's table the delights of a succession of Auslese Rieslings from the man's private reserve. He recovered in a split second. "Oh, you're right!" he shouted quickly and with unnatural fervor, mentally writing off a year of his life as if it meant no more than a sock absent without leave in the washing machine.

In August '97, on a perfect day—the bay, glittering blue, was as thick with Sunday sailboats as a Raoul Dufy canvas—I celebrated another milestone with a lunch in my own dining room. We started as we meant to go on. With glasses of Taittinger Comtes de Champagne Blanc de Blancs '88 in hand, we leisurely compared two caviars: one, jet black, produced from the roe of a wild sturgeon taken from the Sacramento River close to the delta some months before; and the other, pale gray, made more recently from the roe of a sturgeon farm-raised farther upstream.

Toward the end of the nineteenth century, sturgeon were harvested in abundance from the Sacramento River and offered free—the flesh smoked and the roe cured as caviar—to lure customers into San Francisco's drinking establishments. Having been seriously overfished, sturgeon was already close to disappearing when the state issued a protection order in 1901. That order was partially lifted fifty-three years later to allow sturgeon to be taken for personal consumption, but California still forbids the sale of this fish—or any part of it—when caught within the state. To taste wild California caviar, one must know someone who is experienced in preparing it (the eggs, washed and freed from any remaining membrane, are drained and mixed with roughly 5 percent of their own weight in salt) and—sine qua non—is himself a fisherman or has a fisherman friend willing to hand over the roe of a freshly caught sturgeon in return for some of the prepared product. Usually composed of small eggs—more like sevruga than beluga—California caviar can taste milder than imported because it is usually fresher when eaten. Its texture is often firmer, too.

Taittinger's Comtes de Champagne, made from selected white grapes only, is one of the most elegant of Champagne's prestige *cuvées*. The 1988, poured from a magnum, had been generously aged on its lees before disgorging. Its color was pale gold; its bouquet mature but lively; and its flavor, with just a hint of lightly grilled almonds, was perfect with the caviar.

When we moved into the dining room, a slightly chilled bottle of the 1959 *vin jaune* of Château d'Arlay, in the Côtes du Jura, was ready for us, along with a powerfully aromatic dish of *donko shiitake* mushrooms. In Japan—and in China, where they've been cultivated on hardwood logs for centuries—*donko shiitake*, sold dried, are considered a great luxury. Rich in vitamins, minerals, and protein, they are sometimes called "the plant of immortality." Just the thing for a milestone birthday. They'd been suggested (and were supplied and cooked as well) by my friend Darrell Corti, the Sacramento wine merchant and carriage-trade grocer, when I'd mentioned to him my intention of serving a mixed sauté of wild mushrooms as a first course. I needed something mild but savory to accompany a slightly fading red Bordeaux intended to prepare the way for an older, but more vibrant, California Cabernet Sauvignon.

As he told me about the intense flavor of the *shiitake* (when, eventually, they were put to soak before cooking, my entire apartment was filled with a succulent, truffle-like aroma) and his own method of braising them with Manzanilla Sherry and *tamari*, I realized we were about to overwhelm a wine I'd chosen for its reticence. But the more he talked about these *shiitake*, the more I wanted them. I explained my reservations. "Well," he said. "Forget the red Bordeaux. I've got the perfect wine for *donko shiitake*: a bottle of 1959 Château d'Arlay. You yourself must have shipped it to California years ago. It has your old London company label on it." I wanted that wine, too.

• • • • • •

Château d'Arlay is in the Jura, an area between Burgundy and Switzerland that has been much fought over for centuries. It's the source of rivers that flow north and east to the Rhine, their valleys giving access to Germany and the low countries, as well as rivers that flow west and south to the Saône, a tributary of the Rhône, the ancient route south to the Mediterranean. To control this important pathway, the Roman emperor Probus established in the third century a fortified camp on a hilltop at what is now Arlay. The vineyard planted on the open and sunny slope below it is still there, crowned now by the massive ruins of the medieval fortress built by the counts of Charlon-Arlay on the site Probus had selected. But there is a great deal of mystery about the Jura's *vin jaune*. Some think its Sherry-like style was introduced when the Jura, along with the Netherlands, was under Spanish domination—the attraction of those trade routes again.

At any rate, when the white Savagnin wine has finished fermenting, it is put into barrels and simply left in them, undisturbed, for several years. No attempt is made to keep the barrels topped up or to rack the wine from its lees. After a year or so, an indigenous yeast invades the wine, gradually covering its surface with a white veil, much like the "flower" that spreads over the surface of young Fino Sherry. In time it knits some of the wine's alcohol with oxygen to form aldehydes that give *vin jaune* its uniquely penetrating bouquet—certainly a match for *donko shiitake*. That aroma develops even more remarkably once the wine is in its traditional squat bottle, but few ever get to taste a *vin jaune* of respectable age—or at all, for that matter. I was being presented with an uncommon, and entirely appropriate, opportunity, and I took it. In tandem with the *shiitake*, that 1959 Château d'Arlay was something I shall never forget.

The pivot of lunch was roast leg of lamb accompanied by *grano al burro*—pearled (husked) and buttered wheat grains—with the Georges de Latour Cabernet Sauvignon Private Reserve '70 of Beaulieu Vineyards. Much of what we were eating and drinking that day had personal associations for me. The vintages of some of the wines were souvenirs of sea-change years in my life; and the dishes, especially the roast lamb, brought to mind other occasions and other places. Roast lamb was a frequent fixture of Sunday dinner when I was a boy, though the meat we ate then was always extra well done. This one, scented with garlic and rosemary, was juicily rare. It reminded me of my early days in France and the satisfying meals one then ate in the Pullman restaurant cars on French trains. It could be that time has added a gloss to those memories (or perhaps I was overly impressed by the comparison with what was available on British Rail), but the service, the food, and the wines— Pullman's specialty was a particularly good Listrac from the Médoc— always impressed me.

* * * * * *

With lamb I like lentils, beans, or barley. These were all staples of the ancient world, and there's something reassuring, even comforting, about them. It was Darrell Corti's suggestion to have the *grano*, a grain of almost equal antiquity. Cooked wheat grain is a dish typical of southern Italy. Cato, the Roman statesman, ever proud of his peasant origins, gave the recipe still in use there today: "Remove the husks with pestle and mortar, wash the grains, drain them, and cook them in water." In the classical world—and even today, around the eastern Mediterranean— pearled grains had associations of life renewed and everlasting. Greek Orthodox Christians take to church on the third Saturday before Easter a pottage made from pearled grains sweetened with sugar and flavored with cinnamon and crushed walnuts; and Claudia Roden, in her *Book of Middle Eastern Food*, describes a dish—*belila*—of whole grains cooked in syrup, flavored with orange-flower water, garnished with chopped nuts, and offered by Sephardic Jews to visitors who come to celebrate a baby's first tooth. *Grano*, cooked in milk and mixed with ricotta, eggs, cinnamon, sugar, and orange-flower water, is also the filling in *pastiera napoletana*, the tart eaten at Easter throughout Campania—a region where many Greek customs prevail from pre-Roman times. But *grano* has a poignant connotation, too. Andrew Dalby points out in his book, *Siren Feasts*—an account of gastronomy in Greece from ancient to modern times—that for centuries it was a dish that divided rich from poor. Those who could afford millstones and ovens ate bread; those who couldn't ate boiled grains. The Swedes have a proverb: We serve up our past every time we cook.

Roast lamb shows off well almost any red wine from Bordeaux or made from the grape varieties (principally Cabernet Sauvignon and Merlot) we associate with that region. Which is why my menu had taken shape around the combination of roast leg of lamb and the Georges de Latour '70—a memorable vintage in Napa Valley, besides being the year I moved from London to New York.

· · · · · ·

Choosing a wine to follow it presented a gastronomic problem. No wine should allow guests to wish they were still drinking the one that preceded it. Which is why my hosts in Bordeaux, following the rule of younger to older, always keep the oldest and finest red wine at lunch or dinner to be presented with—and therefore confronted by—the cheese board. But that runs the risk of the wine being overpowered by the cheese, and in this case I knew I needed something vigorous to accompany a particularly fragrant Beaufort, a pyramid of Valençay, an Explorateur, and a ripe sheep's-milk cheese from the Cévennes. I dodged the issue by moving to Bordeaux. Here I knew I could find a younger wine that would not overwhelm with sheer exuberance our memory of the Georges de Latour, as a young California wine might have done; and could, if picked with care, confirm the specifically California characteristics of the older wine. I had some 1985 Château Ducru-Beaucaillou, still youthful but satin-smooth, with a fine bouquet and flavor that would, I thought, take the cheeses in stride and give much pleasure without detracting from the Georges de Latour. And that's exactly what it did.

We ended with a series of treats, chief among them a reminder of that surprise dinner fifteen years before—a bottle of Château d'Yquem '67, the vintage considered by the owner, Comte Alexandre de Lur Saluces, to be one of the best of this century. The wine had a deep golden color, an extraordinary bouquet, and a flavor that seemed to suggest, with every sip, unimaginable riches. With it we ate *sacripantina*, a confection of air, cream, and magic unique to San Francisco, with golden raspberries from a farm above Santa Cruz Bay.

At about four o'clock, we were ready for coffee, a taste of Valrhona's Guanaja chocolate, and the kind of benevolent conversation that comes with contentment. The day was becoming another memory to savor.

AUSTRALIA:
SUNNY-SIDE UP

ESPECIALLY WHEN FEBRUARY IS AT ITS BLEAKEST AND SUMMER IS
half a world away, it's a comfort to remember that there are bottles of
Australian sunshine at your nearest wine store. As long as I can remember,
I've had this image of Australia as a place where summer goes into bottles
and cans. It started, I think, when I was a schoolboy in wartime England.
In those days of food rationing, tins of Australian apricot jam were rare
and luxurious treats. They were packed solid with lusciously ripe, whole
fruit; even the apricots of the Garden of Eden (of *course* there were apricots in the Garden of Eden) could not possibly have had such a heady
flavor. Most thrilling of all, it was impossible to spread that jam thinly,
though we were constantly nagged to "make it last." To an eleven-year-
old boy, the sensation of piling that fragrant, orange-gold jam on new-
baked bread and sinking the teeth into it was beyond the merely voluptuous. When I finally went to Australia for the first time, confident I
would be allowed to recapture that incredible feeling of sensuous triumph, my disappointment in finding that Australia now makes apricot
jam like most other apricot jam—a mix of goop and little rags of fruit
that might, perhaps, be apricot—made me doubt my own remembered
childhood. I was devastated.

But I found consolation in Australia's wines—they offered qualities
not entirely dissimilar to those I'd enjoyed in the apricots: generosity, a

concentration of ripe flavor, and a sunny accessibility—and, of course, in Australia itself. For a start, and particularly in Victoria and South Australia, I was astonished to see a countryside lifted straight from eighteenth-century canvases. With immense grass borders for herding animals, gravel and sand roads wind past mannered trees—gracefully inclined and just smudged here and there with a suggestion of painterly foliage—under which perfect rent-a-flock sheep peacefully graze. Most of the time I seemed to be driving through a series of picture frames, and I half expected John Constable to jump out from behind a hedge waving his brush and palette.

I was unprepared for the charm of Australia's small towns. At Mudgee, for example, in the hills of New South Wales, the municipal buildings and railway station were designed and built, even at that remote edge of empire, from the same plans and drawing boards as town halls and railway stations all over Victorian England. The clock turned back a hundred years for me, and I saw the firm hand of the Colonial Office. In Victoria, the town of Bendigo, once a gold rush metropolis, is decorated with a profusion of cast-iron frippery that makes New Orleans' French Quarter look chaste. And, if Australian moviemakers have back lots, I am sure a replica of the main street of Rutherglen is on one of them.

Australia's vineyards are spread through all six states, but mostly they are in New South Wales, Victoria, and South Australia. At the last count, in 2000, there were roughly 336,000 acres of bearing vines, including raisin and table grapes. (The comparable figure for California was 760,000.)

Though the first Australian attempt to plant vines—in 1788 in what is now called Sydney—was unsuccessful, by 1822 an Australian red wine shipped to London had earned a silver medal from the Royal Society of Arts. The medal was awarded by way of encouragement (the wine was "by no means of superior quality" the Society's archives record), but that could hardly have been true of the gold medal awarded the same grower for a wine shipped six years later.

By then, however, the settlers in general and the medal-winning grower, Gregory Blaxland, in particular had had the benefit of James Busby's *A Treatise on the Culture of the Vine and the Art of Making Wine*, published in Sydney in 1825. Busby, son of the colony's newly arrived water engineer, had studied viticulture in France before accompanying his father to Australia, and the *Treatise* drew on what he had learned there as well as on the published works of others. After teaching viticulture for a while to boys in an orphans' farm school near Sydney, Busby left in 1831 to travel through Spain and France, reviewing techniques there while collecting vine varieties that he hoped would flourish in Australia. The carefully packed cuttings of the more than a hundred varieties shipped back were propagated to provide a basic stock from which many of Australia's early vineyards sprang.

Though Busby himself moved to New Zealand in 1932 to take up a government appointment and remained there until he died some forty years later, his book and the cuttings had a lasting effect on viticulture in Australia. Certain rare French varieties thought to be relics of Busby's collection (the Crouchen, for example) are planted commercially in Australia but no longer exist in France; and a preferred clone of Chardonnay now spreading through Australia from the small and viticulturally isolated wine region around Mudgee is believed to be directly descended from cuttings taken by Busby from vines within Clos Vougeot more than 150 years ago. Above all, he is credited with the introduction of the Syrah, known in Australia as Shiraz.

After their initial flourish, both interrupted and sustained by a rush to the gold fields, Australia's vineyards lapsed into mediocrity from the turn of the century until the end of World War II. Australians at that time ate and drank with no particular interest in either food or wine. Overseas, the United Kingdom, Australia's principal market, had a structure of Imperial duty preference that favored high-strength Australian red wine sold there as Invalid Port (labels promised cures for everything from liver troubles to loss of willpower) or blended with thinner stuff to create a cheap flagon wine called Australian Burgundy. In short, neither home nor export markets offered much encouragement to Australian vintners to produce anything but alcoholic red wine and high-strength white suitable as a base for Sherry.

There had always been exceptions, of course, to serve as reminders of what was possible. But a renaissance started when Max Schubert, winemaker at Penfolds in South Australia, returned in 1950 from a visit to Bordeaux. Working with Shiraz rather than Cabernet Sauvignon, Bordeaux's key grape variety, and with more obstruction than support from the Penfolds board, he translated what he had seen in France into a wine now considered an Australian classic—Penfolds' Grange.

Inspired in part by his success (which took some years to be recognized as such) and in part by the ideas that had influenced him, others followed. Changes initiated during the sixties gathered momentum in the seventies and have since led to a worldwide respect—and success—for Australian wines.

* * * * * *

Max Schubert's urge to do better would not have been enough to change the tide had there not been strong complementary currents. Since the war, new immigrants to Australia (until then most immigrants were from the British Isles) had arrived from Italy, Greece, Yugoslavia, and other parts of Mediterranean Europe. Increasing numbers were arriving from Asia. By the 1960s, Australia was changing. And, because almost 90 percent of Australians live in twelve major cities, the changing produce markets and restaurants rapidly affected the eating habits of *all* Australians. (It is ironic that the country many Americans perceive as a wild new frontier should have the most urban population in the world.) *Souvlaki* bought from a Greek butcher would appear on the barbecue along with the customary chops; marinated chicken wings and stuffed quail, Indonesian *satés*, and grilled bell peppers became part of the regular family backyard menu. Neighbors talked about food. And drank wine.

Demand created by those used to drinking simple red wine with their meals could not have come at a more opportune time, because it was clear the United Kingdom outlet for Australian high-strength blending wines would disappear with the loss of preferential rates of duty accompanying Britain's entry into what was then the European Common Market.

Australia had, for decades, selected warm sites, chosen vine varieties appropriate for them, and used winemaking techniques directed at producing wines valued in the United Kingdom for their bulk and their alcohol. At first the vintners were obliged to combine ingenuity with what they already had in order to transform these same grapes into new-style wines with the required freshness, flavor, and zest for table wine consumption. Gradually equipment caught up with the winemakers' changed needs, and vineyards spread into cooler areas, especially at higher elevations. Hill-Smith, for example, a veteran winegrowing family in Barossa Valley, elected to plant its new Heggies vineyard at fifteen hundred feet; David Wynn, the man credited with reviving Coonawarra as a region for Cabernet Sauvignon, has now developed eighty acres of vineyard at two thousand feet on what was virgin pastureland; and Brian Croser of Petaluma Winery has created a series of temperate vineyards from a slice of the steep Adelaide Hills, once given over to foggy market gardens. New acreage of previously scarce varietals—Cabernet Sauvignon, Pinot Noir, Sauvignon Blanc, and Traminer—advances as fast as Grenache and Palomino retreat. Whereas there were fewer than a hundred acres of Chardonnay in all Australia just twenty-five years ago, there are now more than forty-four thousand.

These European varieties, familiar to us, will grow in all of Australia's wine regions. But in each region some do better than others. Even Shiraz, a grape that adapts to conditions just about everywhere, gives a completely different *style* of wine from region to region. The taste of Shiraz from Hunter Valley, for example, especially a Tyrrel or a McWilliam's, with full-throated flavor and a typical tarry, leathery bouquet that hangs in the air (known to local connoisseurs as "sweaty saddle"), hardly resembles the rich, concentrated fruit of a Mudgee Shiraz from Huntington Estate, Miramar, or Botobolar, let alone the elegant, scented versions produced in central Victoria at Mount Avoca and at Château Tahbilk (my idea of how the Garden of Eden must have been), or the intensely berry-flavored wine produced by Kay Brothers Amery Winery from McLaren Vale Shiraz vines planted in 1892.

To help Australian vintners establish new priorities in making this transition from fortified wines, where errors were more easily accommodated, to light, crisp table wines, where they are not, the Riverina College of Advanced Education at Wagga Wagga introduced courses in the early seventies with a highly structured approach to winemaking. (Wagga Wagga is aboriginal for something like "place where many crows screech together," not entirely inappropriate for a College of Advanced Education.) Inevitably the highly technical Wagga methods, relying heavily on an appropriate installation, left little room for rule of thumb and seemed, on the face of it, opposed to the pragmatic approach of several generations of Roseworthy Agricultural College graduates, who still made wine from the vineyard up rather than forward from a computer console.

Roseworthy graduates still pretend to be a little scornful of their Wagga peers, who are unnerved, say the former, if placed in a winery without every conceivable electronic aid; and Wagga graduates are quick to identify as flaws what their Roseworthy colleagues treasure in their wines as idiosyncratic characteristics. In fact, though everyone has some kind of ax to grind, by asking each winemaker to explain, step by step, what he actually did to make his wine, I found a greater uniformity of view than either side admits. Theoretically, for example, the Wagga school believes in cleaning white grape juice by mechanical means—filter or centrifuge—before fermenting it, whereas Roseworthy allows the juice to stand so that grape solids can fall and leave the juice (more or less) bright. Wagga worries about such things as stuck fermentation in its nice, clean juice, but Roseworthy says: "What do you expect when you take all the yeast's nutrients away?" In practice, however, Roseworthy graduates are as eager as anyone else to benefit from the latest filters and bladder presses; and some Wagga graduates, on the other hand, are happy to leave young Chardonnay wallowing on its yeast-lees for months after fermentation.

· · · · · ·

Brian Croser, who set up the Wagga courses after graduating from the University of California at Davis, says he wanted to give positive instruction instead of taking what he felt was California's remedial approach. An influential guru to those he has taught, Croser describes sound wine-making as "causing least aberration to fruit received from the vineyard." Though others would differ, at least in degree, he refers to the options of winemaking as condiments and maintains that a wine's structure, as well as the length and style of its flavor, are established in the vineyard. "The rest is spice, and, if it is allowed to dominate, it is because the fruit wasn't good enough."

In reaching back to the vineyard, Croser demonstrates that, though he and others might place emphasis differently and even hold divergent opinions on everything from the width of vine rows to the aeration of grape juice, all sides of the Australian industry accept that fermentation and aging are steps in a winemaking process begun when a vine is planted. In Australia, it is the vineyard rather than the winery that presently absorbs most attention.

Croser's vines are labor intensive, requiring careful control of the leaf canopy to advance grape maturity and retain an appropriate bite of acidity. But vineyard labor in Australia is expensive and not always available. Not only is there greater reliance on mechanical picking, proportionately, than seems to be the case in California, but pruning, too, is often mechanical, carried out with equipment resembling monster hedge cutters. Mechanical pruning leads to growth at the head of the vine as dense and as convoluted as the coils on Medusa's head, and sometimes as dangerous. Though small bunches held within the tangle present no problem to mechanical pickers, which shake the vine vigorously to cause ripe grapes to fall onto receiving track belts, they are difficult to reach with protective sprays during the growing season and therefore become subject to molds and rot.

To resolve this, in 1973 Australia's official Commonwealth Scientific and Industrial Research Organization (CSIRO) initiated trials with vines pruned so minimally that for all practical viticultural purposes they could be considered not pruned at all. Contrary to the hedge-pruned vines, grown in upon themselves, these vines—left virtually untouched for years except for something resembling a haircut along the bottom each year after the fruit had set, just to keep the aisles clear from trailing growth—form for themselves an arbor of old wood as a supporting trellis, just as an unpruned rosebush would. Bunches close to the surface ripen evenly with better sugar and better acid than do those on either mechanically or conventionally pruned vines.

These studies are highly controversial. They destroy traditional bearings (in my mind I saw woodcut images of hundreds of generations of little men, from Noah on, all with secateur in hand and all about to be proved wrong), and there are these winemakers who suggest that the very qualities claimed for the fruit of such vines (more but smaller bunches, meaning more skin for flavor and color relative to juice) would be detrimental to fine wine because of the greater measure of harsh tannins they would all contribute. On the other hand, though comparative taste tests among Coonawarra Cabernet Sauvignon wines made from the test block of vines and from neighboring vineyards pruned normally can be no more than sketchy indicators due to the limited nature of the experiment, wine made from the minimally pruned vines gave the best result. (The CSIRO block is part of the Coonawarra Rouge Homme vineyard owned by Lindemans.)

Coonawarra, a thin layer of red clay over a freak bed of limestone a mile wide and about eight miles long, has five thousand acres of potential vineyard land, of which four thousand are already planted. It is always described as fertile, but with my own eyes I saw vines producing more prolifically on the black earth at its perimeter. Coonawarra shares, however, with the Médoc and Napa Valley an affinity for Cabernet Sauvignon and produces from it wines with tightly focused flavor. As a result, more Cabernet Sauvignon is planted here than anywhere else in Australia.

Because of the prestige of Cabernet Sauvignon and the variety's concentration in Coonawarra, most major wineries own vineyards or buy grapes there. Seppelt, of Barossa, and Petaluma grow Cabernet Sauvignon in Coonawarra; Orlando uses Coonawarra grapes for its St. Hugo Cabernet Sauvignon; and even Rosemount and Hungerford Hill grow grapes in Coonawarra and then lug them, chilled, all the way to their home wineries in New South Wales. Some wineries own satellite or subsidiary establishments in Coonawarra. Lindemans, also of New South Wales, owns the Rouge Homme vineyard and winery, where its St. George Vineyard Cabernet Sauvignon is produced, and Penfolds owns Wynns, which makes the outstanding John Riddoch *cuvées* of Cabernet Sauvignon.

Not all Coonawarra wineries and vineyards have far-flung connections, however. Hollick's wines, Bowen Estate, and Katnook Estate were among several that I particularly liked.

* * * * * *

Apart from its success in Coonawarra, Cabernet Sauvignon also does well elsewhere in South Australia. In McLaren Vale, south of Adelaide, it is firmer (Wirra Wirra and Pirramimma produce good examples of the local style). In Clare (best known for Riesling), it's lighter. Clare has a cool climate, despite its location to the north of Coonawarra; Australia is topsy-turvy, remember. Cabernet Sauvignons produced there by Grosset, Knappstein, and Mitchell wineries in particular are Bordeaux-like in the way they combine depth of flavor and grace of structure. Tim Knappstein sold his interest in the winery that bears his name and is now installed at Knappstein-Lenswood in the Adelaide Hills—an even cooler region. "I don't think we try to make Bordeaux copies," he told me. "But we do strive for classic dimensions in the wines."

In central Victoria, Cabernet Sauvignon has a firm and, to my taste, even severe style, the best example of which is produced at Taltarni. At Blue Pyrenees Estate, a few miles away, this style is broadened by the addition of Shiraz and Merlot for the estate's red wine.

Combinations of Cabernet Sauvignon and Shiraz are common in Australia and, though they might seem bizarre, they have an honorable antecedent in the blending of Syrah-based Hermitage wine from the Rhône with Bordeaux wines in the nineteenth century. Writing in his *Journal of a Tour Through Some of the Vineyards of Spain and France*, a record of his 1831 trip, James Busby wrote: "The finest Clarets of

Bourdeaux [*sic*] are mixed with a portion of the finest red wine of Hermitage, and four-fifths of the quantity of the latter which is produced are thus employed." The best, and most expensive, red wines of Bordeaux at that time, including the first growths, were those improved in this way and listed as *Hermitagé*.

I found the combination works especially well in Hunter Valley (where the Cabernet Sauvignon is softer and tames the boisterousness of Shiraz without greatly changing it) and in Coonawarra, in Lindemans' Limestone Ridge Vineyard blend and in Penfolds' Coonawarra Cabernet-Shiraz blends. There, when Cabernet Sauvignon character becomes too aggressive, Shiraz mellows in.

New South Wales has been less successful then either South Australia or Victoria with Cabernet Sauvignon (honorably excepting the elegant Cabernet Sauvignon from Lake's Folly—Max Lake, now retired, played Bach to encourage the yeast in its work—and the outstanding wines made at high elevation by Mudgee wineries such as Montrose— now Poet's Corner—and Huntington Estate), but it produces Chardonnay and Sémillon of a scale unmatched elsewhere. Rosemount Estate produces internationally acclaimed Chardonnays in a voluptuously complex style, and the Rothbury Estate produces similarly intense Sémillons that age magnificently. Petersons is also known for the scale of its Chardonnay, and there are others, less assertive perhaps, produced at Brokenwood, McWilliam's, and Wyndham Estate. Murray Robson's fine, spare Chardonnay is quite distinct from others in the region.

If South Australia has Cabernet Sauvignon and Riesling as its specialties, and New South Wales its Shiraz, Chardonnay, and Sémillon, Victoria's climate (or climates) makes possible an even wider range of wines. Near Rutherglen, in the northeast, are rich, aged Muscat wines with the dense flavor of hazelnut praline. Victoria is where the best examples of Pinot Noir can be found, at Balgownie winery in the center of the state and at Yeringberg, Yarra Yering, and Diamond Valley Vineyards, all in Yarra Valley, northeast of Melbourne. Yarra Valley suffered severe setbacks earlier in the century, when prohibitionist sentiments in

Victoria did much to damage the state's wine industry. It is, however, rapidly recovering and producing outstandingly balanced Chardonnays at Coldstream Hills and Yarra Burn and deliciously forthright Cabernet Sauvignons at Mount Mary and Seville Estate.

• • • • • • •

Many wineries were kind enough to show me treasures: an 1886 Port at Seppelt, aged in barrel for a century so that it had become less like a vintage Port and more like a rich, very old Oloroso Sherry; fine old Liqueur Muscats at the Morris and Campbells wineries at Rutherglen; and luscious old Tokays at Baileys. I was introduced to wines I had not seen before: flowery whites made at Lindemans, Hungerford Hill, and Hardy's from the Verdelho grape of Madeira; pure Marsanne (in France it is usually blended with Rousanne) at Mitchelton and Château Tahbilk; and Tarrango, a cross of Tarrigo and Thompson used at Brown Brothers to produce a dry white wine with raspberrylike aroma.

What impressed me particularly, however, was to find some of the best wines of all within the facilities of the largest wineries. Orlando, Penfolds, Mildara, Wynns Coonawarra, McWilliam's, and Seppelt are far from anyone's idea of boutique wineries. Robin Day, development director at Orlando, where I tasted one of the most perfect Traminers in years, said that small wineries are snobbish about the volume of bag-in-box wines turned out by the major wineries.

"Apart from the fact that bag-in-box wines have made Australia a wine-drinking country, their success means we have the resources as well as the will to run small wineries where premium wines are made within our large wineries." What he said held true even for the giant Berri Estates cooperative in the Riverland of South Australia, which clunk-clunks its way through the largest production of any winery in Australia but manages to produce Chardonnay and Shiraz that would be the envy of many hands-on winemakers.

Small wineries in Australia are more idiosyncratic than ours in California and are less likely to bulge with expensive equipment. ("A small winery doesn't have to be like a large winery reduced in scale," one small-winery owner explained with irrefutable logic.) Ian Macrae, whose 1985 Mudgee Chardonnay was among the finest I tasted, had surrounded his winery with what I can only describe as an acre of existential junkyard so that he can design and make his own equipment to get his wine the way he wants it. (He is now the wine maker at Miramar.)

Others successfully adapt simple domestic appliances and equipment or learn, appropriately, to think small. One grower overcame the cost of installing sealed steel tanks for carbonic maceration (to keep grapes in an atmosphere of carbon dioxide generated by their own fermentation) by picking the bunches off the vines and putting them directly into huge, tough plastic bags. The maceration takes place as the sealed bags sit between the rows of vines. Tipping the contents into the winery's crusher later is a lot easier than transferring the mass of grapes from a tank.

A "waste not, want not" attitude applies to Australian wine-region food, too. In country restaurants I could usually order the bits that don't go to market—kidneys, lamb brains, tongue—all imaginatively and well cooked. I also had hot smoked leg of young lamb at the Knappsteins', and I remember with special pleasure barbecued fillets of kangaroo at Coldstream Hills.

A few days before I came home I lunched with the owner of a small Clare winery and his wife. We were drinking a bottle of his Cabernet Sauvignon with stuffed quail straight off the grill in a small restaurant—more a glassed-in lean-to, really—set in a thicket of aromatic trees off one of those unpaved roads. We were eating late, and there were no other customers, and so the cook, a quite young woman, put a Mozart aria on her record player in the kitchen. I can't remember now who the singer was or what she was singing, but I remember thinking that, for all we hear about Australia, no one ever bothers to say how poetic the place is.

CHILE:
A NEW GOLDEN AGE

IN THE YEAR 2000, CHILE SHIPPED THE EQUIVALENT OF ALMOST thirty million cases of wine to more than eighty countries around the globe, double the volume shipped in 1997. The most remarkable thing, however, is that just twenty-five years ago Chile exported next to no wine at all.

Spain's sixteenth-century conquistadors brought the first vine cuttings to Chile. They were mostly País, a simple black grape, rather like the Mission in California, that crops abundantly but makes dull wine. According to family records, Gregorio Ossa, founder of Viña La Rosa in the Cachapoal Valley, ninety miles south of Santiago, brought cuttings of French vines to Chile as early as 1824. What they were is not clear; Cabernet Sauvignon and other specifically Bordeaux varieties are thought to have been introduced only in 1851 by Silvestre Ochagavia, who planted them on his family estate at Talagante, about thirty miles from Santiago. In 1856 the influential Cousiño family—at various times its industrial empire has reached into every aspect of economic activity in Chile—acquired the Macul hacienda, and some years later replanted its vineyards, renowned since colonial times, with French vines. Other growers, too, began to plant French vines, culminating in a great surge of new vineyards in the 1870s and 1880s, about the time Chile went to war with Peru and Bolivia to gain sole possession of the nitrates and copper in a disputed desert on their common border.

Chile's subsequent dominance of the Pacific coast of South America (Chilean troops had actually occupied Lima from 1881 to 1883) brought enormous wealth to the country's governing families. For them it was a golden age. The specific impetus to plant vineyards at this time was probably the outbreak of phylloxera in France; there was widespread speculation that French wine production would never recover from it. But the appearance of so many handsome new wineries attached to elegant residences—all of them within a carriage ride of the capital—was clearly intended to display more than an interest in agricultural pursuits.

But the golden age didn't last. The nitrate boom ended when German scientists discovered, under the exigencies of World War I, how to fabricate nitrates industrially. And then Chile put a spoke in its own viticultural wheel. An anti-alcohol law of 1938, intended to curb the production of cheap País wine sold by small farmers in the impoverished south, imposed draconian controls nationwide that made any extension of the area under vines virtually impossible (a move not entirely unwelcome among the families with extensive vineyard holdings). It also fixed a ceiling on the annual national wine production at sixty liters a head. Over the next forty years, however, Chile's population doubled and wine production was allowed, within the limits of the 1938 law, to follow suit. But the area under vines remained the same. The predictable decline in quality was made worse by import controls imposed at the start of World War II. These blocked the acquisition of winemaking equipment and, for decades, effectively cut Chile off from the technical advances made elsewhere. Fermented in concrete tanks at high temperatures and then aged for excessively long periods in wooden vats that had seen better days, most of the wines were increasingly dull, oxidized, or both.

"It wasn't that the producers *wanted* to keep their wines so long in wood," Arturo Cousiño, of Cousiño-Macul, explained to me. "Bottle supplies were totally inadequate and deliveries were irregular and unpredictable. We had to scrounge for old bottles and reuse them. To have hoped to keep stocks of wine in bottle would have been to dream of an unattainable luxury."

Not surprisingly, Chileans turned away from wine to the fresher, cleaner taste of bottled beers and soft drinks, newly available in the 1970s. And they increased substantially their consumption of *pisco*, a young white brandy usually taken with lemon juice—an ironic consequence given that the 1938 law had been designed to promote sobriety. Through that decade and the next, Chile's annual consumption of wine dropped steadily from sixty liters a head to fifteen. The prices paid for grapes collapsed, and many growers left crops unharvested. Between 1980 and 1985, more than a third of the country's vineyards were ripped out and replaced by fruit orchards, and by the end of the 1980s all but two of the family-owned wineries—founded with such pride more than a century before—had been sold for cash.

In 1979, in the midst of this period of decline, Miguel Torres, of the well-known Spanish wine family, came to Chile and bought at auction an abandoned vineyard year Curicó, some 110 miles south of Santiago. "Curicó is cooler than Maipo, and I saw possibilities," he told me when I met with him at his winery. "The vines were in poor shape. It took two or three years to bring them back. In the meantime, I bought grapes to make wine and released my first—a light, fruity Sauvignon Blanc of the 1980 vintage—as soon as it was bottled."

That wine took Santiago by surprise. Compared with the clumsy, throat-grabbing white wines the city had then become used to, it seemed indecently frivolous. "They called it a ladies' wine," Torres told me. "I told them it was a wine for discriminating drinkers—men or women. But whatever they said, they all wanted to taste it. The enologists flocked to Curicó." What they found were stainless-steel tanks, a refrigeration plant that allowed Torres to control fermentation temperatures, new French oak barrels, and, most important of all, a meticulous approach to winemaking.

"They were particularly impressed by the low temperatures my equipment made possible. But the winery owners were reluctant to spend money. And there were still restrictions—permits, high duties— which made it difficult for them to import the equipment they needed, even had they wanted to. But local reaction was not important to me, really. My efforts were export-directed, and in England, especially, our wines sold well. Other wineries paid attention. They understood what I was doing, and by the late 1980s many of them were making an effort to improve the wines they were hoping to sell abroad."

Rafael Guilisasti, of Concha y Toro, confirmed that his winery had adopted such a strategy. "When we started looking for new markets, we realized that things had to change. The wines the world was drinking were brighter and fresher than those we had to offer. We needed different varieties, too. Chardonnay, for example, rather than Sauvignon Blanc; Merlot as well as Cabernet Sauvignon.

"By then there were no longer restrictions on vineyard development. The business environment had changed, too. Import duties on capital goods had fallen, allowing us to buy the equipment we needed, and corporate taxes had been lowered to encourage investment. Everything changed very quickly, not only in the wineries but also in the vineyards. Where we had used trellis systems for the vines—they allow heavier yields—we changed to wire-trained cordons for better exposure of the fruit. The lower yields we wanted called for tighter control of irrigation, difficult when our system was basically row flooding. The installation of drip irrigation meant we could move onto the hillsides—better for vines anyway—and use water to improve quality rather than just boost quantity."

In a few years, the structure of the wine industry itself evolved. Faced with the possibility of selling their crops at prices that would barely cover the cost of cultivation, if that, many growers began to build wineries of their own. At the beginning of the 1980s there had been fourteen or fifteen wineries. There were soon sixty, even seventy. Meanwhile, the family ownership of wineries founded in the golden age had dispersed over the years among cousins of the fourth or fifth generations who could not agree on how to finance the costly changes necessary for survival, and so sold their properties. Fortunately, new owners brought enthusiasm as well as money to the industry. Previously untapped areas were opened up to vineyards—the cool Casablanca Valley, for example, between Santiago and the port city of Valparaiso; new clones were introduced from both

France and California; and more thought was given to which varieties should be planted where. The producers looked more closely at the differences among Chile's wine regions and started adding distant vineyards, sometimes in the face of logistical efficiency, so that each of the varieties they produced could be grown in an appropriate environment. Everything was monitored. Every vineyard in Chile became a work in progress.

Change had come with a rush that had Chile's youthful winemakers both ecstatic and confused. There was an influx of experts from California and France, most of them involved in joint or new ventures, who brought valuable experience but tended to define the personality of Chilean wines in terms of the markets they were used to. And so, at first, the renaissance was completely market driven. We are now seeing the reemergence of individual winery mannerisms and a freer expression of Chile's regional characteristics. Chile's producers realize that only by showing the distinctiveness of their wines and the nuances of their origins can they break through price barriers that would otherwise keep them forever in the bargain bins of commodity varietals.

"The variety should always be clear," Alvaro Espinoza, the energetic young proprietor of the Antillal vinyard told me. "But our *reserva* wines should also reflect the valley, even the vineyard, where the fruit was grown."

He let me taste a pair of Sauvignon Blancs he had made as former winemaker at Viña Carmen to illustrate his point. One of them, from moderately warm vineyards in the Rapel and Maule valleys, had a deliciously honeyed, ripe-melon character; the other, made from grapes grown in the Casablanca Valley, was crisper, brighter, and had the slightly green tones that many find attractive in this varietal. Both wines had the direct appeal typical of Espinoza's style, yet their regional differences could not have been more obvious.

I was aware of other distinctions. For instance, I thought I could detect a difference of style between wines made from Chardonnay vines that had been around in Chile for some time and those made from clones recently introduced from California. There probably *is* such a difference, but I eventually realized that I was picking up the variance between fruit from recently—and therefore densely—planted vines, and fruit from vineyards planted earlier, at a time when there had been a vogue to copy California's wide rows. (When planted densely, the individual vines need ripen fewer bunches for the same yield per acre, but cultivation costs are higher.) I eventually met what was without question Chile's older Chardonnay clone in Santa Carolina's Reserva de Familia. Made from Chardonnay grapes grown on old vines—some of them planted a century ago—at Santa Rosa del Peral in the cool upper Maipo Valley, close to the Andes, the wine had a tender elegance that masked a firm structure. Its flavor was delicate but long. "The crop is very small," winemaker Pilar Gonzalez told me. "The vineyard's on a slope, and the soil there is thin. Years of open irrigation have eroded much of what there was."

That Maipo Chardonnay stood in startling contrast to another Chardonnay, produced at the Santa Carolina winery by Ignacio Recabarren, an enologist now deeply involved with production at his own Viña Peñalol and Viña Quebrada de Macul but who led much of the recent viticultural reform in Chile, popping up all over the place—as consultant here, winemaker there, special-project director somewhere else. His Chardonnay from the Santa Isabel vineyard in Casablanca Valley, made from vines replicated from cuttings recently brought in from Davis, California, was intense, bold, and lively. The clone, the soil (gravel and limestone), the climatic conditions of a valley completely open to the Pacific, and Recabarren himself must all have contributed something to that wine. Yet even though the valley can give quite fat Chardonnay when the conditions are right, the lively acidity and the intensity of fruit flavor at the core of that Recabarren wine are the qualities most characteristic of Casablanca Valley Chardonnays. Others I especially like, not least for these same regional traits, included the Wild Yeast Cuvée from Errázuriz and the Medalla Real from Santa Rita.

"The Casablanca Valley had been ignored," Agustin Huneeus told me as we toured Veramonte, his imposing new winery overlooking the main highway to Valparaiso. Huneeus, a native of Chile, now lives in California, where he was responsible for building up the group of wineries associated with Franciscan Vineyards of Napa Valley. "We're beyond the reach of irrigation from the Andes here," he said, "so one is obliged to dig for water; the climate is difficult—there is a high frost risk; and because the vintage is always later here, there is always the danger of rot if the autumn rains arrive early. As a result, cultivation costs are high, and one must be content with limited yields. But when everything is right the wine is magnificent, and that is what makes the risk and the costs acceptable."

* * * * * *

When Silvestre Ochagavia and his peers brought their cuttings from Bordeaux to Chile, it had been their intention to use a mix of vines of Bordeaux origin to make wines with characteristics similar to those of the Médoc. It would not have occurred to them to make a wine from any single kind of vine: Each one was valued for what it contributed, not for what it was. They were jumbled together in their vineyards, and the wines were sold as proprietary blends. In recent years, when growers needed to identify their individual vines so that cuttings could be taken to create single-variety vineyards for the production of "varietal" wines, they had great difficulty doing so. Some varieties still flourishing in Chile were never replanted in France after the devastation of phylloxera, so even the French, when called in to help, couldn't do much better. Carmenère, for example, is a vine not used anymore in Bordeaux. In Chile it was at first misidentified as Merlot. As a result, many vineyards in Chile planted as Merlot are now known to contain a mix of Merlot and Carmenère, or even Carmenère alone. The vines are being sorted out and several wineries in Chile are now making a Carmenère cuvée. Undurraga made an exciting one in 1997. It has a big, wild flavor.

Malbec, too, is being sold as a varietal wine. The best I've tasted— more assertive than the few I've come across in California—was the 1997 made by Patricia Inostroza, then winemaker at Montes Wines. Its aroma was of violets, very pure and very intense. Cabernet Sauvignon had played a minor role in Bordeaux in the early nineteenth century, and Carmenère and Malbec quite important ones. If a Chilean producer could be persuaded to produce a wine that combined just these two varieties, we might have a chance to taste what an early nineteenth-century Médoc was really like.

In any case, it is with classic Bordeaux varieties, chiefly Cabernet Sauvignon and Merlot, that Chile is making its greatest impact. It is also among these wines that regional distinctions become clearest. Merlots, for instance, bring out the opulence of the Maipo Valley (as in the Santa Rita 1996 Reserva), the elegance of the Rapel Valley (as in the impressive Merlots from Viña La Rosa), and the lean intensity of Casablanca. There are narrower geographic comparisons, too. I'm sure, for example, that the difference between Cabernet Sauvignons from Santa Rita and those from Concha y Toro, both based in Maipo, has more to do with their vineyards than with anything that happens in the winery after the fruit is picked. Concha y Toro Cabernets have a strong eucalyptus or cassis element; Santa Rita shows in its Cabernets the chocolaty character of very ripe tannins.

The most memorable wine I tasted when I visited Chile in 1998 was a 1995 blend of 60 percent Cabernet Sauvignon and 40 percent Merlot. It was Cousiño-Macul's Finis Terrae, a *cuvée* first produced by the winery in 1992. A deep-colored wine, it had a distinction beyond the sum of its component varieties and a lithe power that owed nothing to mere technique and everything to the vineyard.

SIMPLE PLEASURES

IT WAS A SATURDAY IN JUNE. THE SUN WAS FLOODING INTO THE apartment. A mass of flowering privet that had caught my eye on one of the stands in the market that morning was making the living room smell green and woodsy.

I had a lazy-day feeling, but I made a pot of *ratatouille* anyway and ate some at midday with quartered eggs that had been simmered in the shell just to the point where they were no longer soft but were not quite hard, either. I ate alone in the dining room, looking through the open window into the studio of the painter across the street. The air was warm and still, and I could faintly hear the rumble of traffic on the Boulevard Clichy.

I was drinking a 1995 red Burgundy—a Mercurey—and the second glass, even better than the first, was just right with a slice of Charollais, a soft goat's-milk cheese that I hadn't tried before, from the hills above the Mâconnais. I picked out a few small ripe apricots—they were sweet and had an intense flavor. It was a simple lunch, but I took my time and there were roses on the table so it seemed quite luxurious. I made some coffee, helped myself to a square of chocolate, and, back in the living room, put on a CD of Carlos Gardel singing tangos he'd composed and recorded in the 1930s.

I like simple food. Keep it simple—*faites simple*—was the constant admonition of Auguste Escoffier, the great French chef who transformed nineteenth-century cooking into twentieth-century food. Escoffier was exhorting us, the late British food writer Elizabeth David suggests in the introduction to her book *French Provincial Cooking,* to avoid "unnecessary complication and elaboration." But *faites simple,* as the novelist Sybille Bedford once remarked, "doesn't mean *faites* slapdash."

It doesn't mean ascetic austerity either, for that matter. The notion of simplicity applies just as well to the uncluttered but cosseted lunch of caviar, *blini,* and bottle of Bollinger that I share from time to time with a son and daughter-in-law in a tiny *salon,* hung in green damask, above Kaspia on the Place de la Madeleine, as it does to the *pan y tomate* with which every meal began at a small hotel in Catalonia I once stayed in for several days.

As soon as I sat down at the table, at lunch as at dinner, I would be served a carafe of robust red wine, some warm grilled bread, a peeled clove of garlic, half a ripe tomato, salt, and a flacon of olive oil. I'd rub the grilled bread with the garlic and then, quite hard, with the cut tomato. I'd drizzle it with oil, sprinkle it with salt, and then munch on it with a glass of wine while deciding what to order. Spanish white bread is bland, but the grill gave it flavor and the applied regimen of garlic, tomato, oil, and salt transformed it into such a savory treat that sometimes, especially at lunch, I half thought of calling for another carafe of wine and more grilled bread and waving the menu away altogether.

The longstanding affinity between bread and wine, with or without tomato and garlic, needs no emphasis. I remember arriving one evening some years ago at an informal dinner hosted by one of Oregon's pioneer vintners to find him offering bread to his guests along with a welcoming glass of wine. It was unselfconscious—he happened to be slicing bread at the time—but perhaps more instinctive than he knew.

The gesture of offering bread and wine is an ancient and hallowed prelude to hospitality, one we've transmuted into a glass of Champagne and a canapé. A friend who has a reputation as a cook, and an enviable cellar, gets the most pleasure from his best bottles (he mumbled something recently about a Château Margaux '61) when he opens them for friends to enjoy with nothing to distract them, just good plain bread.

Bread, one of the simplest as well as one of the most satisfying of pleasures, can't be taken for granted, however. Even Paris has for some time been in the throes of a quiet revolution over the quality of its bread. Most blame the deterioration of the standard baguette on flour from new high-yielding over-fertilized strains of wheat. Many Paris bakers now offer, for a small premium, bread made from flour milled from the old-fashioned kind. "Bread as it was in the thirties," claims the baker at the corner of my street (in a recent survey his baguette was justifiably ranked among the city's best).

In an attempt to meet the demand for better bread, yet another *boulangerie artisanale* with a wood-fired, stone-built oven opens in the neighborhood every few months, and in no time at all there are lines as people stop to buy a loaf on their way home from work. Recently I noticed one baker announcing that bread warm from the oven is available at his shop every evening at five, a subtle reminder that it is freshly baked, on the premises, not only for breakfast and again for lunch but also for dinner. "What is that supposed to mean?" my neighbor said with a sniff when I pointed the sign out to her. "Every Paris baker offers oven-warm bread at five o'clock. They always have."

But that baker is shrewd: He knows that even the *promise* of warm, freshly baked bread goes straight to the heart. Writing of the harvest in Sicily in her book *On Persephone's Island,* Mary Taylor Simeti describes her husband wrapping his sweater around a loaf just out of the oven while they race home to dip the warm bread in their newly pressed olive oil and enjoy it with a glass of their own, barely fermented, red wine.

◆ ◆ ◆ ◆ ◆ ◆

In my previous life as a wine merchant, one of the occasional rewards of the annual dash along leafless French roads in bleak January weather to get first pick of the latest vintage was to find a young wine already in bloom—a Beaujolais-Villages, perhaps, or an aromatic young Chinon—and taste it with a crust of warm bread. A white Sancerre I used to select in good years had an irresistible aroma of white peaches when taken straight from the vat. The grower I bought it from in Verdigny would join me, once the deal had been struck, in drinking a glass from whichever lot I'd chosen. As if on cue, his wife would appear with bread hot from the oven and a tray of *crottins*, the local Chavignol goat cheeses—nutty, firm, and fresh.

Simple pleasures make us content, and that's when happiness creeps up on us. An occasional evening in a gastronomic temple is something I look forward to and remember long afterward, but my day can be made just as easily by a lunch of beer and a baguette sandwich (*rosette* sausage with Beaufort cheese is my favorite) with a friend at a neighborhood café near the Buci market; by coming to terms with a well-stuffed burrito at *the* Taqueria on Mission at 25th Street in San Francisco (please note: not just *any* taqueria); or by eating pizza almost anywhere with my grandchildren.

Along my road to personal contentment is the dense ham from the village of Jabugo in the remote wooded hills of northern Andalucía, where native Ibérico pigs forage for their diet of acorns and truffles; a glass of aged Tawny Port and a dried Smyrna fig after dinner; See's chocolate-covered ginger—one of the least-publicized treasures of California; and the thick white asparagus that dominate restaurant menus in Germany from early May until late June. In the evening I am comforted by Jerusalem-artichoke soup spiked with a dollop of Fino Sherry, and on gray winter mornings in San Francisco by a mug of rich hot chocolate and a brioche from the Noe Valley Bakery. (I discovered in Italy, long ago, that a little cornstarch thickens drinking chocolate so voluptuously that with every sip I get a better grip on how the world must have looked to a seventeenth-century cardinal, propped up in his Roman bed under a scarlet silk baldachin.)

Satisfactions less precise than these are the subject of *La Première Gorgée de Bière—et Autres Plaisirs Minuscules* (The First Mouthful of Beer—and Other Insignificant Pleasures), the slim collection of reminiscences published in Paris a year or so ago by the writer Philippe Delerm. It sold in huge numbers despite having been condemned by the French literary critics, who could smell a popular success—horrors!— from the title alone. Delerm articulates pleasures we hardly ever acknowledge: driving alone on a clear night on a deserted freeway with a favorite music program on the radio; the invitation to stay for pot-luck lunch that suddenly signals tacit acceptance into another family; pulling on a favorite sweater and realizing, with a sense of anticipation, that the season has changed; having the luxury of time to read the morning paper at breakfast, the world's woes kept at bay by the coffee cups and marmalade jar.

Mildly surprising, however, even to me (a man who sometimes has difficulty remembering what game it is the 49ers actually play), Delerm includes no discussion, either as participant or observer, of sporting activity among his accounts of minor pleasures. Other than obscure references to bicycles, the only physical exertion he describes is walking home with the family breakfast on a cold morning and eating one of the warm croissants straight from the brown paper bag. Has he never sat in a boat, I wonder? Or skied on new snow?

I learned to ski in the Vorarlberg, the western tip of Austria, so long ago that our varnished wooden skis were fixed to laced leather boots—an inner boot and an outer boot, in fact—with straps as well as "safety" bindings. We were taught to keep our knees tightly together as we moved, something virtually impossible today with those man-on-the-moon ski boots. *"Zusammen! Zusammen!"* Herr Schilli, our instructor, would yell if we cheated with just a little snowplow to slow our progress as we made our way gingerly down the mountain. For me, skiing was a pleasure like no other.

I began skiing again when I moved to San Francisco and could drive up to Lake Tahoe. I discovered, though, that the point of skiing in California, back in the early seventies at any rate, was to get up the mountain and down again as many times as possible in the day. So there were always lines for the ski lift. There were lines, too, for the rather wretched, cafeteria-style food. In Europe, skiing had been a social activity. There was usually a modest restaurant with stews and soups at the top of the lift and often a cabin or two somewhere on the mountain where one could stop for coffee and cake or a glass of mulled wine and hot sausages. Everyone liked to ski fast, but no one was in a hurry. In

Austria, in the postwar years, the food was simple—mostly veal, veal, and mystery veal—but it was good, and we would linger over our meal. There was no choice in any case: Everything stopped for lunch. And in the late afternoon, as we drifted in from the slopes, the bars had music and we would clump about on the dance floor in our leather boots before changing for dinner.

Having once again slipped on ski pants and parka, I soon moved on from Tahoe to Taos Ski Valley in New Mexico—difficult skiing, but delicious, homey French food from chef Claude Gohard at the Hotel St. Bernard (where he has been cooking for nearly thirty years). And then to Deer Valley, Utah, which opened with impeccably manicured ski slopes, no lift lines, and food orchestrated by Bill Nassikas, son of Jim Nassikas, at the time still president of the Stanford Court Hotel in San Francisco.

But my most vivid memory of skiing has nothing to do with food or wine. It's of a day spent on a remote slope in the Sawtooth Range of Idaho, north of Sun Valley. Three of us (I was in the company of a *Gourmet* photographer and a guide) were set down by helicopter on the flat spur of an isolated ridge. Once the engines were out of hearing range, we stood there in absolute silence with nothing around us but snow-covered mountaintops. The photographer did his work, and then we all set off for our distant rendezvous, gliding quickly over the fresh snow with hardly a sound except for the occasional light swish from a tight turn. I noticed among the trees the bright eyes of small animals watching us go by.

◆ ◆ ◆ ◆ ◆ ◆

My clearest recollections of food and wine usually involve the surprising or the unexpected: drinking new—still fizzy—Brunello with hot roasted chestnuts on a damp November day in Montalcino; the burst of flavor in a glass of Joseph Phelps Napa Valley Délice du Sémillon dessert wine; and the texture of tender young fava beans eaten raw, straight from the pod, with an apéritif of cool white Tuscan wine. A surprisingly fine *blanquette de veau* served with a well-aged Vouvray at an otherwise ordinary roadside restaurant outside Tours has become the standard by which I judge all others. A delicious salad of chickpeas in a village café on the way to Draguignan, and an exquisite dish of *cèpes,* just in season, that I had with a carafe of red Côtes de Bourg at what was little more than a bar off the *place* in Bourg itself have also taught me that good food needs no *Michelin* star.

A sauté of rabbit eaten in the mountains of Crete on a day when the sun had finally emerged after a week of depressingly continuous rain was particularly unforgettable. The restaurant was really not much more than a ramshackle kitchen; its yard was populated by a troop of cats and filled with flowers growing in old, massed, multicolored cans. It held half a dozen tables, and we chose one in the shade of an arbor.

I was traveling with a friend from Athens, and we knew it would be a while before the meal would be ready. "You should have let me know you were coming," the elderly proprietor had said, with a clear implication that her preparation would now have to start from ground zero with a visit to the hutches.

We ate bread and *hummus* and black olives and poured a sweetish, amber-pink wine for ourselves from a plastic jug. She had filled it by dipping it directly into a large terra-cotta pot. We talked and time passed. Eventually, a salad of cucumber, tomato, onion, and feta appeared, and I knew we were getting close.

And so did the cats. Long and thin, and with small, sleek heads, they quickly gathered around us in a circle, sitting upright on their haunches. They made me uneasy: Many of them had white in their eyes, which gave them a strange stare. When the woman came with more wine I asked about them. "Many of the cats on Crete are albino," she replied, adding patiently, as if explaining the riddle of the sphinx: "They came from Egypt long ago."

There could hardly have been time for her to marinate the rabbit, but it was deliciously tender, and aromatic with garlic, lemon, and the generous quantity of herbs she must have used. The "sauce," I guessed, was just a reduction of wine with the juices in the pan. We sopped it up with more of the bread. She brought us melon and offered us coffee. We sat there quietly content. Through a gap in the clutter around us we could see the slope of the mountain falling away toward the shore where that morning we'd visited an all-but-deserted monastery, at one time a way station for escaping British servicemen after Crete had fallen to the Germans in World War II.

Perhaps it was the warmth of the sun after a week's deprivation, or the effect of the wine and our modest but delicious lunch, or just the spirit of the place—of Crete itself—that brought to mind a particular scene in Nikos Kazantzakis' novel *Zorba the Greek*. Zorba and the narrator are sitting on a beach late at night—drinking wine, talking, and warming themselves by a brazier on which they're roasting chestnuts. The narrator is marveling at how uncomplicated happiness really is. A glass of wine, he thinks to himself, the warmth of the coals, the sound of the sea. That's all. But enough to make a man happy, if his heart is simple enough to recognize what he has and to seize it.

INDEX